105

Puvis de Chavannes and the Modern Tradition

Puvis de Chavannes

and

The Modern Tradition

Richard J. Wattenmaker

Art Gallery of Ontario

October 24—November 30, 1975

Contents

List of Supplementary Illustrations

Grateful acknowledgement is made to the following for copyrighted material:

ARTnews Magazine: excerpts from Meyer Shapiro, *New Light on Seurat*, Vol. 57, no. 2, April, 1958, ©
1958, reprinted by permission.

Boni and Liveright: excerpts from *Paul Gauguin's Intimate Journals*, translated by Van Wyck Brooks,
New York, © 1921, reprinted by permission.

Charles Scribner's Sons: excerpts from J. G. Huneker, "Puvis de Chavannes," *Ivory, Apes and Peacocks*,
New York, 1915, reprinted by permission; excerpts from Percy Moore Turner, *The Appreciation of
Painting*, New York, © 1921, reprinted by permission.

Crown Publishers, Inc.: excerpts from Leo D. Stein, *Journey into the Self*, edited by Edmund Fuller. ©
1950 by the Estate of Leo D. Stein. Used by permission of Crown Publishers, Inc.

Farrar, Straus & Giroux, Inc.: excerpts from René Gimpel, *Diary of an Art Dealer*, © 1960, reprinted by
permission.

Lund Humphries Publishers Ltd.: excerpts from *The Correspondence of Berthe Morisot*, London, © 1957,
reprinted by permission.

Harper & Row, Publishers, Inc.: excerpts from Walter Pach, *Ananias or the False Artist*, New York and
London, © 1928, reprinted by permission.

McClelland and Stewart Limited, Toronto: excerpts from *The Complete Letters of Vincent van Gogh*, ©
1958, reprinted by permission.

McGraw-Hill Book Company: excerpts from Klaus Berger, *Odilon Redon: Fantasy and Color*, New York,
Toronto and London, © 1965, reprinted by permission.

The Museum of Modern Art, New York: excerpts from Alfred H. Barr, Jr., *Picasso: Fifty Years of his
Art*, © 1946, The Museum of Modern Art, New York. All rights reserved. Reprinted by permission.
Excerpts from Andrew Carnduff Ritchie, *Edouard Vuillard*, © 1954, The Museum of Modern Art, New
York. All rights reserved. Reprinted by permission. Excerpts from Alfred H. Barr, Jr., *Matisse: His Art
and His Public*, © 1951, The Museum of Modern Art, New York. All rights reserved. Reprinted by
permission.

The New York Times: excerpts from Hilton Kramer, *Rediscovering Puvis de Chavannes*, Vol. CXXI, July 16,
1972, © 1972, by The New York Times Company. Reprinted by permission.

Pantheon Books, a Division of Random House, Inc.: excerpts from Camille Pissarro, *Letters to his Son
Lucien*, edited by John Rewald, translated by Lionel Abel, New York, © 1943, reprinted by permission.

University Art Museum, Berkeley: excerpts from Peter Selz, *Ferdinand Hodler*, © 1972, University Art
Museum, Berkeley, reprinted by permission.

University of California Press, Berkeley: excerpts from *The Diaries of Paul Klee, 1898-1918*, edited by
Felix Klee, copyright © 1964, by The Regents of the University of California; reprinted by permission
of the University of California Press.

Yale University Art Gallery: excerpts from Robert L. Herbert, "Seurat and Puvis de Chavannes,"
Yale University Art Gallery Bulletin, XXV, October, 1959, reprinted by permission.

Photographic credits: Herb Ball: cat. no. 10; H.B. Beville: cat. nos. 8 and 9; Photographie Bulloz,
Paris: cat. nos. 41, 42, 43, 44, fig. no. 18; Caisse Nationale des Monuments Historiques, Service
Photographique, Paris: fig. nos. 8, 30, 36; Geoffrey Clements: cat. nos. 12, 13, 55, 67, fig. nos. 15, 42;
Peter A. Juley & Son: cat. no. 27; Joseph Klima, Jr.: cat. no. 45; Lauros-Giraudon, Paris: fig. nos. 2,
3; Lodder Photo Service: cat. no. 86; Michael Parks: cat. no. 19; Philadelphia Museum of Art, A.J.
Wyatt, Staff Photographer: cat. no. 82, fig. no. 6; Ed Roseberry: cat. nos. 39, 47; Walter Rosenblum:
cat. no. 71; John D. Schiff: cat. no. 77; Taylor and Dull, Inc.: cat. no. 66; Charles Uht: fig. no. 38;
Wildenstein and Company: frontispiece. All other photographs provided by the owners.

Abbreviations

Daix and Boudaille
Pierre Daix and Georges Boudaille, *Picasso: the Blue and Rose Periods, a Catalogue Raisonné of the Paintings, 1900-1906* (catalogue compiled with the collaboration of Joan Rosselet), Greenwich: New York Graphic Society, Ltd., 1967

Denis, *Journal*, *I, II, III*
Maurice Denis, *Journal I (1884-1904)*, Paris: Editions La Colombe, 1957; Maurice Denis, *Journal II (1905-1920)*, Paris: Editions La Colombe, 1957; Maurice Denis, *Journal III (1921-1943)*, Paris: Editions La Colombe, 1959

van Gogh, *Letters*
The Complete Letters of Vincent van Gogh, three volumes, Greenwich: New York Graphic Society, 1959

Goldwater, *Some Reasons*
Robert Goldwater, "Puvis de Chavannes: Some Reasons for a Reputation," *Art Bulletin*, XXVIII, March, 1946, pp. 33-43

de Hauke
C. M. de Hauke, *Seurat et son oeuvre*, Paris: Paul Brame et C. M. de Hauke, two volumes, 1961

La Plume
La Plume, no. 138 (special number), 15 January, 1895, pp. 27-61

Malingue
Lettres de Gauguin à sa femme et à ses amis, ed. Maurice Malingue, Paris: Grasset, 1946

Pissarro, *Letters*
Camille Pissarro, Letters to his son Lucien, ed. John Rewald, translated by Lionel Abel, New York: Pantheon Books, a Division of Random House Inc., 1943

Redon, *A soi-même*
Odilon Redon, *A soi-même, Journal 1867-1915, Notes sur la vie et les artistes*, Paris: Floury, 1922 pp. 151-152

Selz, *Hodler*
Peter Selz, *Ferdinand Hodler*, with contributions by Jura Brüschweiler, Phyllis Hattis, Eva Wyler; Berkeley: University Art Museum, 1972

Sterling and Salinger
C. Sterling and M. Salinger, *French Paintings, a Catalogue of the Metropolitan Museum of Art*, Vol. II, XIXth century, 1966

Vuillard, *Entretien*
Henri Puvis de Chavannes, "Un Entretien avec M. Edouard Vuillard: Contribution à l'histoire de Puvis de Chavannes," *La Renaissance de l'art français et des industries de luxe*, February, 1926, pp. 87-90

Vuillard-Roussel
Edouard Vuillard/K.-X. Roussel, Haus der Kunst, Munich, Orangerie des Tuileries, Paris, 1968

Wehrlé, *Lettres*
L. Wehrlé, "Lettres de Puvis de Chavannes, 1888-1898," *La Revue de Paris*, XI, February 1, 1911, pp. 449-477

W
Georges Wildenstein, *Gauguin, Vol. I, Catalogue*, Paris: Les Beaux-Arts, 1964

Lenders to the Exhibition

Arthur G. Altschul
B. Gerald Cantor
Coe-Kerr Gallery, New York
Mr. and Mrs. Nathan Cummings
Davis and Long Company, New York
Gilbert M. Denman, Jr.
Mr. and Mrs. Richard L. Feigen
M. Knoedler and Company Inc., New York
Nanette Fabray MacDougall
The Estate of Henry Pearlman
Perls Galleries, New York
Mr. and Mrs. Daniel Saidenberg
Maud Hill Schroll
Dr. and Mrs. Howard D. Sirak
Arthur Tooth and Sons, London
Vose Galleries of Boston Inc.
Gwen Weiner
Wildenstein and Company, New York
Ian Woodner Family Collection
Anonymous lenders

Albright-Knox Art Gallery, Buffalo
The Baltimore Museum of Art
University Art Museum, Berkeley
Museum of Fine Arts, Boston
The Brooklyn Museum, New York
Museo de Bellas Artes, Caracas
Museum of Art, Carnegie Institute, Pittsburgh
The Art Institute of Chicago
The Chrysler Museum at Norfolk
The Cleveland Museum of Art
Musée Gustave Moreau, Paris
Indiana University Art Museum, Bloomington
John G. Johnson Collection, Philadelphia
The University of Kansas Museum of Art
Rijksmuseum Kröller-Müller, Otterlo
Marion Koogler McNay Art Institute, San Antonio
The Metropolitan Museum of Art, New York
Museo de San Carlos, Instituto Nacional de Bellas Artes y Literatura, Mexico City
The Museum of Modern Art, New York
Nasjonalgalleriet, Oslo
National Collection of Fine Arts, Smithsonian Institution
The National Gallery of Canada, Ottawa
Nelson Gallery — Atkins Museum, Kansas City
Art Gallery of Ontario
Philadelphia Museum of Art
The Phillips Collection, Washington, D.C.
Memorial Art Gallery, Rochester
Smith College Museum of Art, Northampton
Sterling and Francine Clark Art Institute, Williamstown
The Toledo Museum of Art
Rijksmuseum Vincent van Gogh, Amsterdam
The Walters Art Gallery, Baltimore
Washington University Gallery of Art, St. Louis
Yale University Art Gallery

I believe in the possibility that a later generation will be, and will go on being, concerned with the interesting research on the subject of colours and modern sentiment along the same lines as, and of equal value to, those of Delacroix, of Puvis de Chavannes — and that impressionism will be their source.

Vincent van Gogh
Auvers-sur-Oise 1890

Foreword

In the spring of 1972, on meeting Richard Wattenmaker, I asked him what would be the nature of the exhibitions he would like to mount if he came to work at the Art Gallery of Ontario as its Chief Curator. Without hesitation he responded, "A show involving the oil sketches of Puvis de Chavannes together with representative paintings by modern artists he influenced—a reconstructed model of the epoch we think we know so well."

I could see from the manner in which he began to elaborate on the form such an exhibition would take, that Dr. Wattenmaker had devoted a considerable amount of thought to the proposal. This was indeed the case, although neither of us could, at that time, foresee some of the difficult and often frustrating problems which would have to be overcome if the concept was to be made a tangible reality.

When one learns about the development of modern art with its succession of "isms": neo-classicism, romanticism, realism, impressionism, post-impressionism, neo-impressionism and symbolism, the artist Puvis de Chavannes is invariably obscured by his relationship to symbolism. But he was not a symbolist. We know that he was admired by post- and neo-impressionist artists but for what specific reasons? If artists like Picasso admired Puvis's work, were they actually influenced by him? The concept of this exhibition became more intriguing the more we talked about it. Here was an exhibition whose scholarly premise was matched with the prospect of bringing together a group of immensely appealing paintings and presenting them within a creatively didactic format; in brief, a rarely achieved balance which could justify both the requests for such important loans and the expense entailed in organizing the show.

Visualized in our new galleries with their flexible spaces, we could see the contents of this exhibition making available not only important works by such artists as Gauguin, van Gogh, Redon and Picasso but also men infrequently exhibited at the Art Gallery, such as Puvis de Chavannes, Whistler, Hodler, Maurice Prendergast and many others, who were certain to appeal to a broad audience. Provided we could obtain the specifically required loans, the show, soon to be named *Puvis de Chavannes and the Modern Tradition*, became one of the images which materialized as our new gallery—at that point not yet constructed—gradually assumed its present form. Indeed, we expressly intend that the exhibition, despite the considerable research which went into its formulation, be of interest to the general public as well as a challenge to artists who rely on institutions such as ours to provide source material for their own investigations into the traditions which preceded them. In a sense, then, our three-fold and equal responsibilities—to the general public, to the advancement of scholarship in the field of art, and to the living art community of which we conceive ourselves to be an active part—are being fulfilled.

While the paintings are here, we feel that the opportunity for firsthand study is of inestimable value. Thus, in order to underscore the educational aspect of the exhibition, the Art Gallery has invited a group of scholars to participate in a symposium devoted to Puvis de Chavannes's art and related problems. These scholars include Louise d'Argencourt, The National Gallery of Canada, Ottawa; Professor Robert Welsh of the University of Toronto; Ann Condron Peterson, Duquesne University, Pittsburgh; Professor Colin Eisler, Institute of Fine Arts, New York University; Professor Alan Bowness, The Courtauld Institute, University of London and Aimée Brown Price, California Institute of Technology. They will present papers and participate in discussions which we shall subsequently publish. If knowledge of the art of Puvis de Chavannes and that of the artists related to him is furthered by our exhibition and subsequent research is aided by what we have assembled, an important purpose of the project will have been realized.

In the three and one half years since the time of the show's initiation, many difficulties, anticipated and unanticipated, have been overcome or accommodated. Not the least of these was the decision of our sister institution, the National Gallery of Canada, Ottawa, to organize, in conjunction with the Musée du Louvre, Paris, a one-man exhibition of the same artist. That we have been able to work within some of the severe limitations imposed by this unexpected turn of events—for example, we agreed to confine our loan requests for paintings by Puvis de Chavannes to museums and collectors in the western hemisphere—is a credit to the perseverance of our Chief Curator.

Finally, I should like to express my thanks to all those museum directors, curators and registrars, collectors and dealers, who have been so helpful to us, who have endured our inquiries, both written and verbal, who have allowed us to reproduce, often for the first time and in colour, the works in their collections and who have made such an indispensable contribution to the first large scale nineteenth century exhibition organized by the Art Gallery of Ontario in its new home. *Puvis de Chavannes and the Modern Tradition* is, we believe, an exhibition which will begin to reshape our conceptions and replace some of our misconceptions about that important and far from fully explored era.

William J. Withrow
Director
Art Gallery of Ontario

Preface and Acknowledgements

The genesis of this exhibition goes back more than ten years when I saw a large oil sketch, *The Woodcutters* (cat. no. 18) by Puvis de Chavannes in an exhibition together with paintings by a number of modern artists.[1] I had first become aware of Puvis de Chavannes's work years prior to that on seeing the artist's *Dramatic Poetry*, the finished oil study for the mural of the same title in the Boston Public Library, hung at The Barnes Foundation in proximity to paintings by modern artists whose work I later came to connect with his.[2] Subsequently, in the home of Duncan and Marjorie Phillips, I saw *Greek Colony, Massilia* (cat. no. 8), *Marseilles, Port of the Orient* (cat. no. 9) and *Sacred Grove* (cat. no. 24), together with various nineteenth and twentieth century paintings, which further aroused my curiosity about Puvis's relationship to the art of that era. Formerly, I had found in Puvis only the reincarnation of the great Italians who were his sources — Giotto and Piero della Francesca — and had considered him the successor in the French tradition to men such as Poussin, Ingres, Chassériau and Corot whose paintings his work recalled. This view provides an instructive wedge backwards into the study of the western traditions and one important aspect of their development from the fourteenth through the late nineteenth centuries. The new context in which I began to perceive his work led forward into the realm of *his* influence on the painters of the modern tradition, whose visions were formed in the last quarter of the nineteenth century and whose styles laid the basis for all that was to come in the twentieth.

The Woodcutters also appeared in an exhibition[3] with Gauguin's *Still Life with 'Hope' by Puvis de Chavannes* (cat. no. 55), Maurice Denis's *Maternity* (cat. no. 58), works by Picasso (*Lady with a Fan* of 1905) and many other painters, which again stimulated my thinking about the evident but yet to be demonstrated links between Puvis and certain late nineteenth and early twentieth century artists.[4] I resolved to undertake a systematic inquiry into the multi-level relationship between Puvis de Chavannes and the modern tradition and was convinced that the task of reestablishing these connections by assembling a specific body of works — supplemented with documentary texts by the artists themselves, as well as a selection of writings by critics and collectors of the period — would be a worthwhile project for a museum exhibition.

My conceptual odyssey continued in 1969-70 when, during a year spent mainly in France, I took the opportunity of seeing as many of Puvis de Chavannes's murals as possible, including those in Paris, Rouen, Bayonne and Marseilles, as well as his smaller paintings wherever I encountered them. The idea was further reinforced by seeing again in 1971 Puvis's *Greek Colony, Massilia*, one of the very works which had kindled my interest, juxtaposed with paintings by Whistler and a variety of other late nineteenth century artists.[5] It seemed as if these paintings were following me. Exactly one year later, *Puvis de Chavannes and the Modern Tradition* was the very first exhibition I suggested, prior to actually assuming my

1. *Important European Paintings from Texas Private Collections*, New York: Marlborough-Gerson Gallery, 1964. The painting, no. 33, was erroneously entitled *La Vie Antique*.

2. Dr. Barnes's unorthodox interspersion of paintings from different periods and traditions was designed to stimulate the perception of such interrelationships.

3. *Seven Decades: 1895-1965, Crosscurrents in Modern Art*, April 26-May 21, 1966. Catalogue by Peter Selz, New York: Public Education Association. *The Woodcutters* (no. 40) was also inaccurately identified as *La Vie Antique*.

4. The choice and inclusion of *The Woodcutters* in a show whose temporal dimensions were 1895-1965 became all the more interesting — and ironic — as the painting dates not from 1895 as given in the catalogue, but from approximately twenty years earlier, *c.* 1870-1875, which adds credence to its having been used to make the point of the exhibition's subtitle, "crosscurrents in modern art."

5. *From Realism to Symbolism: Whistler and His World*, organized by the Department of Art History, Columbia University and the Philadelphia Museum of Art. The exhibition was held in New York at Wildenstein and Company and at the Philadelphia Museum of Art in the spring of 1971.

current position at the Art Gallery of Ontario and, even before arriving in Toronto, I began to map out the show.

After the Art Gallery of Ontario had made known the fact that we were actively preparing this exhibition — by that time scheduled for late 1975 — we were informed that the National Gallery of Canada, in conjunction with the Louvre, was planning to undertake the organization of a one-man retrospective of both paintings and drawings by Puvis de Chavannes to be held in Paris and Ottawa in the latter part of 1976 and early 1977. Although work had not yet begun on that second exhibition which was planned for approximately one year after ours, this information posed possibly serious conflicts, since it would inevitably place a strain on the limited amount of loan material available.

Due to the specific aims of our exhibition, which were confined from the outset to a well-defined sphere of interest, and with regard to what effect double demands on museum and private collections would have, we agreed to confine our loan requests for works by Puvis de Chavannes to institutions in the western hemisphere, foregoing that portion of the artist's *oeuvre* in European, mainly French, collections. Within these limitations we were aware that many of Puvis's most significant paintings were in North American collections, even though we would also have to work around those which, by terms of their bequests, were unavailable for loan. We believe that we have fully succeeded in meeting our objectives and that we have assembled a representative body of work by Puvis de Chavannes, with emphasis on his oil sketches, which enables us to make the points we seek to demonstrate. No systematic attempt has here been made to explore the sources of Puvis's art or to discuss its iconographical or philosophical content.

Having based my ideas almost exclusively on visual observations supplemented by occasional reading, I also had the benefit of several discussions with Professor Robert Goldwater who had, in 1946, written a thought-provoking article on Puvis[1] and who agreed wholeheartedly that not only was the investigation of his relationship to modern artists worth pursuing, but that an exhibition based on that premise would have a beneficial effect in stimulating such study, in addition to being valuable in itself.[2] We have brought works together which we hope will lead both public — including working artists — and scholars alike to develop, confirm or reevaluate their ideas about Puvis de Chavannes and his relationship to the modern tradition.

The literature on Puvis de Chavannes is extensive. Scholarly interpretations of his work were well underway during the latter part of his lifetime and many critics of that period recognized his influence on certain modern artists. We shall try to show how important this was and to what extent the consciousness of Puvis's widespread influence among modern painters, which was also reflected in some of the early collections of modern art, has been dissipated over the last several generations. In recent years new critical approaches to his art have taken several forms. The first of these has been the attention shown Puvis's work in both studies and exhibitions devoted to such moderns as Seurat, Gauguin, Denis, Redon, Hodler, Picasso and many others. Although Puvis's influence frequently assumes but a minute part of the main focus of attention in these investigations, when assembled, considered and augmented by other data they form a substantial amount of commentary on the relationship he bears to modern art.

Another source of information about the artist, especially but not exclusively biographical, bibliographical and iconographic, includes a number of unpublished masters' theses and doctoral dissertations. Among the most notable are: *A Reevaluation of Puvis de Chavannes* by Ann Condron Peterson (University of Pittsburgh, 1961); *The Art of Puvis de Chavannes: Its Sources, Development and Influences* by Patricia A. Railing (University of Kansas, 1964); *Puvis de Chavannes: A Study of Le Bois Sacré cher aux Arts et aux Muses* by Salvatore Porcellati (Queens

---

1. Goldwater, *Some Reasons.*

2. Professor Goldwater played no role in its organization and therefore bears no responsibility for the opinions advanced in this study.

College, City University of New York, 1972); *Les Peintures murales de Puvis de Chavannes au Musée de Picardie* by Louise d'Argencourt (University of Paris, 1973) and *Puvis de Chavannes: Aspects of his Art before 1883* by Sara B. Webster (University of Cincinnati, 1974). These studies are available for consultation and several of the authors have been gracious enough either to augment what they have written or to supply specific information which has been extremely useful. Another dissertation, *Puvis de Chavannes: The Easel Paintings* (Yale University, 1971) by Aimée Brown Price has not been made available for consultation. I requested from Mrs. Price specific data concerning the histories of works which entered American collections prior to 1930, although I had been able to locate much of this material from my own sources, including the records of the respective lenders. Mrs. Price informed me that she was in the process of revising her dissertation and preparing it for eventual publication but she was able to provide some factual information on thirty-six paintings, of which seventeen are included in the present exhibition. I want to acknowledge Mrs. Price's assistance and at the same time we hope that the facts we have been able to develop in the course of our study prove useful in furthering her research. With the exception of the Art Gallery's recent acquisition of a painting by Puvis de Chavannes, we have foregone lengthy histories of ownership because it is outside the purpose of our project.

Among those to whom I should like to express my thanks are Mrs. Ann Condron Peterson whose observations on the philosophical background of Puvis's art comprise an imaginative approach to his work; and Mrs. Sally Webster who has been extremely gracious and enthusiastic in supporting our exhibition. Of all the assistance I have received from informed specialists who have made detailed studies of various aspects of Puvis's art, that of my colleague, Mlle. Louise d'Argencourt, Assistant Research Curator, the National Gallery of Canada, has been most informative and generous. She has shared her broad knowledge of the artist and we have frequently discussed a wide range of problems confronting our respective exhibitions. Mlle. d'Argencourt's astute work is surely laying the foundation for much of the serious scholarly investigation that will follow her research and I want not only to thank her but also to wish her every success in the preparation of her study of Puvis de Chavannes which forms the basis of the Ottawa-Paris exhibition.

The selections, evaluations, analyses and descriptions of the works of art which make up this exhibition, as well as the context in which they have been placed, are my own and are grounded upon whatever I have been able to observe in the paintings themselves which, after all is said and done, are the ultimate reference.

We should like to thank the lenders to the exhibition, including those who wish to remain anonymous, for their generosity in allowing their works of art to travel.

To the following persons I should like to express my sincerest thanks for their cooperation, suggestions, information, encouragement and constructive disagreement over the past three and a half years: Warren Adelson; Arthur G. Altschul; Dennis Anderson, Curator of Twentieth Century Art, Chrysler Museum at Norfolk; Leon Anthony Arkus, Director, Museum of Art, Carnegie Institute, Pittsburgh; Miguel G. Arroyo C., Director, Museo de Bellas Artes, Caracas; Timothy Bathurst; Graham Beal, Director, Washington University Gallery of Art, St. Louis; Huguette Berès; Jean Sutherland Boggs, Director, The National Gallery of Canada, Ottawa; Michael Botwinick, Director, The Brooklyn Museum; Harry Brooks; James Bruce; Robert T. Buck, Jr., Director, Albright-Knox Art Gallery, Buffalo; James Cahill, Director, University Art Museum, Berkeley; Anselmo Carini, Assistant Curator, Art Institute of Chicago; Charles Chetham, Director, Smith College of Art, Northampton; Walter P. Chrysler, Jr., Director, Chrysler Museum at Norfolk; Barton Church; Charles F. Church; Geoffrey Clements; Lili Couvée-Jampoller, Librarian, Rijksmuseum Vincent van Gogh, Amsterdam; H. van Crimpen, Rijksmuseum Vincent van Gogh; Charles C. Cunningham, Chief Curator, Sterling and Francine Clark Art Institute, Williamstown; Barry Deane; A. Denis; Claire Denis; Gilbert Denman, Jr.; Charles Eldredge, Director, University of Kansas Museum of Art, Lawrence; Richard L. Feigen; Richard S. Field, Curator, Davidson Art Center, Wesleyan University, Middletown; Richard Finnegan; Jacques Foucart, Musée du Louvre; Tom L. Freudenheim, Director, The Baltimore Museum of Art; the Frick Art Reference Library; Dolores Giannuzzi, Registrar, Memorial Art Gallery of the University of Rochester; Sister Ellen Glavin; Michael Greenwood, Director, York University Art Gallery, Toronto; J. H. Guttmann; George Heard Hamilton, Director, Sterling and Francine Clark Art Institute; Robert Herbert; Norman Hirschl; McAllister Johnston; William R. Johnston, Assistant Director, Walters Art Gallery, Baltimore; Gerard de Klerk; Terry Korell; Antoinette Kraushaar; Felipe Lacouture F., Director, Museo de San Carlos, Mexico City; Robert H. Lafond, Registrar, The Art Museum, Princeton University; Richard Larcada; John P. Leeper, Director, Marion Koogler McNay Art Institute, San Antonio; Simon H. Levie, Director, The Rijksmuseum, Amsterdam; Guy Loudmer; Laura Luckey, Assistant in the Department of Painting, Museum of Fine Arts, Boston; J. Patrice Marandel, Curator of Classical and Post Renaissance Painting, Art Institute of Chicago; E. R. Meijer, Director, Rijksmuseum Vincent van Gogh; Jo Miller; Philippe de Montebello, Vice-Director for Curatorial Affairs, The Metropolitan Museum of Art, New York; Jane E. Nitterauer, Registrar, Albright-Knox Art Gallery; R. W. D. Oxenaar, Director, Rijksmuseum Kröller-Müller, Otterlo; Mrs. Henry Pearlman; the late Henry Pearlman; Mr. and Mrs. Klaus Perls; Marjorie Phillips; Marshall Phillips; Brenda Richardson, Curator of Painting and Sculpture, The Baltimore Museum of Art; Joseph J. Rishel, Curator of Paintings before 1900, Philadelphia Museum of Art; David M. Robb, Jr., Curator, Kimbell Art Museum, Fort Worth; Allen Rosenbaum, Assistant Director, The Art Museum, Princeton University; Samuel Sachs II, Director, The Minneapolis Institute of Arts; Daniel and Eleanore Saidenberg; Eleanor Sayre, Curator of Prints and Drawings, Museum of Fine Arts, Boston; Alan Shestack, Director, Yale University Art Gallery; Gridley Smith, Curator, University of Kansas Museum of Art; Thomas P. Solley, Director, Indiana University Art Museum, Bloomington; Jennifer Stephens; Ross E. Taggart, Chief Curator, William Rockhill Nelson Gallery, Kansas City; Jack Tanzer; Maurice and Carol Taylor; Herdis Bull Teilman, Curator of Paintings and Sculpture, Museum of Art, Carnegie Institute; Johannes Tjaardstra; Richard Took, Head of Rights and Reproductions, The Museum of Modern Art, New York; Nicholas Tooth; Mrs. George Trosk; William Truettner, Associate Curator, National Collection of Fine Arts, Washington, D.C.; Evan Turner, Director, Philadelphia Museum of Art; Elizabeth Usher, Chief Librarian, The Metropolitan Museum of Art and her staff; The Engineer V. W. van Gogh, Vincent van Gogh Foundation, Amsterdam; Stephen Vickers; Robert Vose, Jr.; Katheryn Votaw; David Ward; Peter Warren; Jane Watts, Registrar, Fogg Art Museum, Cambridge; Robert and Bogomila Welsh; Deedee Wigmore; James N. Wood, Associate Director, Albright-Knox Art Gallery; Ian Woodner.

No exhibition can be realized without a cooperative effort. Many tasks, seemingly minor and unrelated but actually integral, are part of a total scheme which becomes more and more apparent as the organization progresses over an extended period. For their diverse and important contributions to this exhibition I should like to thank the following members of the staff of the Art Gallery of Ontario: Alvin Balkind, former Curator of Contemporary Art; James Chambers, Head Photographer; Kenneth Churm, Traffic Manager; Michael George, Secretary-Treasurer; Lee Greenough, Administrative Secretary to the Librarian; Marta Hejlova, Curatorial Assistant; Claudette Kernaghan, Secretary to the Director; Gaynor Kotchie, Secretary to the Traffic Manager; Darlene Lamothe, Assistant to the Librarian; Charles McFaddin, Registrar; Roald Nasgaard, Curator of Contemporary Art; Larry Ostrom, Assistant to the Head Photographer; Sybille Pantazzi, Chief Librarian; Eva Robinson, Assistant Registrar; John Ruseckas, Chief Preparator and his staff; Mary Squario, Secretary, Publications Department; Maia-Mari Sutnik, Head of Photographic Services; Nancy Tousley, Acting Assistant Curator; Eduard Zukowski, Conservator.

I should like to make particular mention of the invaluable aid received from four of my associates at the Art Gallery: Katharine A. Jordan, Assistant Curator in charge of Prints and Drawings, for her painstaking help in gathering research material for the exhibition; Mairi MacArthur, Secretary to the Chief Curator, who has contributed significantly to the organization of the exhibition by her energetic work on a broad range of essential matters: we are also indebted to her for the translations from French and German which appear herein; Olive Koyama, Head of Publications, for having devoted herself to all aspects of this publication; and William J. Withrow, Director, for having furthered the organization of the exhibition in a number of ways too various to specify.

Richard J. Wattenmaker
Chief Curator
Art Gallery of Ontario

Biographical Chronology

1824 Pierre-Cécile Puvis de Chavannes born December 14, son of Ambroise Puvis de Chavannes (1780-1861) and Françoise Bertalon de la Vanerie (died 1840), in Lyons. Father a prosperous mining engineer who provides lifelong income for Puvis.

1840 After attending the Lycée in Lyons, Puvis goes to Paris where he is enrolled in the Lycée Henri IV. He prepares for the Ecole Polytechnique but does not take exams. Also takes courses at the Faculty of Law.

1840s Spends several years in Macon with his sister.

1847 First trip to Italy with indeterminate effect on later painting. Works in studio of Henry Scheffer (1798-1862), brother of Ary Scheffer, less than one year.

1848 Second trip to Italy lasts approximately one year. Travels with painter Bauderon de Vermeron (1822-1898) who was acquainted with Delacroix. Two weeks in studio of Delacroix.

1849 Three months in studio of Thomas Couture (1815-1879)—"I slept in his studio for three months and when I woke up I left it." Meets Marcellin Desboutin.

1850 *La Pietà* first painting accepted at Salon (*Société des artistes français*—the official Salon).

1851-58 Paintings refused at Salon. This had lasting effect on Puvis's attitude toward young painters and official art organizations. He works steadily on his own despite official rejection.

1852 July 15, takes studio at 11 Place Pigalle which he retains as his domicile until a year before his death. Several years later he takes a large studio in Neuilly, Boulevard du Château, no. 40, where he works on large murals.

1854-58 Series of ten paintings for the interior of his brother Edouard's house, *Le Brouchy* near Cuiseaux (Saône-et-Loire). Influence of Théodore Chassériau paramount during this period.

1855 *Exposition Universelle*, Paris; large exhibition of paintings by Ingres, Delacroix, the Barbizon painters, the English Pre-Raphaelites and German Nazarenes. Courbet erects and exhibits in his *"Pavillon de réalisme."* Puvis admires the work of Corot.

1858 *Ecce Homo*, church at Champagnat.

1859 *Return from the Hunt* accepted at Salon. Puvis gives painting to the Musée des Beaux-Arts, Marseilles. Hereafter, Puvis exhibits regularly at the Salon.

1861 *Concordia (La Paix)* and *Bellum (La Guerre)* exhibited at Salon. Puvis wins second class medal for history painting. *Concordia* is purchased by the state and donated to the city of Amiens. Puvis, not wishing to see his compositions separated, donates

Bellum to the city, where both murals are installed in the newly-built Musée de Picardie. He admires Degas's work.

1863   *Le Travail* and *Le Repos* exhibited at the Salon. Puvis donates them to the city of Amiens, Musée de Picardie. Four compositions are painted *"à la cire,"* an oil and wax mixture on canvas applied directly to the wall.

1864   Paints *Ave Picardia Nutrix*, commissioned by the city of Amiens through the architect Diet, who admires his work. *L'Automne* (Musée des Beaux-Arts, Lyons) at the Salon.

1865   Two compositions comprising *Ave Picardia Nutrix—La Cueillette des Pommes* and *La Rivière*—completed and exhibited at Salon. Puvis admires Degas's *Scène de Guerre du Moyen Age* and later exchanges drawings with him.

1866   *La Vigilance* and *La Fantasie* (Musée de Tourcoing) exhibited at Salon. Puvis now *hors concours* which means he no longer is forced to submit his work to the jury to gain entry to the annual salons.

1867   Exhibits *Le Sommeil* (Musée des Beaux-Arts, Lille) at Salon. Commissioned by the city of Marseilles to paint murals for the Musée des Beaux-Arts in the Palais de Longchamps. Puvis made *Chevalier de la Légion d'Honneur*.

1868   Around this time Puvis establishes friendship with Berthe Morisot; he advises on her painting and they remain friendly until her death in 1895. Through Berthe Morisot Puvis meets Manet and other young painters such as Fantin-Latour.

1869   Two compositions for Marseilles, *Massilia, colonie Grecque* and *Marseille, porte de l'Orient*, completed and exhibited at the Salon. Paints *La Madeleine au désert* (Staedel Kunstinstitut, Frankfurt) and *Décollation de saint Jean-Baptiste* (National Gallery, London). Compliments Bazille on his work *(View of the Village*, Musée Fabre, Montpellier, Bazille's entry at Salon that year).

1870   *La Madeleine au désert* and *Décollation de saint Jean-Baptiste* exhibited at the Salon.

1870-71 Puvis joins National Guard and serves with Manet, Tissot, Braquemond, Carolus-Duran and Meissonier during the war of 1870. Stationed at Versailles, he works out ideas for *The Balloon* (1870) and *The Carrier Pigeon* (1871) during the German occupation. Studio in Neuilly partially destroyed. Paints first version (nude) of *Hope* (Musée du Louvre) as third of the group of patriotic allegories. Corresponds with Berthe Morisot.

1872   Appointed one of five "supplementary" jurors on jury of twenty for Salon and is one of only two who vote against rejection of Courbet's work. Meissonier leads opposition to Courbet on political grounds. Puvis resigns from jury and in retaliation his *Les Jeunes filles et la mort*, 1872, is also rejected. He shows only *Hope* (clothed version) of 1872. The artist is commissioned by the city of Poitiers to decorate new Hôtel de Ville.

1873   Exhibits *L'Eté* (Musée des Beaux-Arts, Chartres) at Salon. Begins showing work at the gallery Durand-Ruel.

1874   Completes two murals, *Charles Martel sauvant la chrétienté par sa victoire sur les Sarrasins* and *Sainte Radegonde donnant asile aux poètes et protégeant les lettres contre le barbare du temps*. The former is exhibited at the Salon. Puvis commissioned to decorate L'Eglise du Panthéon in Paris with murals on the life of Saint Genevieve.

1875   Exhibits second of large murals for Poitiers and *Fisherman's Family* at the Salon.

1876   Exhibits *Childhood of Saint Genevieve* at the Salon.

1877   Made *Officier de la Légion d'Honneur*. First series of murals on the life of Saint Genevieve. These comprise four large segments:
—*Sainte Geneviève en prieure*
—*Rencontre de Sainte Geneviève et de Saint Germain d'Auxerre*
—*L'Enfance de Sainte Geneviève*
—*Saint Germain et Saint Loup bénissant Sainte Geneviève.*

1878   Decorative frieze, *Les Saints légendaires de France* and *La Foi, L'Espérance et La Charité veillent au berceau de Geneviève* completed. Entire Saint Genevieve series installed in Panthéon.

1879   Final commission for the Musée de Picardie, *Ludus Pro Patria*. Exhibits *The Prodigal Son* (Bührle Collection) and *Girls by the Seashore* (Musée du Louvre) at Salon. Accepts commission from Chamber of Commerce, Bordeaux, to paint murals for the Bourse but refuses to accept dictated programme and declines commission.

1880   *Jeunes Picards s'exerçant à la lance,* part of *Ludus Pro Patria,* exhibited (under "art monumental") at Salon.

1881   Exhibits *Le Pauvre Pêcheur* (Musée du Louvre) at Salon.

1882   Commission from painter Léon Bonnat for mural decoration for his home in Paris, *Doux Pays* (now Musée Bonnat, Bayonne). Exhibits *Ludus Pro Patria* and *Doux Pays* at Salon and receives medal of honour.

1883   Exhibits *Le Rêve* (Musée du Louvre) and *Portrait de Mme. Marie Cantacuzène* (Musée des Beaux-Arts, Lyons) at Salon. Paints *Orphée* and begins commission to decorate the staircase of the Palais des Arts, Lyons. May 3, attends Manet's funeral.

1884   Exhibits *Le Bois sacré, cher aux Arts et aux Muses,* at the Salon.

1885   Admires work of Claude Monet.

1886   Exhibits *La Vision Antique, L'Inspiration chrétienne* and *Le Rhône* and *La Saône,* completed murals for Lyons, at Salon. Invited to participate in Durand-Ruel's first exhibition in the United States but refuses.

1887   May. Durand-Ruel exhibits ten paintings by Puvis together with impressionists in New York. Puvis exhibits cartoon for mural, *Allégorie des lettres, des sciences, et des arts,* destined for the amphitheatre of the Sorbonne, at the Salon. Durand-Ruel holds major one-man show—84 paintings, pastels and photographs of the large murals—from November 11 through December 11. Musée du Luxembourg acquires *Le Pauvre Pêcheur.*

1888   Paints *La Fileuse.* Works on mural for Sorbonne. Does not exhibit at Salon.

1889   Completes mural for Sorbonne. Made *Commandant de la Légion d'Honneur.* Does not exhibit at Salon. Contributes to subscription to purchase Manet's *Olympia* for the Luxembourg.

1890   *Inter Artes et Naturam, La Poterie* and *La Céramique* for the Musée des Beaux-Arts, Rouen. Breaks with the *Société des artistes français* and founds, together with Rodin and Meissonier, the *Société nationale des beaux-arts (Salon du Champ-de-Mars)* where he exhibits *Inter Artes et Naturam.* Commissioned to paint series of murals for the Hôtel de Ville, Paris.

1891   Accepts commission to paint nine murals for the Boston Public Library on which he works from 1893-1896. Many contacts with younger artists. Exhibits *L'Eté,* mural for the Hôtel de Ville, at the *Salon du Champ-de-Mars.* Admires Hodler's *Night* and encourages him.

1892   Exhibits *L'Hiver,* mural for the Hôtel de Ville, at the *Salon du Champ-de-Mars.* He invites Burne-Jones to exhibit and also receives gift of drawing from Aubrey Beardsley.

1893   Completes *Victor Hugo donnant sa lyre à la Ville de Paris,* ceiling painting for the *escalier du Préfet de la Seine,* Hôtel de Ville, Paris. Paints *La Normandie.*

1894   Completes Hôtel de Ville commission with twelve architectural decorations: *Paris Moderne, Paris Ancien, L'Enthousiasme, L'Industrie, La Fantaisie, L'Urbanité, L'Intrépidité, L'Esprit, La Charité, L'Ardeur artistique, L'Etude* and *Le Patriotisme.* Durand-Ruel shows six paintings in November and holds one-man show in New York, December 15-31. Participates in first exhibition of *La Libre Esthétique* in Brussels, showing three paintings, *L'Enfant prodigue, La Mort d'Orphée* and *Etude de Femme.* Begins *Pastoral Poetry, Dramatic Poetry, History* and *Astronomy* for the Boston commission.

1895   January 16, banquet in honour of Puvis's seventieth birthday, presided over by Rodin and attended by more than five hundred artists and writers including Zola, Renoir, Carrière, Forain, Gustave Geffroy, Gauguin, Raffaelli, Roger Marx, Monet, Antonin Proust, O. Mirbeau, Signac, Boudin and Bourdelle. Exhibits *Les Muses inspiratrices acclamant le Génie messager de lumière,* mural for Boston, at the Salon. Presides over banquet June 8 honouring Marcellin Desboutin, attended by 200 artists and writers. Visits Cézanne exhibition at Vollard's Gallery. Commissioned by André Marty to make lithograph for *L'Estampe originale.*

1896   Boston Public Library commission completed and installed. Puvis exhibits five of the eight upright panels at the Salon: *Virgil, Eschyle, Homère, L'Histoire* and *Astronomie.* Makes it possible for Henri Matisse to become a *membre associé* of the *Société nationale des beaux-arts.* Exhibits two paintings, *Charity* and *The Shepherd's Song* in the first Annual Exhibition of the Carnegie Institute, Pittsburgh.

1897   Marries Princess Cantacuzène who has been his companion for forty years. Begins work on the last series of four murals on the life of Saint Genevieve for the Panthéon. Completes first of this final series, *Sainte Geneviève ravitaillant Paris.* Vollard commissions lithograph of *Le Pauvre Pêcheur* for the second series of *L'Album des Peintres-Graveurs.* Becomes founding member of editorial board of *Art et Décoration.* Moves from Place Pigalle to 89 avenue de Villiers, so as to be close to his studio.

1898   Exhibits *Geneviève dans sa pieuse sollicitude veille sur la ville endormie* at the Salon. Honorary member of newly-founded International Society of Sculptors, Painters, Gravers (Whistler president). Exhibits one painting and one drawing in first show. Madame Puvis de Chavannes dies during the summer. Commissioned by the state to prepare a tapestry cartoon for the house of Jeanne d'Arc in Domrémy (project never undertaken). Puvis completes remaining two murals in the Panthéon series, leaving only the last frieze incomplete, and dies on October 24.

1899   Memorial exhibition held at Durand-Ruel.

1904   Retrospective memorial exhibition, *Salle Puvis de Chavannes,* at the *Salon d'Automne,* October 15—November 15: forty-three paintings, drawings, pastels, cartoons and caricatures. Cézanne, Redon, Toulouse-Lautrec and Renoir also have special rooms.

1910   Exhibition organized by The Friday Club, London.

1912   Louvre buys *L'Espérance* at the Rouart sale, first painting by Puvis de Chavannes to enter the museum.

1913   "Armory Show," New York. Fifteen paintings, pastels and drawings exhibited.

1915   *The Balloon* and *The Carrier Pigeon* "rediscovered" by Bryson Burroughs, Curator of Paintings at the Metropolitan Museum of Art, New York. They are exhibited together with six other paintings by Puvis including loans from John Quinn of *The Beheading of Saint John the Baptist, Cider* and *The River* (studies for *Ave Picardia Nutrix,* Amiens) as well as paintings owned by the museum and by Mrs. Havemeyer.

Pierre Puvis de Chavannes
Self-Portrait, circa 1887
Oil on canvas; 22 x 18¼ in. (56 x 46 cm.)
Unsigned
Private Collection (not in exhibition)

Puvis de Chavannes and the Modern Tradition

The primary purpose of this exhibition is to bring a representative group of paintings, both independent compositions conceived as easel paintings, and oil sketches for and replicas of Puvis de Chavannes's larger mural compositions, together with pictures by modern artists whose work was influenced by Puvis. At the same time we are laying the basis for further research into this aspect of late nineteenth and early twentieth century art by encouraging the examination of the works themselves for evidence of interrelationships between Puvis de Chavannes and the modern tradition which have hitherto gone unexplored and undetected. The exhibition is a type of control experiment by which we are exposing vast numbers of relationships which enable the visitor to explore and enrich his own perceptions.

Unlike the public of seventy-five to a hundred years ago, neither the current generation of scholars nor of museum visitors has grown up in a period which has either valued Puvis's work or, more importantly, provided easy access to it; so the natural linking of many of the qualities found in his art, which were taken for granted by artists, critics and collectors on both sides of the Atlantic three generations ago, has been neglected and even lost as new values and new priorities have been stressed. We are not claiming that the well-established objectives of the modern artists were different from what has heretofore generally been conceived. What we are trying to establish is that Puvis de Chavannes was a pervasive and vital part of the environment in which these artists moved, that he provided a totally realized artistic vision, a simplified conceptual framework to which his younger contemporaries could relate. To reinstate what has been relegated to the background is to restore some semblance of the balance that must be perceived if we are to understand the formation of the revolutionary developments which carried beyond impressionism on into new realms of personal vision in the closing years of the last century and the opening decades of our own. The reconstruction of a historical perspective must begin with a fresh look at the works of art of the period which are here, for the first time, brought together with a varied body of paintings by Puvis. This physical juxtaposition has been accompanied by the introduction of some new documentary material and some reinterpretation of other well-known facts in a new context which supports the visual evidence of the works themselves.

However, with renewed interest in symbolism amounting to a full scale revival, museums throughout the world have also been active in attempting to demonstrate certain relationships between Puvis and the symbolist movement. That effort is quite different from our objective, for we do not conceive of Puvis as a symbolist, nor of many of the so-called symbolist painters as truly innovative or even creative modern artists. Nevertheless, the public has been increasingly exposed, within a highly specialized and even misleading context, to his work, by two exhibitions held in London and Madrid in 1972: *French Symbolist Painters: Moreau, Puvis de Chavannes, Redon and their Followers*[1] and *El Simbolismo en la Pintura Francesa*.[2] In the first of these, the organizers sought to elucidate a complex and highly speculative thesis comprising "an alternate tradition of modern art—a line of succession that leads us from the Romantic period (when the modern world seems to begin) directly into the preoccupations of the 20th century."[3] But, while recognizing Puvis's crucial importance to the young paint-

1. Arts Council of Great Britain, London and Liverpool, 1972. Introduction by Philippe Jullian, pp. 7-13; "An Alternate Tradition?" by Alan Bowness, 14-20, 333 works (twenty-three paintings and twelve drawings by Puvis). See Hilton Kramer, "Rediscovering Puvis de Chavannes," *The New York Times*, CXXI, Sunday July 16, 1972, section 2, p. 17. The author, in his review, perceived Puvis as the only artist of real substance in the show, stating: "The disinterment of symbolist painting continues on its merry, necrophiliac course . . . what Puvis is up against in this exhibition . . . is not painting of a high order but the iconography of a perverse dream world."
2. Museo Español de Arte Contemporaneo, introduction "El Simbolismo, casi un siglo despues" by José Vergara (twelve paintings, seven drawings and one watercolour by Puvis).
3. Bowness, *op. cit.*, p. 14. This is not the place to argue the thesis of the show; a good case could be put forward, on a somewhat more modest but nonetheless applicable scale, for the work of Monticelli as exemplifying a parallel or "alternate" tradition in the second half of the nineteenth century, although that much admired and influential painter was not included in the show.

ers of the last two decades of the nineteenth century, they had trouble comfortably fitting the artist into the context of their show. Professor Bowness quotes Puvis himself at length, saying "In all my work, let it be clearly understood, there has been no deliberate seeking after symbolism." He then concludes, in contradiction to the show's own premise (as stated in its mistakenly exclusive sub-title): "One might argue then that Puvis is not a symbolist at all."[1] Since the artist made known his intention and said he was not a symbolist, one would think it would not require argument. No one would gainsay the fact that Puvis had an impact on the French symbolist painters, but he influenced as well the really important innovators of modern art, men such as Seurat, Gauguin, Vuillard and Picasso and many others who, it is clearly stated, were not a part of the show.[2] Therefore no opportunity was present for the investigation of Puvis's relationship to the modern tradition other than that part of the symbolist movement which is construed to be "modern."

The second exhibition covered ground very similar to that of the British show and its organizers also had difficulty in knowing where to place Puvis in the context of its symbolist theme. José Vergara in his introductory essay is forced to draw the identical conclusion as Bowness, to wit: "In reality, Puvis is not a symbolist."[3] He then goes on to say, "The major influence in Picasso is that of the least symbolist painter, Puvis de Chavannes. The 'Blue' and 'Rose' periods of the Spaniard's art are so impregnated, plastically, by the work of the Lyonnais that it can be said that Puvis owes his popular survival to his early follower."[4] Nevertheless, it is symbolism which is used as the link that causes Puvis to be exhibited in the context of the exhibition, denials of his role notwithstanding. The same is true as well for a number of earlier exhibitions in which works by Puvis appear in a symbolist context. These include *From Realism to Symbolism: Whistler and his World*, 1971;[5] *The Sacred and Profane in Symbolist Art*, 1969;[6] *Visionaries and Dreamers*, 1956;[7] and *Eugène Carrière et le Symbolisme*, 1949-50.[8] Clearly there has been so much emphasis on trying to link Puvis with the symbolists and even to wrench a connection with their aims that we are in danger of losing sight of Puvis's staunch independence and his much more significant links to the formation of important modern painters who were not a part of the symbolist movement. Charles Chassé wrote in 1947, "At times one comes in fact to the point of wondering if Puvis's art is symbolism in the full sense of the word."[9] And as Puvis's friend and associate Léonce Bénédite had written, "He has always been detached and independent, reluctant to submit to any regimentation, shunning all discussion and fuss."[10]

1. *Ibid.*, p. 17. The author goes on to add, "There is no underlying meaning to it all—these are essentially subject-less pictures, which evoke a mood that allows us the luxury of reverie and private association . . . Puvis's most successful and characteristic works do have a remarkably meaningless quality" [sic]. The accompanying essay by Philippe Jullian is not worthy of serious discussion.

2. Only one "token" painting by Paul Gauguin was included.

3. "El Simbolismo, casi un siglo despues," *op. cit.*, p. 27. Vergara continued "It is certain that in 1895 he accepted a banquet with 500 participants, at which the whole of the symbolist movement attended" implying a connection which did not exist and which was staunchly denied by Puvis. The banquet in Puvis's honour was attended by artists and writers from all segments, including Renoir, Monet, Boudin, Signac and Zola. etc. It was presided over by Rodin and organized under the auspices of the *Salon du Champ-de-Mars* (*Société Nationale des beaux-arts*) of which Puvis was President. It was not controlled by the symbolists even though certain publications at the time made it appear so.

4. *Ibid.* p. 31. The author also notes the influence of Puvis at that time on the early work of the Uruguayan painter Joaquin Torres-García. For an example see his *Composicion* of 1902 (Museum of Modern Art, Barcelona).

5. *Op. cit.*

6. Galleria Civica d'Arte Moderna, Turin and the Art Gallery of Ontario, 1969, organized by Luigi Carluccio. Another show in which Puvis was included was *Die Nabis und Ihre Freunde/Les Nabis et leurs Amis*, Kunsthalle, Mannheim, 1963.

7. The Corcoran Gallery of Art, Washington D.C. ("An exhibition illustrating the influence of the French symbolist artists on succeeding generations"). In his catalogue essay, "Symbolist and other Visionaries" Henri Dorra states, "Puvis had a place in the symbolist movement for much the same reason as Moreau" (p. 19) and he claims, "Puvis succeeds in giving his compositions a sub-conscious appeal, an obsessive quality . . ." Both claims we find unsupported in the artist's work or writings.

8. *Orangerie des Tuileries*, "Introduction à l'esprit symboliste du XIXᵉ siècle" by Michel Florisoone; introduction by René Huyghe.

9. *Le Mouvement Symboliste dans l'art du XIXᵉ siècle*, Paris: Floury, 1947, p. 42.

10. *Art et Décoration*, Vol. IV. July-December 1898, p. 17.

The confusion of categories and values was deplored by Puvis in his own time. Perhaps the earliest indication is found in a letter of 1888 in which he writes:

> . . . you know how I much prefer to paint some lovely, natural and eternal scene which expresses a human feeling. How little they know me, these dreadful connoisseurs who, forgetting the deep and loyal love I have bestowed on the things of nature, confine me hypocritically to a few rare incursions into the sphere of philosophy—something I abhor![1]

The first public denial of a link with symbolist aims comes in response to an article by Sâr Péladan which appeared in *Le Figaro*, September 2, 1891 in which were announced the plans for the first *Salon de la Rose + Croix* the following March. The founder and organizer of the group stated that "the great Puvis" was "nearly an adherent" to his cause. Puvis replied to the editor the following day and his letter was printed, as had been the article, on page one with this introduction by the newspaper:

> No luck for Sâr Péladan. His manifesto had hardly appeared when the protests began. One of the artists enlisted by him under the banner of the *Rose + Croix*—and by no means the least—wrote to our chief editor:
> "Dear Mr. Magnard, I most strongly protest the mention of me in the article which appeared this morning: *Le Salon de la Rose + Croix*. I would be very grateful if you would allow me to express this protest and thanking you in advance, I remain yours sincerely, 2nd September, P. Puvis de Chavannes."
> Bad luck, Sâr![2]

This confusion, begun to Puvis's immense displeasure in his own day, has been perpetuated by a kind of selective perception advocacy in order to bolster the work of lesser men, whether they be symbolists or many of the legions of other *fin-de-siècle* painters floundering on the fringes of the world of serious painting, and whose work in itself merits no consideration if isolated from its artistic movement. These overstressed dependencies have, in a sense, done Puvis a disservice and further obscured the broad spectrum of his work as if it consisted only of a few select, endlessly repeated—and one-sidedly interpreted—examples.[3] Puvis commented in 1893, after having been bored to stupefaction (*"J'ai été assommé"*) by a performance of Wagner's *Valkyrie*, "It almost amounts to ingratitude, for a number of people, through their extreme goodwill towards myself, have coupled my name with that of Wagner. And throughout my life I have had a horror of things obscure or hazy! Judge from that."[4] In a more positive statement, quoted by Maurice Denis, Puvis said:

> For all clear ideas there exists a plastic thought which translates them. But ideas most often come to us muddled and confused. We should therefore first untangle them to be able to view them purely and simply with the inner mind. A work is born from a kind of confused emotion within which it is contained, like the bird in the egg. The thought which lies within this emotion, I turn it over and over until I can view it as clearly and intelligibly as possible. So, I look for a spectacle which interprets it precisely . . . This is symbolism, if you wish . . .[5]

1. Wehrlé, *Lettres,* p. 451.
2. Redon, mentioned in Péladan's article, also declined the dubious honour of participating.
3. E. g. *The Poor Fisherman,* (Musée du Louvre), *The Prodigal Son* (Bührle Foundation, Zurich), *The Dream* (Musée du Louvre), *Hope* (Musée du Louvre). Puvis laughed when esoteric sources for these compositions were suggested, saying, for example, that *The Prodigal Son* was a pretext for painting the pigs which actually interested him. See Marius Vachon, *Puvis de Chavannes,* Paris: Braun Clément et Cie., 1895, pp. 72-73.
4. Wehrlé, *Lettres,* p. 468. The symbolist critics, especially but not exclusively Téodor de Wyzewa who admired Puvis, were also great admirers of Wagner. See Goldwater, *Some Reasons,* p. 38, where he terms de Wyzewa "Wagnerite and propagandist for symbolism, who discovered in Puvis a style and an intention in harmony with [Wyzewa's] symbolic conception of what art should be." See also *ibid.* note 35.
5. Maurice Denis, *Nouvelles Théories sur l'art moderne, sur l'art sacré,* Paris n.d. (1922) p. 28.

We have quoted extensively from various sources expressly in order to counteract this mis-apprehension without weakening at all the symbolists' genuine claim to having been influenced by Puvis. But they are neither his sole nor his most important progeny, as many writers today would have us believe.[1] The symbolists were merely the most literary and therefore the noisiest in claiming Puvis's paternity. In short, Puvis was made into a cult figure by the symbolists and the exhibitions of the last twenty-five years have tended to per-petuate that attitude. This narrow view stems, I am convinced, in large measure from the mistaken idea that art is an alternative form of literature—visual literature—to be "read" and "translated;" when we see such ideas promulgated in exhibitions and various publica-tions we can only deplore them. It is highly doubtful that the artists of the modern tradition looked at Puvis's art in that way.

Puvis's closest friends and associates were neither amused by the *littérateurs* who made silly remarks about the artist nor were they gentle or circumspect in their ripostes. Well meaning or no, Puvis did not want to be associated with such wilful misinterpretations of his work as were circulating in the nineties and it is evident that he consulted and approved of the state-ments made by such intimates as the painter Ary Renan (1858-1900), who wrote at the same time as the above mentioned banquet:

> But he has really swept away any inherited illusions from the vision of modern artists and, in the whole school, he is launching an appeal to spir-ituality and to emotional observation. In good faith, one could not hold him responsible either for the gropings of impressionism or for the unheal-thy mania of the false painters of the soul. You will always find him op-posed to nonsense, mystery, quintessences and symbolism ... No school monopolizes him, no sect can call him their own. Pseudo-idealism is not, thank God, viable and the little groups of all kinds who share our litera-ture have no more right to keep him to themselves than will the guardians of official formalism have one day, much much later.[2]

And exactly a year later, reviewing Marius Vachon's newly published monograph on Puvis, Renan wrote:

> It would seem difficult for these paltry modern schools to dispute work as naive and personal as his. However, we have witnessed attempts of this nature. They have already wanted to shelter behind this banner; they have taught the astonished master and his friends that he was the head of a spiritualist, mystic, symbolist and ethereal school. He replied that in art he only preached one pure, healthy doctrine, free from all mystery.[3]

Emile Zola, who had also attended the banquet in honour of Puvis, reviewing the *Salon du Champ-de-Mars* of 1896 in which Puvis exhibited five of the vertical panels for the Boston Public Library (see cat. nos. 38 and 39), pulled no punches:

> It is a lamentable outburst of mysticism. Here, I believe that the guilty party is the very great and very pure artist, Puvis de Chavannes. His fol-lowing is disastrous, even more disastrous perhaps than that of Manet, Monet and Pissarro. He himself knows what he wants and does it. There is nothing more clearly forcible and healthy than his tall, simplified figures.

1. An extreme example of this distortion of Puvis's aims is contained in Edward Lucie-Smith, *Symbolist Art*, New York and Wash-ington: Praeger, 1972, a popular history of the movement in which he states: "Intellectually, as well as temperamentally, Puvis was attuned to Symbolist ideas, though he sometimes refused to recognize the fact" (p. 84). The author then goes on to the fol-lowing absurdity: "In his concern for the unity of the picture-surface, Puvis is the real forerunner of Cézanne" (p. 86).
2. Ary Renan, "Puvis de Chavannes," *La Revue de Paris*, I, January 15, 1895, p. 447.
3. Ary Renan, "Puvis de Chavannes, à propos d'un livre récent," *Gazette des Beaux-Arts,* Vol. XV, January 1896, p. 82. Camille Pis-sarro wrote to his son Lucien, February 6, 1896: "Another symbolist has failed miserably! ... All the painters worth anything, Puvis, Degas, Renoir, Monet and your humble servant, unanimously term hideous the exhibition held at Durand's of the sym-bolist named Bonnard." (Pissarro, *Letters* pp. 281-282).

They seem not to exist in our everyday world, they have nonetheless a life of their own, logical and complete, submitted to the laws laid down by the artist. I mean that they evolve in this world as immortal creations of an art made up of reason, passion and will.

But his following, good God! What scarcely formulated stutterings, what a chaos of the most annoying pretensions! The arrival of English aestheticism has ended up by throwing into disorder our straightforward and solid French genius. All sorts of influences, which it would take too long to analyse here, have accumulated and driven our school of thought to this defiance of nature, this hatred of the flesh and the sun, this return to the primitives' expression of ecstasy; and yet the primitives were ingenuous, sincere imitators, whereas we are dealing with a fashion, with a whole band of wily fakers and shammers eager to create an uproar. Trust is lacking, all that is left is the flock of the powerless and skilful.

I am well aware of all that can be said and the origin of this movement, which I shall call idealist to give it a simple label, is a natural protestation against the triumphant realism of the previous period. It was also apparent in literature and is a result of the law of evolution where any overactive movement calls for a reaction. One must also admit the necessity for young artists not to become immobilized in existing precepts but to search for what is new, even extravagant. And I am far from denying that there have been curious endeavours and interesting finds in this return of the dream and the legendary, of all the delightful flora of our ancient missals and stained glass windows. From the decorative point of view especially, I am enchanted with the reawakening of art, though not, alas, for fabrics, furniture and jewels! A modern style may have been created, but because in fact we have been in the process of rediscovering the incomparable tastes of the past in life's common objects.

But oh! for pity's sake, no painting of the soul! Nothing is more tiresome than the depiction of ideas. That an artist place a thought inside a head, yes! but that the head be there, solidly painted and in such a way that it will defy the passage of centuries. Only life speaks of life, from beauty and truth emerges only living nature. In a material art such as painting especially, I defy anyone to leave an immortal figure, if it is not drawn and painted in a human manner, as simplified as one would like, still retaining the logical anatomy and the normal proportion of the form. What dreadful procession have we been witnessing for some time now, those sexless virgins who have neither breasts nor hips, these girls who are almost like boys, these boys who are almost girls, these larva-like creatures emerging from limbo, flying through colourless space, tumbling about in the confused regions of grey dawns and soot-tinted twilights! Ah! the ugly world, it is turning to sickening disgust!

Happily, I believe that this masquerade is beginning to sicken everyone and it has seemed to me that the current Salons have included many fewer of these fetid lilies, grown in the swamps of the present day's false mysticism.[1]

In reading Zola we must take into account his feelings about the literary origins of symbolism, but those ideological antagonisms do not necessarily negate his conclusions. A final statement in the same vein:

1. *Le Figaro*, May 2, 1896, reprinted in *Emile Zola, Salons, recueillis, annotés et présentés par F. W. J. Hemmings et Robert J. Neiss*, Geneva and Paris: E. Droz, 1959, p. 155. The first half of this article contains Zola's renunciation of support for Cézanne and the aims of the impressionists.

Puvis has been caricatured in the pen-portraits of the long-haired aesthetes and neo-mystics, the scullions let loose from the kitchens of Montsalvat, which appeared during the last years of his life . . .

. . .They saw, or pretended to see, in Puvis a great initiate, a revealer of the "sense of mystery," the wonderful mystery of which they pretended to have the key, though . . . they have never been able to make it very clear. No, Puvis had no thought of disentangling any "ulterior" or "hidden" or esoteric meaning from Nature . . .[1]

American painter-critics also took an active interest in Puvis and the Boston Public Library commission had reinforced both critics' and collectors' concern for placing the artist among his contemporaries, something which, as we have seen, was difficult to do. Americans had been buying Puvis's work for nearly a decade when Kenyon Cox wrote in 1896, "A classicist of the classicists, a primitive of the primitives, a modern of the moderns, Puvis de Chavannes is above all, an individual and original artist, and to copy his methods would be to learn ill the lesson he teaches. His style is indissoluably bound up with his message; his manner is the only one fit to express what he alone has to say. It would be but an ill-fitting, second-hand garment for another . . ."[2] However, John La Farge, perhaps better than anyone before or since, summed up two years after Puvis's death:

Nothing could be farther from literary ideas than his simple types of meaning. They were all rebuilt from an inner consciousness and appreciation of what is purely plastic, and an intention as general as the very words which we use to designate general ideas. In a certain sense, therefore, his allegories and representations of ideas are nearer to the representation of ideas than the allegorical figures of most painters. They resist the wish of the critic to bring them to a definite limitation, in the same way that all general ideas have resisted the attempts at classifying them, made by thinkers from the time when man first divided his thoughts.

The very manner in which he has avoided the enclosing of a definition has probably had a great deal to do with his gradual appreciation by intelligences living outside of the practice of plastic art. The literary mind, the poet, the writer has found in Puvis de Chavannes, a stimulus or an excuse for other methods of feeling. Because the writer and the literate began to like him, the artists living in technique alone, and their coadjutors, objected to him as painting literature. But it was not so—no writing, no verse, no phrase could claim to be the origin of the life of his figures. They were parallel to literary expressions which remain entirely outside the meaning of plastic art. Like nature, they read differently according to the looker-on.[3]

Goldwater, in a similar context, wrote, "In other words, and this is not without its importance, Puvis insisted upon being the simple uncomplicated artist."[4]

Because there has been admiration for Puvis's work among diverse segments of the art world makes of him neither a member of any school nor even a specifically modern artist. The mutual regard which existed between Puvis and the impressionists, Berthe Morisot in particular, and also Monet; the esteem of Degas, Whistler, Redon, Seurat and Gauguin, to whom can be added Maurice Denis, Maillol, Vuillard, Roussel, Vallotton, Hodler, Picasso and the Americans Arthur B. Davies and Maurice Prendergast, as well the above quoted

1. André Michel and J. Laran, *Puvis de Chavannes,* Philadelphia and London: 1912 pp. IX, XIII-XIV. Michel, who wrote these words, had been an admirer and commentator on Puvis's work since the 1880s.
2. "Puvis de Chavannes," *The Century Magazine,* LI, 1896, p. 569.
3. John La Farge, "Puvis de Chavannes," *Scribner's Magazine,* XXVIII. 1900, p. 673.
4. Goldwater, *Some Reasons,* p.38.

men, is ample evidence that Puvis cannot be characterized as a part of one or another group merely because they respected, even lionized him. These artists looked to Puvis as individuals, not as representatives of any movement or advocates of esoteric theory. Likewise, critics of a broad spectrum of viewpoints, the academics who disdained the moderns[1] and vice versa, as well as collectors of various inclinations, praised and bought his work. In addition to their paintings, one has only to peruse the written legacies of artists such as Redon, van Gogh, Pissarro, Gauguin, Signac, Hodler, Denis, Vuillard and many many others to learn how much in their consciousness Puvis de Chavannes was and we have cited where appropriate statements on him by these and other artists. However, many artists were not of theoretical or literary bent, men such as Picasso or Maurice Prendergast, for example, and so it is always the work itself which bears witness to the extent and specific nature of each artist's borrowings and adaptations from Puvis. The tendency is almost irresistible to overstress the relationships where journals, letters, interviews and articles make reference—often repeatedly and in great detail—to Puvis and we must always bear in mind that this fact may not necessarily correlate with the extent of influence exerted.[2] Nor does the fact that an artist made a copy after Puvis, as we know was done by Seurat, Gauguin, Redon, van Gogh, Toulouse-Lautrec, Maillol, Picasso and Maurice Prendergast, to name just some, in one medium or another at various stages in their careers, automatically signal the degree of influence which can be observed.

Not every painter who was influenced by Puvis is included in our show. Indeed, this would be an impossibility, so far-reaching was his impact, and we have for the most part confined our investigations to those artists who made creative contributions to or were in some respect a part of the tradition of modern art. A few men, such as Moreau and Ryder, are also included for the light they may shed on influences perhaps transmitted through them from Puvis to certain modern artists. However, they play a decidedly minor or peripheral role in our exhibition. Direct imitators of Puvis's style, or followers such as Edmond Aman-Jean, Alphonse Osbert or Alexander Séon, contribute nothing new or qualitatively significant to the traditions and so they, and painters of their type, are not included. Properly speaking they do not fit into the modern tradition, nor do other painters with as diverse styles as Augustus John, Charles Conder or Hans von Marées, however much influenced by Puvis they might have been. This is true as well for the even more numerous provincial and academic imitators of various aspects of Puvis's style throughout Europe and America at the end of the last century. Any systematic investigation of such influence would fall into the category of revisionist history which attempts, in the process of seeking to recreate the historical era, to resurrect insignificant painters, elevating them to the level of "forgotten masters" in order to provide artificial self-justification for paying attention to them at all. Recreating the historical milieu, a legitimate goal, does not serve a useful purpose if it becomes confused with the search for what is genuinely new and creative in the art of the period. Although this phenomenon of "rediscovery" has not occurred in the sphere of academic painting in anywhere near the proportions of the interest in symbolist painting, the groundwork for this revisionism has been laid in such shows as *Le Musée du Luxembourg en 1874*.[3] These will surely be followed by solemn pronouncements of reputations called from the dead, provincials overrated for brief periods in their own time, and for whose benefit distinctions of quality will be blurred or even ignored. We leave this work to those who cannot—or will not—make the effort to distinguish between creative art and mere painting, that is, historical and aesthetic values.

Puvis de Chavannes did not disdain to participate in the exhibitions of his time with the young painters. From 1873 on his painting could be seen side by side with the impressionists

1. Léonce Bénédite, curator of the Luxembourg Museum, to cite one example, played an active role in discouraging acceptance of the Caillebotte bequest, of which more than half was ultimately rejected.
2. E.g. van Gogh, see pp. 110, 114.
3. Paris, Grand Palais, 1974.

at Durand-Ruel and later permanently on display at the Panthéon, the Sorbonne, and the Hôtel de Ville. After he broke with the official Salon in 1889 to found the *Salon du Champ-de-Mars,* painters of a variety of styles were encouraged to participate. His studio was always open to those young artists who were sufficiently interested to seek him out. Five months before Puvis's death, Camille Pissarro wrote to his son Lucien:

> My *Avenue de l'Opéra* series is hanging at Durand-Ruel's. I have a large
> room devoted just to my things. . . . In the neighbouring rooms there is a
> group of admirable Renoirs, another room has some superb Monets, a
> room is devoted to Sisley and the last small room to Puvis de Chavannes.
> So the gallery is filled with impressionist works. My *Avenues* are so clear
> that they would not suffer alongside the paintings of Puvis.[1]

When we consign Puvis to be hung with his academic contemporaries of the late nineteenth century, we have done him a great disservice. His work does not fit beside that of Bouguereau, Gérôme, Bastien-Lepage, Regnault, Vibert, Chabas and others among the slick hucksters of popular escapist imagery where, if hanging at all, it is now placed in many of our major North American institutions. In Pissarro's day this was clearly understood. Puvis had a room set aside for forty-three of his works in the *Salon d'Automne* of 1904, along with special rooms for Cézanne, Redon, Toulouse-Lautrec and Renoir. The academics had no place in that environment. At the "Armory Show" in 1913, whose purpose was to introduce the newer trends of modern European art to this continent, it was Redon who showed the greatest number of works—seventy-five[2]—and Puvis, dead for nearly fifteen years, was represented by fifteen.[3]

To reiterate, the basic concept of the present exhibition is to provide the material for a demonstration of the powerful influence of Puvis de Chavannes on painters of the late nineteenth and early twentieth centuries and to show that while this idea was probably taken for granted seventy-five years ago, it has lost currency, but not accuracy, because Puvis's work has dropped from public view and the opportunity to see him with his descendants has been removed. The reestablishment of a major and pervasive source of many ideas seen in the works of the modern masters could not be achieved by isolated photographic comparisons of a figure borrowed here or a compositional motif there. What little of this has already been done has not served at all to reinstate Puvis's important position. The comparison both obvious and subtle of his special colour tonalities, paint handling, atmospheric qualities, scale and other palpable, pictorial qualities are more important but no more elusive to trace, once the paintings are before us, than the obvious illustrative borrowings.

It is useful to bear in mind that Puvis's paintings are decorations without many of the qualities commonly associated with the *decorative.* Although relatively flat, they are subdued rather than intense in colour, static rather than animated in composition, premeditated and placid rather than curvilinear in line. What, for example, Matisse and his generation made the substance of their decorative simplifications Puvis eschewed. His decorations consisted of relationships suited to the surroundings for which they were designed, particularly in scale, and in their rhythmic ebb and flow of outline and pose. The compositional continuity between figures and setting had a sedate, even sober, but intriguing harmony which exploited a range of decorative values more akin to the fourteenth or fifteenth century Florentines than to his late nineteenth century contemporaries and younger followers. Thus, for Puvis, decoration did not imply or entail loss of permanence, complexity and intellectual substance. Indeed, he was the artist who reinstated its credibility among the younger generation.

1. Pissarro, *Letters,* p. 325, letter of May 29, 1898. See also George Lecomte, *L'Art impressioniste: d'après la collection privée de M. Durand-Ruel,* Paris: 1892, pp. 36-37.
2. Forty-two paintings and pastels, twenty-six lithographs, seven etchings.
3. Three paintings, ten drawings and two pastels.

Puvis de Chavannes played a special role in the formation of the modern tradition; his art, independent as it was personal, led several generations of younger men to see in his work a reservoir full to the brim with intelligently formulated plastic ideas which *were of use to painters*—as well as supplying false leads to the literarily inclined theorists and sentimentalists who claimed, without any encouragement from Puvis himself, to be his legitimate progeny. It was Puvis's irreducible and undogmatic individuality, those tangible qualities which mark his vision—his special approach to decorative painting—which were so broadly appealing as to attract a wide following among the young individualists of his later years. Puvis holds a unique place in the history of the period; if it is hard to identify that place, so it is equally difficult to envisage the period without him. For to subtract Puvis de Chavannes from the last forty years of the nineteenth century and ignore the network of interconnected links between his art and that of the younger men is both not to fully understand them and to bypass a potent force in the great period of French art between 1875 and 1914.

> Almost alone among the painters of the middle of the nineteenth century, Puvis foreshadowed a major development of the twentieth: the simplification and reduction of the means of the artist. . . . His was really a restriction of the means employed, and however short the distance he travelled, his direction was the direction of later art. That this was often felt without being understood does not detract from its importance.[1]

When Robert Goldwater wrote these words in 1946, Puvis de Chavannes was at the nadir of his critical reputation among artists, critics, collectors and those who directed the affairs of the museums of the western world. This was not always the case. But a generation of neglect, resulting in the withdrawal of a considerable number of paintings, particularly but not exclusively, from the walls of the museums in North America, resulted in a lack of familiarity and respect on the part of the art-interested public which had, twenty years earlier, considered Puvis one of the most important and influential painters of his day. The lapse in appreciation of Puvis's art which, despite the renewed scholarly interest which Professor Goldwater's article gradually began to awaken, has lasted to the present, has obscured Puvis's true place in the art of his time—the second half of the nineteenth century—and virtually obliterated awareness of his immense impact on the art of the young painters and sculptors of the late nineteenth and early twentieth centuries who created what we now know as "modern art." As Goldwater recognized, "there were . . . aspects of his art which were part of, and above all gave inspiration to the beginnings of a new tradition."[2]

As popular awareness of art, especially modern art, has burgeoned in the last thirty years, and the names van Gogh, Gauguin, Toulouse-Lautrec and Picasso have become as familiar as those of any politician, scientist or inventor—and in many cases much more so—the name Puvis de Chavannes draws little or no response. This is so not because of any negative reaction but because of absolute lack of familiarity with pictures still today to a large extent in the storage rooms in many of our major museums, or otherwise inaccessible to the public. Before we demonstrate that the art of Puvis de Chavannes was a major catalyst in the formation of modern art and moreover that this fact was clearly recognized internationally by the artists themselves, it should be stated that although we are emphasizing that particular

1. Goldwater, *Some Reasons*, pp. 41-42.
2. *Ibid.*, p.43. "Puvis's reputation, with such a high point to fall from, disappeared into an abyss of forgetfulness, pushed by the 20th century's enthusiasm for Impressionism and dislike of less colorful art," Robert L. Herbert, "Seurat and Puvis de Chavannes," *Yale University Art Gallery Bulletin*, XXV. Oct. 1959, p. 23.

aspect, Puvis is not important for that reason alone. Because we value so highly the work of the modern men he influenced, it would be as totally unfair and inaccurate to see in Puvis's art merely a forecast of things to come, rather than something also worthy in and of itself, as it is to look upon the Old Testament as only a series of cryptic prophesies of revelations contained in the gospels of the New. Puvis was a creative force in his own right, and the artists who learned and borrowed from him were interested in both his vision and especially in the means with which he formed it because they were attracted to the unique character of his art.

Puvis was specifically instrumental in affecting the younger generation because of the widespread respect in which he was held. Goldwater, in touching upon those aspects of the modern tradition which Puvis anticipated, makes a point which is frequently overlooked: namely, the "simplification and reduction of the means of the artist,"[1] that is, the dramatic shift of the aims of painting toward goals primarily decorative. Two broad tendencies developed in the art of the late nineteenth century: the first of these may be termed the constructive tendency, a tradition best exemplified in the work of Paul Cézanne, who simplified and, as it were, dismantled the constituent means of the artist in order to reconstruct with those means a more solid, colourful and powerfully direct vision of nature than had previously existed in the traditions. In this aim Cézanne was influenced by men such as Daumier, Courbet and Manet, all of whom anticipated or shared to one degree or another in the objectives of simplifying in order to make more powerful their plastic statements. Cézanne was paralleled by other artists—notably Degas, Renoir and Seurat who also shared in different personal terms, and varying degrees, certain of these constructive objectives. In contrast to these men, the impressionist painters Pissarro, Monet, Sisley and their followers were interested in momentary aspects of nature although they also made use of colour as the fundamental pictorial element in recording their sensations. Nonetheless, by its very nature, impressionism discounted volume and compositional complexity, stressed surface and on-the-spot spontaneity and eliminated almost entirely subject content extrinsic to the immediate scene before them.

A younger group of painters, centred around Paul Gauguin and also including such men as Vincent van Gogh, Odilon Redon, Maurice Denis, Edouard Vuillard and their followers, in the late eighteen eighties and early eighteen nineties sought to merge these newly developed decorative colour discoveries of the impressionists and neo-impressionists with an illustrative content which they felt was lacking in the purely impressionist paintings created since the late 1860s by Monet, Pissarro and their companions. The emphasis on decoration, on simplification, on the flattening and silhouetting of illustrative matter—also given great impetus by the widespread influence of Japanese woodblock prints in the latter part of the century—led them to find in Puvis, the only great large scale decorative artist of his time, guidance as well as some of the means of reintroducing figurative content into an overall decorative context. Thus, the aims of these younger artists, while they also respected Cézanne, Renoir and Degas and employed or tried to adapt many of their ideas in their own work, departed markedly from the visions and goals of these older men who were mainly concerned with permanence and monumentality and who relegated decoration to a secondary objective in their work, while not disdaining it. Lautrec, Forain and early Picasso all used Degas as a model but none of them ever achieved the level of substance of Degas's work; Renoir had many imitators and Bonnard, among others, creatively applied some of his ideas in a more overtly decorative vein; Cézanne had countless imitators and despite the unparalleled extent of his influence not one of them succeeded in taking his discoveries further along in the expressive direction of his art. Puvis was to have immense impact because art was moving towards a dominantly decorative presentation of ideas in the field of painting, even when, as it often did at this time, it embodied varying degrees of illustrative con-

1. Goldwater, *Some Reasons*, p. 41.

tent and complexity. Gauguin, Redon, Denis, Vuillard and Picasso were able to enhance this trend of decorative illustration by merging it with the colour concepts of the impressionists. Cubism, Cézanne's unwitting progeny which, even though it stressed planes and minimized—even at times eliminated—illustrative content, moved away from the solidity, massiveness and power which were at the heart of Cézanne's quest and achievement. With fauvism and other movements of the early part of this century, painting decisively gravitated in the direction of decorative expression.

Puvis's art, in its relative flatness, its majestic large scale impressiveness and dramatic pattern simplifications, its rational departures from naturalistic appearances without abandoning compositional and linear rhythmic continuity so important to the *fin-de-siècle* aesthetic—especially as it was revealed in the pervasive forms of *l'art nouveau*—as well as its subdued, atmospheric colour harmonies, attracted a wide circle of admirers. Puvis's comprehensible complexity, his impeccable mastery over a wide variety of means, the logical but human intellect accessible behind the classic detachment of his work, attracted the younger men. On the other side, the tranquil, at times dreamlike harmonies of his paintings were fused with a rigorous lucidity, a mastery whose very intellect seemed to absorb the immaterial, the enchantment of another world, without losing hold on our own. These and other qualities held great fascination for the younger painters. Also, Puvis relied on no academic technical tricks, which were anathema to these artists. The new generation saw him as a creative individual who had confronted officialdom, been rejected and ultimately came to terms with and was honoured by it without surrendering his individuality. Then, at the height of his success, he turned his back on the Salon. Many of the young painters, such as Denis and Sérusier, were devoutly religious, others such as Signac and Cross were anarchists who saw in art a means of significantly entering into and even affecting in quasi-practical ways the life of the modern world around them. Some, like Denis or Signac, thought that if they could substitute religious or "modern" (i.e. soldiers, workers) thematic content for Puvis's classical repertoire and apply his rules, they would have found their own solutions for achieving an artistic personality.[1]

In a word, Puvis's work gave these decoration-oriented artists a framework, both conceptual and physical, which was more easily adaptable than the complexities of Cézanne's experiments, while at the same time providing them with access to the past traditions—Poussin, the Florentines, Greece—by showing them a simpler method of absorbing them. Puvis played down to a bare minimum the contrast found in Manet and Daumier, he stressed modulations of tones within a relatively confined range, easier to handle in his broad technique than the varied technique of the impressionist painters who sought to grasp elusive, momentary effects, an objective as difficult to carry out as it was limited. So the appeal was both conceptual and physical; flatness required less effort than solid volume; large scale mural formats could be adjusted to any size and were easily adaptable to a variety of decorative objectives—posters, tapestries, scenery, as well as easel paintings; and the narrow range of tonalities mingled with white for overall greyish harmony rather than the infinitely more ambitious and complex colour qualities of Cézanne, gave access to a conception of art which was neither academic nor revolutionary but remarkably self-contained and formulated in every respect. Interestingly enough, even the neo-impressionists Signac, Cross, Petitjean and others took over Puvis's compositional formats and illustrative orientation while couching his ideas in a totally different colour and technique. Gauguin in the eighties consciously attempted to absorb Cézanne's objectives and even copied his technique for a time, but in his mature work he was closer to Puvis's basic statement. Likewise, Maurice Denis, who began under the influence of Puvis, turned to Cézanne, who throughout his life remained a source of theoretical inspiration, but his forms

---

1. As an example of Signac's application of this idea see *Au temps d'Harmonie*, 1894/95 (fig. 23, p. 154). (See also Françoise Cachin, *Paul Signac*, Greenwich: New York Graphic Society, 1971, pp. 69-71.)

never diverge from the impact of Puvis. They retain always the pale, light and decorative character which Denis made into something distinctly his own. In 1899 he wrote in his *Journal:*

> Exhibition of sketches by Puvis de Chavannes. One must not feel one's way around on a large surface: fix and specify the main lines and colourings. Great importance of the melodic line in the decoration. Locate it pure and certain and hold to it without hesitation. For the colour, be concerned especially with the general harmony, that is to say with a relationship between two or three tones which should be illustrated and strictly determined in the sketch. The subject can be as summary as one wishes—qualities which I sense in myself but my feelings are more complex, my will hesitant. Become solid.[1]

But he was never able to achieve the Cézanne-esque solidity he sought. It was not in tune with his personality. Essentially, while the modern painters claimed Cézanne as their preceptor, none of them was able to carry on his central aim of making something solid and durable out of nature. One by one they came to terms in a decorative vein with isolated aspects of Cézanne's art: for example, the cubists' use of radical distortions or the fauves' adaptation of the patchwork paint application in his later landscapes. Cézanne had coordinated these devices and applied them to his specifically constructive objectives. In the hands of his followers, Cézanne's personal means took a decorative direction which coincided with what Puvis had sought as his end from the beginning. So, the decorative interests to which the modern painters, by a variety of routes, came back in one form or another, became almost exclusively the substance of twentieth century art however varied and unlike Puvis's art the new styles may have been. In the background, Puvis was always a painter to be reckoned with, he was too omnipresent to be ignored. He simplified, he flattened, he discarded without losing sight of the classical shoreline of French painting at any one time in his career. Indeed, in certain works he stayed too close to it and had he not done his free sketches and smaller easel paintings, it is questionable whether the interest of certain moderns would have been as intense as it was. However, if Puvis did not venture far off the coast, he left his academic contemporaries far behind. If it remained for an artist such as Cézanne to really explore the uncharted regions of the artistic horizon and to lead many to try to follow his newly created paths, Puvis cannot be faulted for his modest innovations; in the context of his milieu they were remarkably adventurous. As Vuillard said in 1926, "[Puvis's] ambition [like that of Cézanne] was also to renew the art of painting and one could say that he achieved it. . . . The researches into stylization and expressive synthesis which characterize the painting of today, are clearly noticeable in his work."[2] Ultimately, many of the modern painters circled back to his decorative aims through channels opened by Cézanne.

Matisse is a perfect example: employing means learned from many sources including Cézanne and the eastern traditions, he adapted Signac's compositions into his *Luxe, calme et volupté* of 1904-05 (fig. 24, p. 154). The thematic content of Signac stems directly from his adaptations from Puvis—Puvis once removed and with powerful camouflage of neo-impressionist colour and technique. Likewise, *Le Luxe I* (see fig. 12, p. 123) would appear to have Puvis's *Girls by the Seashore* as its spiritual ancestor (see fig. 11, p. 122). By the time, 1931-1933, Matisse painted the murals, *La Danse,* he was very far away from the Cézanne *Bathers* which inspired him and nearer to Puvis's murals, even though his aims were formulated in Cézanne's terminology. He said, "My aim has been to translate paint into architecture, to make of the fresco the equivalent of stone or cement. This, I think, is not often done any more. The mural painter today makes pictures, not murals."[3] Asked about Puvis, Ma-

---

1. Denis, *Journal I,* p. 152 (March, 1899). The very last entry in his *Journal,* October 13, 1943 was "Lyons. No way of seeing the Puvis works; they would have taught me so many things! Caught sight of the *Bois sacré:* solidity." (*Journal III,* p. 242.)

2. Vuilllard, *Entretien,* p. 90.

3. Henri Matisse, quoted in Dorothy Dudley, "The Matisse Fresco in Merion, Pennsylvania," *Hound & Horn,* Vol. VII, no. 2, January-March, 1934, p. 299. It is interesting that Matisse refers to his mural, painted like Puvis's in oil on canvas, as a fresco.

tisse replied, "He approaches it, yes, but does not arrive perfectly in that sense. The walls of the Panthéon, for example, are of stone. Puvis's paintings are too soft in feeling to make the equivalent of that medium . . ."[1] Nonetheless, for all of their fundamental differences from Puvis's art, their linear arabesques versus Puvis's static effects, Matisse's murals are large scale, decorative in intent and in effect, restricted in colour range to only four colours—grey, pink, blue and black—and in that basic sense closer to Puvis's aims than to Cézanne's. This is underscored by the reactions to the mural after the artist had seen it *in situ.* Matisse said, ". . . in my studio . . . it was only a painted canvas. There in the Barnes Foundation it became *a rigid thing, heavy as stone, and one that seemed to have been spontaneously created at the same time with the building . . .*"[2] Matisse continued, "Barnes said, 'One would call the place a cathedral now. *Your painting is like the rose window of a cathedral.*' "[3] Matisse, showing his interviewer a photograph of the mural in place, concluded, "And when one looks from this angle [i.e. from below], one would say, too, *it is like a song that mounts to the vaulted roof.*"[4] There is a considerable difference between "a rigid thing, heavy as stone" and "a song that mounts to the vaulted roof." Cézanne aimed to recreate the power and solidity of the cathedral itself, not the rose window and not the song which graces its vaults. Matisse, therefore, despite himself, is closer to what Puvis achieved in the Panthéon than to what Cézanne realized in a ten by twelve inch painting of apples on a table. In pointing out this apparent discrepancy between what he wanted his mural to be and what it is, we do not denigrate Matisse's achievement in the least. We seek merely to objectify by this example that the orientation of the mural by Matisse, who possessed the greatest repertoire of *decorative* forms of any painter of the twentieth century, corresponds specifically to what Goldwater observed about Puvis when he wrote that "his direction was the direction of later art. That this was often felt . . . does not detract from its importance." It should also be pointed out that Matisse might not have been painting such a mural in a secular building had it not been for Puvis's murals in similar structures. Matisse and Puvis were faced with analogous problems in Boston and Merion; each was familiar with the architecture, Matisse firsthand and Puvis by way of a cutaway scale model of the library which he kept in his studio while painting the murals. In Boston, the main staircase leads to a landing opening out by way of large windows onto a courtyard. The same illumination which partially gives light to the murals on the side staircase and to the long mural on the second floor landing, also throws into deep shadow the two murals on the first landing. Likewise, in order to see the entire second floor mural, *The Muses,* one is forced to look from below or at an oblique angle in order to try to see the mural at once, which is virtually impossible. The same is correspondingly true with the Matisse mural at Merion which can either be seen from below at a steep angle, or from the balcony directly across from it. As well, the light pouring in from below, when one looks from below at the mural, has some of the effect of the light from the windows opposite the staircase in Boston.[5]

1. *Ibid.* This part of the interview took place in Matisse's studio before he saw his mural installed.
2. *Ibid.* p. 303, emphasis added.
3. *Ibid.,* emphasis added.
4. *Ibid.,* emphasis added.
5. Matisse's familiarity with mural painting and his ties to Puvis de Chavannes can be summarized as follows. In 1896 at the *Salon du Champ-de-Mars* Matisse exhibited four paintings. After a dispute over whether or not to admit Matisse as a member, Puvis de Chavannes, President, proposed his appointment over the objections of Jean Béraud, Secretary, and Matisse became a *membre associé* of the *Société nationale des beaux-arts.* In 1897 Matisse exhibited five paintings which he succeeded in entering solely because he was entitled to exhibit as a member. (See R. Escholier, *Matisse: A Portrait of the Artist and the Man,* New York: Praeger, 1960, pp.

Puvis de Chavannes was one of the great self-formed artists of the nineteenth century. Like Corot, Daumier, Courbet, Pissarro, Cézanne and Gauguin, he rejected the mechanical channelling of vision in the schools and fiercely guarded his own while seeking to develop the technical and expressive means to make it manifest. During the 1850s when Puvis was excluded from the official Salon, he continued to work out his ideas and his method, observing nature and the traditions systematically and with evident insight. His experiments with *peinture à la cire,* by which he mixed wax into the oil paint, allowed him the kind of control of his medium and at the same time produced the kind of semi-matte surface the artist desired for his large mural compositions. In this technique the brush stroke has a sharper edge than with normal oil paint and a textural surface is achieved more directly. Puvis was a persistent experimenter and the work of other artists—not merely those in the past but his contemporaries and the younger men as well—was the object of his close scrutiny both in the annual Salons and at the art galleries. Moreover, Puvis kept his studio on the Place Pigalle open and encouraged other artists to visit and talk with him. At the time of the banquet held in his honour on January 16, 1895, for which Rodin was the main organizer, Monet and Renoir among those on the organizing committee, a flurry of interviews and articles in the journals and newspapers revealed not only how revered was Puvis among his fellow artists (the number in attendance had to be "limited" to approximately 500 and Puvis's brief speech acknowledging the homage was interrupted ten times by applause) but just how accessible he was to artists and others interested in his work. "Everyone knows that, despite his considerable position, his imposing work, the great painter is the most open, the most welcoming of the contemporary masters towards the young. So, youth should also be invited to salute the artist."[1]

We know also from his writings and those of his contemporaries, both artists and critics, that Puvis was in close touch with the latest developments. Having begun his career as a student of Chassériau, Delacroix and Couture, Puvis was an admirer of Degas, aspects of whose early compositions paralleled certain aims of his own and had perhaps influenced him. Puvis complimented Frédéric Bazille on his *View of the Village* (1868) at the Salon of 1869 and Bazille's *Men Bathing* (fig. 1, p. 55) may have been one of the first paintings by the younger generation to show strong affinity to or even influence of Puvis.[2] He admired the work of Manet and often praised that of Berthe Morisot who describes in her letters, among other things, accompanying Puvis to the Salon; he valued Corot's work and Courbet's. Exhibiting with Durand-Ruel, the impressionists' dealer and tireless advocate, Puvis could not but have consistently come into contact with their work—and they with his—and he admired Monet, referring to him in a letter to Berthe Morisot (June 5, 1885) as "that inspired painter of water."[3]

38-39.) Matisse therefore was undoubtedly familiar with the Boston Library murals which Puvis exhibited in 1895 and 1896 at the Salon and if he ever met his sponsor or visited his studio it would have been at the time of their production. Matisse, with Albert Marquet, had worked painting decorations in the Grand Palais in 1900. Alfred Barr states that "Matisse had proposed doing some decorative panels for a relative's house in Bohain about 1902. But the only canvas Matisse had painted explicitly as a decoration was the large *Harmony in Blue* (1908) which Shchukin . . . lent to the Autumn Salon of 1908 where it was listed as a 'Decorative Panel for a Dining-Room'. " *(Matisse: His Art and His Public,* New York: The Museum of Modern Art, 1951, p. 133). Barr believes that after *Harmony in Blue* was transformed into *Harmony in Red* of 1909, Shchukin may have had the idea to commission *Dance* and *Music* from Matisse. *Dance* is the forerunner of the mural at The Barnes Foundation. When, in 1910, the Muscovite patron seriously considered rejecting the completed canvases which he came to see at the *Salon d'Automne* that year, he thought of replacing them with a large mural by Puvis de Chavannes. (He already owned *The Poor Fisherman,* 1879, by Puvis.) Matisse's dealer, Bernheim-Jeune, asked the artist to propose the purchase of the Puvis and to advise Shchukin on how the fifteen-meter-long mural (a cartoon study for *Ludus Pro Patria* in Amiens which had been exhibited at the *Salon d'Automne* in 1904, no. 3) could be made to fit the stairwell in the collector's house. At the last minute, Shchukin changed his mind, cancelled the purchase of the Puvis and accepted Matisse's panels. (See Barr, *ibid.,* p. 134 and especially note 6.)

1. Philippe Auquier, *Le Figaro,* December 26, 1894, p. 5. See also *Le Figaro,* January 17, 1895, "Le Banquet Puvis de Chavannes," p. 3 (unsigned).
2. See Kermit S. Champa, *Studies in Early Impressionism,* New Haven and London: Yale University Press, 1973, pp. 81, 88-89.
3. *The Correspondence of Berthe Morisot,* ed. by Denis Rouart, London: Lund Humphries, 1956, p. 126.

14

In the later stages of his development, when many younger men openly admired and were influenced by his work, Puvis fostered the exchange and when he broke with the official Salon in 1889 to found the following year the *Société nationale des beaux-arts,* he made sure that the new generation was not excluded from its annual exhibitions as he had been forty years earlier, but rather actively encouraged to participate. Puvis accepted invitations to exhibit with *La Libre Esthétique,* avant-garde successor to *Les XX* in Brussels at its first exhibition, where in 1894 he showed three paintings together with Pissarro, Sisley, Gauguin, Redon, Lautrec, Maillol, Denis and Ensor among others.[1] He was one of the original members of the editorial board of *Art et Décoration* in 1897 which published numerous articles on a great variety of contemporary artists and craftsmen.

Degas had long admired Puvis's art; both his painting and drawing and his compositions showed a parallel interest to those Puvis was developing.[2] Degas's biographer, P.-A. Lemoisne, wrote: "Concerning Puvis de Chavannes whom he valued enormously and whose paintings he admired for their conscious arrangement, 'No one but he has found the exactly right placing of figures in a composition. Try to move one of his figures by one line or point and you will not succeed, it is impossible.' "[3] It was, however, the younger artists who sought out Puvis for guidance and it is not unreasonable to believe that they were confident in doing so partly because they realized that the modern masters they modelled themselves after, Degas, Monet, Pissarro and many others, also respected and valued his art. In the eighteen eighties, the experience related by Maillol serves to elucidate Puvis's position of respect. Maillol, who came to Paris in 1882 and remained a student at the *Ecole des Beaux-Arts* under Cabanel and Gérôme for five years, stated:

> I received no counsel, I was forced to find it myself in the work of great artists and that is why I asked advice from Puvis ... Puvis! It is to him that we owed the greatest emotions about art in the time of our youth; these compositions of pretty style and fine design filled us with an impression of poetry through their knowledge of vast decor and their harmony. The work of Puvis has provided good counsel for our inexperience ... Degas, who withdrew from the Salon, said that in order to work Puvis had need of the successes which he achieved there. He had no enemies ... if we had looked only to him we would perhaps have turned this great advice to good account; unfortunately we also went to see Laurens, Bonnat, the whole Institute.[4]

Maurice Denis, at age seventeen, visited Puvis's one-man exhibition at Durand-Ruel in 1887 and recorded in his *Journal:*

> Yesterday I visited the exhibition of works by Puvis de Chavannes. I found the decorative, calm and simple aspect of his paintings very fine: a wonderful mural colour; there are marvellous harmonies of pale tones. The backgrounds are very interesting as decoration; backgrounds like this are very preferable to the golden backgrounds of some frescoes. The broad, discreet, ethereal composition surprises me: it has to be extraordinarily clever. It is this, no doubt, which produces this quiet and mysterious impression on the spirit, both restful and elevating.[5]

It is significant to record Denis's thoughts since he was already acquainted with many of the young men who were to make up the various modern movements of the next

---

1. See M. Octave Maus, *Trente Années de lutte pour l'art: 1884-1914,* Brussels: L'Oiseau Bleu, 1926.

2. See, for example, *Jeunes spartiates s'exerçant à la lutte,* National Gallery, London; *Semiramis construisant une ville,* Musée du Louvre; *Les Malheurs de la ville d'Orléans,* Musée du Louvre; and *The Daughter of Jephthah,* Smith College Museum of Art.

3. *Degas et son oeuvre,* Paris: Plon, 1954, p. 126.

4. Quoted in Judith Cladel, *Aristide Maillol: sa vie, son oeuvre, ses idées,* Paris: Editions Bernard Grasset, 1937, pp. 39-41. Maillol at this time made copies of *The Poor Fisherman* and two figures from the Saint Genevieve murals in the Panthéon, see *ibid.,* p. 40 (see cat. no. 63).

5. Denis, *Journal I,* p. 67.

generation—Vuillard, Roussel, and the following year at the Académie Julian he met Sérusier and Bonnard as well as in 1889, Gauguin and Redon. Years later he would recall in an article commemorating the centenary of Puvis's birth, "I insist . . . on the fact that [Puvis] is a modern painter. He did not archaize, he did not repeat; he is not an end, he is a beginning . . . in my time he passed for a revolutionary."[1] Edouard Vuillard, Denis's school-mate at the Lycée Condorcet, whose family came from the same village as Puvis's and who noted the fact when asserting his enormous respect for Puvis's art, early responded to it. Both his pale, matte colour tonalities and the flat, processional disposition of figures in his compositions show his basic indebtedness to the older man. Throughout his lifetime, he re-turned time and again to study Puvis's paintings and in 1926 an interview with Puvis's nephew was arranged so that Vuillard could record some of his feelings about Puvis which he was concerned should be conserved for posterity.

> I was received by the artist's mother. . . . we talked of the terraced villages of Haute-Bresse . . . "I lived in Cuiseaux!" she said, "I knew your family well; my son's admiration for Puvis de Chavannes dates from a long time ago; at the Lycée Condorcet in Paris he formed a friendship with Xavier Roussel and the spontaneity of this affection can be traced to the happy surprise which the two children and future artists felt at the discovery that they shared the same admiration for the great Puvis . . ." And here is what Edouard Vuillard said to me: "The slightest gesture of Manet or Renoir have—and quite rightly—been carefully noted and described. There is nothing of the sort as far as your uncle is concerned. Since his death, noth-ing has really been able to help us to delve deeper into his way of thinking. Now I consider him, and I am not the only one, as one of the greatest in-tellects of his time.
>
> "*La Revue de Paris* published in 1910 two admirable letters of his. But there must certainly be others which should absolutely be made known, as well as his pencil and pen drawings for the decoration of Amiens, Rouen, Lyons, Paris, Marseilles, Boston: these are marvellous and substantial sources . . .
>
> "Puvis de Chavannes was passionately interested in all expressions of art; at Cézanne's first exhibition at Vollard's he was the most attentive of visitors. For his ambition was also to renew the art of painting and one could say that he achieved it. For example, has he not dealt with all the subjects which had previously attracted Chassériau? But what a breath of inspiration, very much his own, has enlivened them!
>
> "As with all men of genius, Puvis de Chavannes was in advance of his time. The researches into stylization and expressive synthesis which char-acterize the painting of today, are clearly noticeable in his art.
>
> "When he started out, he was prey to very contradictory tendencies. How did he know to choose between so many influences, free his powerful personality, discipline his extraordinary imagination which sometimes bordered on extravagance? That is what would be interesting and ex-tremely useful to reveal and demonstrate.
>
> "His compositions often spring from an idea still cloudy and obscure: look at the lack of precision in his first sketches. Then his mind sets to work and instead of diminishing the evident charm of the piece, as happens with so many others, on the contrary he enlivens it and adds to the freshness of the initial impression. Puvis de Chavannes, although an illustrious figure,

1. Maurice Denis, "Puvis de Chavannes," *La Revue Hebdomadaire*, December 1924, no. 49, p. 10.

16

remains in twilight; a thorough study is imperative in order to shed full
light upon him . . . and to teach us a great deal."[1]

Puvis was not a dreamer in an ivory tower as he has been pictured by many hostile but
misinformed critics. A man of the world, open when it came to matters of art—but not in
politics—curious and persistently searching, and above all an artist interested in seeking in
nature—not books—the sources of his visual ideas. He gave instruction at several private
studios in Paris where young students came to learn art and also in his own studio.[2] His attitude toward nature and drawing is revealed to some extent in this story related by the
American illustrator Henry McCarter (1864-1942) who came to Paris in 1887 at the age of
twenty-three. He was a year too young to enter the *Ecole des Beaux-Arts* and so he enrolled in
a small school where "Léon Bonnat and Puvis de Chavannes were the masters." There was
a class of fifty and ". . . the masters came irregularly." Nevertheless, they invited the students to call at their homes and McCarter related to his biographer: "These men were most
courteous and intimate—often they would talk to you about your own work . . . Puvis de
Chavannes, who was kind to his students—Puvis said, 'Go to the country, get a fisherman
and all his family to pose—draw one after the other, sit close to them when you draw, close
enough to touch them, your eyes will see round them—but draw! draw! draw! all the
time!"[3] Some insight as to why Puvis did not have an even wider following among the
young is provided by Maillol: "Puvis de Chavannes had been refused as a professor, this
man of genius blackballed at the age of 60! They said he didn't know how to draw. Some
like Forain thought the *Beaux-Arts* could have been saved with Puvis at its head."[4] "I received no counsel, I was forced to find it myself in the work of great artists and that is why I
asked advice from Puvis . . ."[5]

While Puvis may not have approved of all the developments being formulated by the
younger artists, he was nonetheless curious and receptive since his close observation of
nature was allied to their own. He himself had said, "Impressionism and what came immediately after have shed light on the studio and cleansed the palette before work begins."[6] In
the late seventies or early eighties Seurat visited Puvis's studio and observed his working
methods firsthand. Aman-Jean's son has written:

> Puvis de Chavannes was their [Seurat's and Aman-Jean's] real lord and
> master. He welcomed the two young people with kindness, brought out
> their talent, adopted them. Thereafter, they came to square off the
> sketches of the *Sacred Grove*, enlarged the studies of allegorical figures,
> watched the master at the top of his ladder painting the periwinkle-blue
> sky of the decoration, the foot of which is rolled up, all the while talking to
> them of Greece and of art. Spiritually and plastically, one can affirm that
> Puvis influenced his two pupils.[7]

Seurat's studies, both in oils and in his charcoal drawings for the large compositions such as
Une Baignade, Asnières, 1883-84 (see fig. 5, p. 103) and *La Grande Jatte*[8] of 1884-86 (see cat. no.
47), correspond very closely to Puvis's customary procedure of making numerous preparatory studies for each phase of his compositions, large or small.[9] From the time they were cre-

1. Vuillard, *Entretien,* pp. 87-90. It might also be pointed out that Vuillard kept a daily journal for fifty years (*c.* 1890-1940) which
   will not become available for study until 1990. We may surmise, however, that there is considerable additional material on Vuillard's feelings about Puvis.

2. See Paul Baudouin, "Souvenirs sur Puvis de Chavannes," *Gazette des Beaux-Arts,* May, 1935, pp. 312-313.

3. Quoted in R. Sturgis Ingersoll, *Henry McCarter,* Cambridge: The Riverside Press, 1944, pp. 24 and 26. McCarter also worked as
   an assistant to Toulouse-Lautrec and was known at that time as a pupil of Puvis de Chavannes.

4. Cladel, *op. cit.,* pp. 34-35.

5. *Ibid.,* p. 40.

6. Quoted by Chassé, *op. cit.,* p. 43.

7. François Aman-Jean, "Souvenir d'Aman-Jean," Paris: Musée des Arts Décoratifs, 1970, p. 18.

8. *Un Dimanche d'été à l'Ile de la Grande Jatte* (Art Institute of Chicago).

9. See Baudouin, *op.cit.,* p. 300.

ated, Seurat's compositions have been associated by informed critics with Puvis. For example, Félix Fénéon, friend of Seurat and the critic who reflected closely the artist's attitude toward his own work, wrote in 1886 of *La Grande Jatte*:

> The subject: through a sultry sky, at four o'clock, the island boats casting off from the side, the movement of a casual Sunday crowd enjoying the fresh air among the trees; and these forty or so persons are invested with a hieratic and summary style, treated strictly from the back or the front or in profile, sitting at right angles, stretched out horizontally, rigidly upright: like a modernized Puvis.[1]

Another contemporary critic, Paul Alexis, had described *Une Baignade, Asnières* in 1884 in the following terms: "*Une Baignade* by M. Seurat . . . is a fake Puvis de Chavannes. But it is painted with so much conviction that it appears almost touching and I don't quite dare poke fun at it."[2]

Alexis's comments were not made with hostile intent and he perceived the connection between Seurat's painting and its primary immediate source, *Pleasant Land* (cat. no. 23) of 1882 by Puvis.[3] Aman-Jean himself wrote in 1890:

> Among the painters who apply their art to the trees and the sky, none other besides him [Puvis] has given this impression of serenity which emanates from the fresh air and the countryside; our modern school owes him a feeling for nature which up until now it has only caught a glimpse of. Everyone works outdoors or by means of studying—they look to him and remember.[4]

Perhaps the most telling and authentic evidence not only of Seurat's interest in Puvis and Puvis's influence on Seurat, but also of how Puvis was looked upon at the time of his one-man exhibition at Durand-Ruel in late 1887, is Gustave Kahn's review of that exhibition which employs the show as a point of departure for a discussion of Seurat.[5] Kahn, the editor-in-chief of *La Revue Indépendante,* friend of Seurat and staunch supporter of neo-impressionism wrote:

> At present neo-impressionism is closely examining colour variation, noting the play of localized colour and searching, in a synthesis of the paintings' lines, for a complete hieratism.
>
> Are these not the very words which best characterize the essence of M. Puvis de Chavannes: hieratism, purity of tones, clarity, harmony provided through noble and lasting lines. One of the young neo-impressionist innovators defined his visions of art to me in this way, "The Panatheneic frieze of Phidias was a procession—I want to make modern compositions move like these friezes, and in their essentials, place them on canvases arranged in harmonized colours, through the direction of the lines, the line and colour set out one for the other."
>
> The differences between these principles and those which we can deduce from the works of M. Puvis de Chavannes are a result of the fact that M. Puvis de Chavannes in no way restricts himself to contemporary life.[6]

1. *Les Impressionistes en 1886,* Paris: Publications de la Vogue, Léon Vanier Editeur, 1886, p. 26.

2. Trublot (Paul Alexis), "A minuit, les indépendants," *Le Cri du Peuple,* May 17, 1884 (translation adapted from John Rewald, *The History of Impressionism,* fourth rev. ed., New York: The Museum of Modern Art, 1973, p. 508).

3. Alexis, friend of Zola and Cézanne, remained close to Seurat since the artist made a drawing of him in 1888 and dedicated it to the writer (de Hauke II, no. 691). Nearly all later critics have observed the relationships of these paintings to Seurat (Goldwater, Soby, Shapiro, Homer and Herbert, see pp. 100-104).

4. "Puvis de Chavannes," *L'Art dans les Deux Mondes,* no. 2, 29 November, 1890 Paris and New York: p.11. See also Baudouin, *op.cit.,* p. 298 and Seurat's charcoal drawing of Aman-Jean, *c.* 1883, Metropolitan Museum of Art, de Hauke II, no. 588.

5. "Exposition Puvis de Chavannes," *La Revue Indépendante,* VI, no. 15, January, 1888, pp. 142-146.

6. *Ibid.,* p. 142.

Kahn then further underscores his linkage of Puvis to the younger contemporaries by closing his review, "The exhibition is far from complete [because the murals were impossible to include], it cannot be otherwise but every scholar and artist knows the work, it is a precious memento."[1]

That Seurat valued Puvis's opinion is documented in this rather poignant incident related by the artist's friend Charles Angrand.[2] In March 1891, less than two weeks before his death, Seurat was in the galleries at the *Salon des Indépendants* together with Angrand when Puvis entered the room studying the pictures intently and looking at some sketches by Maurice Denis. Believing Puvis would look at his *Cirque*, on exhibition though incomplete, hanging nearby, Seurat remarked to Angrand that Puvis would find fault in the drawing of the horse. But Puvis passed Seurat's paintings by without a glance and the younger man was deeply pained.[3]

Kahn's judgement was not a temporary one. He himself attended the banquet in honour of Puvis in 1895 and had contributed a poem to the *Album des Poètes*[4] and he subsequently discussed Puvis in the context of Seurat's work in two later books.[5] In the first of these he reinforced the remark in the above mentioned review that everyone in the field of art knew Puvis's work by saying, "A sympathetic admiration for Puvis was the rule among the great impressionists."[6] He continued:

> The new torchbearers Seurat, Signac, respected this. Seurat in fact said, on the subject of Puvis's pictorial grandeur, "He achieves it through the brightness of the studio." An allusion to a pictorial construction term. No one is faultless. Seurat did not press the point. The grouping of Puvis's figures, moreover, could not help but please him. All of impressionism admitted and praised it. Other groups also. Puvis was the one great painter on whom we were most unanimous. Integrity, noble ambitions, a new and delicate artistic harmony! He was not challenged. . . . Puvis was eternal. Those who disparaged him died, enthusiasts were born. Puvis became incontestable, national. There were no more monuments except to him.[7]

As if to stress the point, Kahn repeated time and again how widespread was the respect for Puvis and he put the impressionists at the forefront, other groups and movements being implicitly less significant. Writing when he did, in 1925, the author must have also sensed with Vuillard the lapse of public interest in Puvis and a lack of understanding about certain attitudes of the impressionist and neo-impressionist artists—as if the growing public esteem for these groups was being custom tailored to fit a streamlined and distorted image of the period in which they flourished.

In the eighties others among the younger generation began to take careful note of what Puvis was doing and respond to it. In 1884, Toulouse-Lautrec painted, in jest, but not without extremely careful observation of Puvis's painting itself, his large scale parody of *The Sacred Grove* (see cat. nos. 25 and 45) which he had seen that year at the Salon.[8] At the same

1. *Ibid.*, p. 146.

2. Charles Angrand (1854-1926) was one of the original founders of the *Salon des Indépendants* in 1884.

3. See John Rewald, *Post-Impressionism from van Gogh to Gauguin*, second ed., New York: The Museum of Modern Art, 1962, p. 412. The story is also related in Gustave Coquiot, *Seurat*, Paris: Michel, 1924, pp. 166-167. See also Rewald, "Extraits du Journal inédit de Paul Signac 1894-1895," *Gazette des Beaux-Arts*, Vol. XXXVI. July-September, 1949, pp. 97-128 in which Signac noted on November 27, 1894: "He [Angrand] prefers Puvis's mural decoration, simple and without showiness, to that of Delacroix, more turbulent and full of contrasts."

4. See La Plume, p.57.

5. *Silhouettes Littéraires*, Paris: Editions Montaigne, n.d. (1925), pp. 112-113; *Les Dessins de Georges Seurat*, Paris: Bernheim-Jeune, n.d. (1926).

6. *Silhouettes Littéraires*, p. 112.

7. *Ibid.*, pp. 112-113.

8. Lautrec had studied in Bonnat's studio in 1882, at the same time of Bonnat's commission of *Pleasant Land* from Puvis. Puvis posed for a full length portrait by Bonnat (also in 1882), ill. Vachon, *op. cit.*, frontispiece.

time, Theo van Gogh, who was acquainted with Puvis, wrote to his brother Vincent about the Salon and about Puvis, receiving this reply: "What you write about the Salon is very important. As to what you say about Puvis de Chavannes, I am very glad you see his work thus, and I perfectly agree with your appreciation of his talent . . . I can become quite absorbed in a Puvis de Chavannes . . ."[1] A short time later he added: "I had not seen *anything* in reproduction from the Salon of '84 and now I at least got some idea of a few interesting pictures from the Salon number. For instance, of that composition by Puvis de Chavannes [*The Sacred Grove*]."[2]

That Puvis himself was attentive to experiments in art which were being shown at the *Salon des Indépendants* is revealed by a curious story related by Bryson Burroughs, which occurred in the mid-eighties:

> When I was a young student in Paris I had been given a letter to Puvis and some days later I met him at the Indépendants, looking at each canvas most attentively. There was just then a much-talked-about artist who had a theory: when a cloud fleeting across the sky had the air of a camel, he had to paint a camel; when a branch trailing to the ground gave the impression of a sea serpent, he felt obliged to paint a serpent!
>
> I in my pride at knowing Puvis and being able to talk to him, went up to him and said how ridiculous I found it all, and Puvis replied: "It's the first time I've seen him and I don't yet feel I can take the liberty of criticizing him."[3]

Puvis was accessible to young Frenchmen and foreigners alike and therefore we have no reason to doubt, as others have seen fit to, that Paul Gauguin was acquainted or at least on speaking terms with him. Having been an early collector of impressionist paintings and an exhibitor at the impressionist exhibitions of 1880, 1881 and 1886, as well as at the *Salon du Champ-de-Mars* in 1891, he would have been at ease in approaching the older artist. By the eighties he was paying close attention to Puvis's work; by 1888 he was borrowing or adapting motifs for his own work from the very compositions which had interested Seurat, Toulouse-Lautrec and van Gogh.[4] Gauguin related the following story to André Fontainas: "Puvis de Chavannes, very distressed at reading an unfavourable criticism, said to me one day: 'But what is it they do not understand? The picture—it was his *Poor Fisherman*—is very simple.' I replied, 'To others it will be spoken in parables so that seeing they may not see and hearing they may not understand'."[5] Although we shall discuss this statement and others related to it further (pp. 120-128), it is significant to observe that this incident, which could have taken place as early as 1881 when *The Poor Fisherman* received mixed reviews at the Salon (Huysmans viciously attacked the painting and Puvis)[6] or in 1887 when it was shown at Durand-Ruel and bought by the Musée du Luxembourg, reveals the broadly based respect for Puvis's work which no later than the early eighties was virtually universal among the younger generation. Puvis by then had become a cornerstone of their artistic education. In 1889, at least a year after motifs borrowed directly from Puvis begin to appear in Gauguin's work (see fig. 9, p. 121), Gauguin composed an article, actually a reply to comments made by Huysmans about Puvis which were contained in the book *Certains,* in which Redon's work, though praised, was misinterpreted in that he was considered an illustrator rather than a colourist.[7] Gauguin also admired Redon, whom he had got to know by 1886,

1. Van Gogh, *Letters* II, p. 290, no. 368, from Neunen, May 1 or 2, 1884.
2. *Ibid.,* p. 349, letter no. 394, from Neunen, March, 1885.
3. Quoted in René Gimpel, *Diary of an Art Dealer,* New York: Farrar, Straus and Giroux, 1960, pp. 165-166 (entry June 7, 1921). Gimpel himself admired Puvis's work enormously (see p. 77).
4. *Enfants Luttant,* 1888 (W 273) and *Jeunes Baigneurs Bretons,* 1888 (W 275).
5. *Malingue,* no. CLXXII. August 1899.
6. In *L'Art Moderne,* Paris: G. Charpentier, 1883 (collected articles) see "Le Salon Officiel de 1881" pp. 178-179. Also cited by Goldwater, *op. cit.* p. 39 note 39 and Charles Chassé, *op. cit.,* p.38.
7. *Certains,* Paris: Tress and Stock, 1889; "Du dillettantisme—Puvis de Chavannes" p. 146 and "Le Monstre" pp. 150-154.

and he wrote, "Nature possesses mysterious and infinite depths, a powerful imagination . . . she reveals herself in ever-varied creations. The artist himself is one of her means and, in my opinion, Odilon Redon is one of her elected few for the continuance of this creative process. With him dreams become reality through the credibility which he bestows upon them."[1] But Gauguin, with not only the work but also undoubtedly the above mentioned encounter with Puvis in mind, took on Huysmans and continued in a somewhat aggressive vein: "On the other hand, Puvis de Chavannes does not attract you [Huysmans]; his impulsive movements do not attract. Simplicity, nobility are out of favour. What do you want, eminent art critic, these people will one day be very much in favour. If not on our planet, on another one more favourable to beautiful things . . ."[2] Coupled with the story about *The Poor Fisherman* and Gauguin's need to assert his strong convictions about Puvis's importance to Huysmans (Puvis was a public figure who had been made a commander of the Legion of Honour that same year and Gauguin was unknown), who, as we have noted, was one of Puvis's most persistently negative critics, we can conclude that Gauguin was deeply impressed with Puvis's art. His work from this period on repeatedly reflects it. Gauguin's staunch adherence to the aesthetic of "simplicity," "nobility" and offbeat rhythmic organizations ("impulsive movements") underlie all of his mature work. Puvis's drawing—considered by academic critics as crude and insufficiently realistic, i.e. simplified and tending towards the abstract—is exactly what had appealed to Seurat in his hieratic placement of figures in *La Grande Jatte* and one of the aspects which made his art most attractive to Gauguin. Gauguin was to build his compositional designs and graceful linear motifs around what the conventional critics considered awkward in Puvis's work—what Henry James, speaking of the Panthéon compositions, had termed their "simplicity at any price."[3] Gauguin sought not a classicism which had been virtually exhausted by Puvis, but a renewed classicism, with a primitive, not Grecian, cast as inhabitants of a realm as yet unexplored—as Puvis's had been—by other artists. He identified with Puvis because, as is true of all creative artists, he was from the outset able to distinguish his own aims and adjust what it was that he was borrowing from the older man's work. It was never so much a question of specific motifs—although Gauguin continued to repeat or reintroduce quotations from Puvis's work until the end of his life—but rather the framework, the formats, the simplifications and the prototype for incorporating a vast repertoire of figures such as Gauguin was able to find in Tahiti into a comprehensible scheme of presentation.[4]

The exhibition of eighty-four works by Puvis at the Durand-Ruel Gallery in November-December, 1887 was a major event in the art world of Paris. In fact it was the sole one-man exhibition mounted that year, due to the fact that the gallery's financial status had been poor for the preceding several years.[5] This retrospective exposure doubtless spread Puvis's reputation among the informed public and served to consolidate it among his fellow artists. For example, Renoir, who had been in a prolonged crisis over the direction of his work, and who had found reinforcement for his interest in Raphael, Roman frescoes and a more classically oriented, drier tonality, in the work of Puvis, would have been most interested in the show (pp. 105-109). Redon, a long-standing admirer of Puvis, in his journal *c.* 1880 wrote:

1. J. Loize, "Un inédit de Gauguin," *Les Nouvelles Littéraires,* no. 1340, May 7, 1953, p. 1 (written in late 1889).

2. *Ibid.* Gauguin had written several years earlier in a sketchbook he used from 1884-88, "Who are the painters we admire at present? All those who removed the schools and those who drew their science from the personal observation of nature." "Synthetic Notes" (Gauguin's title), *Paul Gauguin: A Sketchbook,* Raymond Coquiot and John Rewald, New York: Hammer Galleries, 1962, p. 64 (facsimile edition).

3. *The Nation,* Vol. XXII, June 29, 1876, p. 415 (unsigned notes).

4. In 1895 Gauguin made a drawing after Puvis's *Hope* which was published together with a poem by Charles Morice in the *Mercure de France* (February, 1895). But Gauguin gave the seated girl distinctly Tahitian features and a slightly "Egyptian" pose. See Richard S. Field, *Paul Gauguin: Monotypes,* Philadelphia Museum of Art, 1973, p. 71, no. 32. See also cat. no. 55, *Still Life with 'Hope' by Puvis de Chavannes.*

5. Lionello Venturi, *Les Archives de l'Impressionisme,* Vol. I, Paris, New York: Durand-Ruel, Editeurs, 1939, p.82 (preface to catalogue by Roger Ballu). See M. Denis quoted *supra,* p. 15.

In the great eras painting was done in fresco; but what of other periods? One can certainly cover the walls with important works; one can also deal with historical painting; in the art of decoration, beautiful things can be attempted; but one will only succeed easily in these elevated genres by treating one's subject in a strictly unpretentious manner, with that spirit of self-sacrifice which knows how to instruct the hand to work in a simplified and concise way. This is what Puvis de Chavannes knows and it is for this reason that, without deviating from his set purpose, he has been able to paint so successfully on stone [sic], a bold and risky task which has been too severely criticized.

One will only fully understand the work of this master by looking at it from his own point of view, which without a doubt is this: model the human figure and the trees and all else as if they were on the tenth or twentieth plane; the key to his work lies there.

Look at an object in the distance and see how the lines become simplified, how the planes are reduced, how the difference in values is scarcely perceptible. The figures have a shade, a light, and the shadow thrown by the body is not visible. On the horizon the mountains will be no more than a ridge, etched sharply against the sky, as in a stage-set.

Puvis de Chavannes is long-sighted through abstraction: he must have reflected a long time before painting and finding his direction, this direction which has been debated and disputed as have all those which reveal an individual intelligence. It was worth it for him, however, to find and follow this path since he has been able to convey to us his unconstrained spirit, depict his dreams and, in a word, create work which will be imitated and will remain: he has found a style.[1]

What better expression could we have than that of Redon, himself searching to find a style, looking for a model on which to support his own long postponed struggle for a painting style which he commenced in the eighties. His transition from the black and white graphic work does not fully occur until the mid or late nineties when his painting in oil and pastels begins in earnest. His interest in Puvis must have manifested itself early in his career since he had accepted in 1870 a commission for a decorative mural of a religious nature and had painted a mural for a chapel in Arras.[2] Moreover, in 1873 his friend Rodolphe Bresdin warned Redon, "Do not consume any more Puvis de Chavannes (violent poison)."[3] Another document is contained in a sketchbook of Redon's,[4] which is datable from this period, 1880, in which there is a sketch after Puvis's *The Prodigal Son* (see fig. 28, p. 160). The show at Durand-Ruel must have been a spur to his future direction. Redon's pale chalky tonalities, his flat almost weightless figures and an ethereal quality which pervades many of his paintings and pastels, especially in the late nineties and after 1900, are substantially derived from his study of Puvis's work.[5] *The Crown* (cat. no. 72), for example, is adapted from the semi-draped figure

1. Redon, *A soi-même*, pp. 151-152, undated entry probably written in the early 1880s. See also entry of May 14, 1888 in which Redon compares Puvis's nudes with those of Giorgione and Correggio.

2. Destroyed in World War I. See *Lettres de Gauguin, Gide, Huysmans, Jammes, Mallarmé, Verhaeren à Odilon Redon*, ed. Ari Redon and Rosaline Bacou, Paris: José Corti, 1960, pp. 58-61. Redon had tried architecture in his early days.

3. *Ibid.* Letter dated February 25, 1873.

4. Art Institute of Chicago, dedicated to René Philippon in 1895 and which contains names of early Italian painters he planned to study on trip to London (see Klaus Berger, *Odilon Redon: Fantasy and Color*, New York, Toronto and London:McGraw Hill Book Company, 1965, p. 86). The existence of this drawing was kindly brought to my attention by Jacques Foucart. Redon's lithographs also reveal influences of Puvis, e.g. *He Raises the Bronze Urn*, 1888; *Beneath her long hair . . . I thought I recognized Ammonaria*, 1889 and *Mystical Conversation*, 1892.

5. E.g. *Pandora c.* 1910-12 (Chester Dale Collection, National Gallery of Art, Washington D.C.) whose pale blue background, lilac textures, drawing in general, weightlessness and ethereality of figure all stem from Puvis (see Redon, *A soi-même*, May 1910, cited herein p. 160).

in the upper background of Puvis's *Dramatic Poetry* in the Boston Public Library (fig. 35, p. 172).

Among the foreign artists who in his lifetime were significantly influenced by his work, (van Gogh's mature work belonging to the French tradition), Ferdinand Hodler (1853-1918) presents perhaps the most dramatic example of Puvis's impact outside of all the types of painting we have been discussing. Hodler was undoubtedly familiar with Puvis's work from photographs and careful firsthand descriptions by the mid-eighties. In 1889 he sent a painting, *Procession of Wrestlers* to the Paris World's Fair where it is claimed by one of Hodler's biographers that Puvis admired it.[1] Two years later Hodler's composition, *Night*, of 1890 was entered in the *Salon du Champ-de-Mars* (May-July, 1891) where Puvis remarked that it was one of the best pictures in the show.[2] Hodler came to Paris and was made a member of the *Société nationale des beaux-arts* of which Puvis was President and he continued to exhibit there through 1895. In his work and in his writings, Hodler makes clear his debt to Puvis; he also paid homage to him on the occasion of the 1895 banquet even though he was unable to attend. Critics linked him with Puvis throughout his life and in what was perhaps his most important statement on his philosophy of art Hodler wrote:

> The deeper we penetrate into the spirit of nature, the more completely we can express her; the better our means of expression, the better we can delineate her image. . . . To aim at unity, at a strong and powerful unity, is to stress one thing above all others, to express it strongly, whether it is a graceful or a powerful subject. But that is not all. The present period proves it. There is a general mad rush toward diversity, except a few who, like Puvis de Chavannes, introduce this harmonious note.[3]

Although other painters in the nineteenth century had utilized the frieze-like disposition of figures across a surface—Courbet, Daumier and Monticelli, for example, employed it from time to time—no one employed the long horizontal formats as conspicuously as a container for their aesthetic forms as did Puvis de Chavannes. From the 1860s in his murals for Amiens, *Ave Picardia Nutrix*, and again in 1879-82 in *Ludus Pro Patria*, Puvis's paintings repeatedly took on the frieze format as a basic geometric dimension for the complex processions and interlocking groups of figures in broad (but not deep) simplified landscapes which characterize his most typical work. *The Childhood of Saint Genevieve* (fig. 8, p.121) of 1876, *The Sacred Grove* (cat. no. 25) of 1884, the *Allegory of the Sorbonne* of 1889, *Inter Artes et Naturam* (cat. no. 30) of 1890 and *The Muses of Inspiration* of 1895, in addition to the actual friezes of saints in the Panthéon of 1877, all indelibly—and publicly—identified the artist's work with the long horizontal layout. This concept was further disseminated in the numerous reductions of these compositions which Puvis painted and which were exhibited repeatedly by Durand-Ruel.[4] A significant part of his influence was determined by how artists identified with his distinctive formats which were a striking part of the appealing novelty to which they were attracted in his art. Without analyzing what this meant for Puvis, or noting the various ancient and renaissance sources of the frieze which made it convenient for him to associate his themes with classical formats, we may note that beginning in the 1880s with Seurat[5]— discounting Lautrec's parody—and accelerating in the 1890s with van Gogh,[6]

1. See Ewald Bender, *Die Kunst Ferdinand Hodlers,* Zurich: Rascher et Cie., 1923, p. 19. The picture won an honourable mention.

2. *Ibid.,* p. 21 (and note 2).

3. *The Mission of the Artist,* lecture written in late 1896 and early 1897, translated and annotated in Selz, *Hodler,* pp. 119-125.

4. Among reductions in this format are *Ludus Pro Patria* (Metropolitan Museum of Art), Sterling and Salinger, p. 288; *Allegory of the Sorbonne* (Metropolitan Museum of Art), *ibid.,* pp. 229-230; *Inter Artes et Naturam* (Metropolitan Museum of Art) cat. no. 30; added to these are, of course, the numerous preparatory drawings and oil sketches.

5. *Une Baignade, Asnières,* (fig. 5, p. 103) and *La Grande Jatte.*

6. See J.-B. de la Faille, *The Works of Vincent van Gogh: His Paintings and Drawings,* Amsterdam: Meulenhoff International, 1970, nos. F770, F771, F773, F775, F776, F777, F778, F779, F793, F809, F811, F816, F819. (See also cat. no. 50.)

Maurice Denis,[1] Vuillard,[2] Roussel,[3] Gauguin,[4] Hodler[5] and later in America, Arthur B. Davies[6] and Maurice Prendergast,[7] numerous artists employed the format as well as other pictorial devices, colour, shallow space, matte tonality, borrowed directly from Puvis. Puvis de Chavannes had led the way and forged the contemporary means of conceiving painting as a fundamentally decorative art, as had the fresco painters of old. He was, in his words, "simply content to decorate the wall." This shift of format by so many of the artists of the nineties was as marked a divergence from the practice of the impressionists as the other departures—in subject content, colour and light. The impressionists rarely employed the long horizontal format. Degas used it on occasion; Monet much later in life and solely for purposes—decorative purposes one might add—which were consistent with expanding those ideas advanced in his earlier, standard-size canvases. The scheme lends itself to decoration; the long walls in Lyons, Amiens, Rouen and Paris required paintings which conformed to the architecture.[8] The younger men, interested in his easel paintings, could have ignored these formats altogether and still could have borrowed the basic pictorial essentials from Puvis. But they conceived of decorating a wall as essential and decorative art as something desirable and not beneath their dignity. Charles Morice wrote in 1891: "At the present time Puvis de Chavannes, Carrière, Renoir, Redon, Degas, Gustave Moreau and Gauguin are, in painting, directing the young artists."[9] Although he surely did not speak for all the young artists of the period, Jan Verkade (1868-1946), a young Dutch follower of Gauguin and member of the Nabi group wrote in his memoirs in 1926:

> Towards the beginning of 1890, a war cry resounded from one studio to the next: "No more superfluous pictures! Down with useless furniture! Painting must not encroach upon the freedom which isolates it from the other arts. The work of the artist begins where the architect considers his as completed. Walls, walls to be decorated! Down with perspective! The wall must remain a surface, and must not be broached by the representation of infinite horizons. There are no pictures, there are only decorations!"[10]

Puvis had a container for his overtly decorative ideas and the younger men felt comfortable with it and found it easily adaptable to a variety of uses. This sentiment was shared by others, including such as Vuillard and Bonnard who were painting posters and stage scenery, as well as Maurice Denis, Paul Sérusier and K.-X. Roussel for whom mural painting came to occupy a significant part of their later output. Vincent van Gogh, judging from the frequent and wholly laudatory references to the artist in his letters, admired the older man with increasing insight as his career developed. Van Gogh never painted a large mural but the long horizontal format of thirteen of his ultimate series of landscapes was strongly tied to Puvis's *Inter Artes et Naturam* (cat. no. 30), the definitive version of which he saw and studied closely at the *Salon du Champ-de-Mars* in May, 1890, two months before he ended his life (see

1. For example, *La Couronne de fiançailles, Le Mariage, Broderie devant la mer, La Naissance* and *L'Enfance ou la Cueillette des pommes* (cat. no. 57) all stemming directly from Puvis. See also *April* (cat. no. 56).

2. For example, the six decorative panels for Paul Desmarais painted in 1892, measuring 189 x 393 ¾ inches each (485 x 1170 cm.) See *Vuillard/Roussel*, pp. 155-157, nos. 33-37. See also *The Dressmaker's Shop, c.* 1893, 18¼ x 45½ inches (fig. 16, p. 136).

3. See cat. nos. 61 and 62.

4. *Where do we come from? What are we? Where are we going?* Museum of Fine Arts, Boston (fig. 13, p. 124) and *Faa Iheihe*, Tate Gallery, London (fig. 14, p. 125).

5. For example, *Night*, Kunstmuseum, Bern (fig. 20, p. 146) of 1890, *The Disillusioned*, Kunstmuseum, Bern (fig. 21, p. 147) of 1892 and *Day II* (Kunsthaus, Zurich) of 1904-1906, among others.

6. See cat. no. 86.

7. For example, *Promenade* (Detroit Institute of Arts) of 1914-1915 and *Figures at the Beach* (The Barnes Foundation) of *c.*1918.

8. *L'Eté* (Musée de Chartres) and the paintings for Marseilles and the Hôtel de Ville, while not friezes, are emphatically horizontal.

9. "Gauguin", *Les Hommes d'Aujourd'hui*, no. 440, 1891 (quoted in Rewald, *Post-Impressionism, op. cit.*, p. 498).

10. Dom Willibrord Verkade, O.S.B., *Le Tourment de Dieu: Etapes d'un Moine Peintre*, Paris: Librairie de l'art Catholique, n.d. (1926) p. 94.

cat. nos. 49 and 50). We shall review his extensive comments on his reaction to Puvis at the 1890 Salon and the impact it began to have on his painting at Auvers in June-July of that year (pp. 110-114). Both Gauguin's *Where do we come from? What are we? Where are we going?* of 1897 (fig. 13, p. 124) and *Faa Iheihe* of 1898 (fig. 14, p. 125) in addition to the numerous motifs he adapted from the sculpture relief friezes of the Javanese temple at Borobudur, all demonstrate his deep interest in pursuing the possibilities of the long format (see pp. 125-128), and the two paintings have been consistently linked to Puvis by critics—as they were by Gauguin himself.[1]

By the time Puvis had reached his sixty-fifth year in 1889, completed the *Allégorie des lettres, des sciences et des arts* for the Sorbonne and been made a Commander of the Legion of Honour and resigned from the official Salon to found the *Société nationale des beaux-arts*, he had reached that stage in his career where commissions flowed in, homage was paid on all sides and the younger generation of painters, sculptors, writers, poets and critics considered him to be the preeminent artist of the day. Hence, in the last decade of his life, with struggles for acceptance behind him, he undertook four major mural decoration projects—Rouen, Boston, Hôtel de Ville, Paris and the completion of the Panthéon cycle on the life of Saint Genevieve—as well as involving himself deeply in the affairs of the *Salon du Champ-de-Mars*, participating in numerous foreign exhibitions, working on easel paintings and collaborating with his first serious biographer, Marius Vachon, the first edition of whose study of the artist appeared in 1895. Short of being canonized, there was nothing remaining for Puvis but to work.

Even before Puvis's death, just short of his seventy-fourth birthday, a flood of articles, interviews and critiques began to appear in French, English and American journals. After 1898, following his death, a number of monographs, articles, selections from his letters, a book devoted to his caricatures and more reminiscences appeared. Paintings and drawings were sold in Germany, England, Russia and most of all in the United States, where the Boston Public Library murals as well as firsthand accounts of his life and art were published.[2]

1. See Robert Goldwater, *Paul Gauguin*, New York: Abrams n.d. (1957) p. 150.
2. See John La Farge, "Puvis de Chavannes", *op.cit.*, pp. 672-684; Kenyon Cox, "Puvis de Chavannes", *op.cit.*, February 1896, pp. 558-569; Kenyon Cox, *Old Masters and New: Essays in Art Criticism*, New York: 1905, pp. 143, 210-226; and Ernest F. Fenollosa, *Mural Painting in the Boston Public Library*, Boston: Curtis and Co., 1896. J. Alden Weir (1852-1919) helped persuade Puvis on behalf of McKim, Mead and White to undertake the Boston Public Library commission (see Dorothy Weir Young, *The Life and Letters of J. Alden Weir*, New Haven: Yale University Press, 1960, pp. 170-171). He was also agent for Alfred A. Pope, one of the earliest American buyers of Puvis and purchased a Degas for Pope's collection in early 1883.

Puvis de Chavannes was naturally admired by those critics who had either direct access to him before his death in October, 1898 or who were in contact with members of the younger generation of artists who were influenced by Puvis and made no secret of it. As we have seen, a number of the artists themselves published writings in which they clearly expressed their respect for Puvis's art.[1]

Leo Stein (1872-1947), collector and scholar, perceived the importance of the two pioneers of twentieth century art—Matisse and Picasso—as early as 1905. His critical evaluations had immense impact upon collectors and connoisseurs whose taste was formed prior to World War I.[2] Leo wrote to Mabel Weeks around the end of 1904 or early 1905:

> ...If this proves to be a treatise ... the responsibility will lie with the obligation that I have been under ever since the Autumn Salon [1904] of expounding L'Art Moderne (you will observe that this is not the same thing as L'Art Nouveau). The men whose pictures we have bought—Renoir, Cézanne, Gauguin, Maurice Denis—and others whose pictures we have not bought but would like to—Manet, Degas, Vuillard, Bonnard, van Gogh for example—all belong. To make the subject clear requires a discussion of the qualities of the men of '70 of whom the Big Four and Puvis de Chavannes are the great men and the inspirers in the main of the vital art of today. The Big Four are Manet, Renoir, Degas and Cézanne. . . .
>
> Renoir, Manet and Cézanne substitute for naturalism the abstraction of the quality of color, and form from the model. . . . Whistler lost it almost completely, substituting for it an artifice so brilliant in its accomplishment as almost to succeed in disguising the loss.
>
> The loss of dramatic quality was a necessary consequence of this devotion to the model and we have an art that is full of ideas and personality, but which does not attempt to render ideas of personality. This was its great limitation. This other side was ministered to most adequately among contemporaries by Puvis de Chavannes, Gustave Moreau and Fantin-Latour. . . .
>
> The influence of all these people, except perhaps Fantin, has been enormous. Practically every young man who counts artistically has undergone it in some place and in all sorts of combinations. . . . Maurice Denis derives from Degas, Puvis de Chavannes and Cézanne. His decorative feeling is of the finest. . . . He has an almost Fra Angelico daintiness yet firmness of religious feeling with an amplitude of conception that makes him a worthy follower of Puvis and while revelling in the grays and pale tones of the latter he has yet at command a palette of ringing intensity. . . . The general drift of this letter will be to indicate what I think of modern art and to repeat that it vitally goes marching on.[3]

From the foregoing we can see that between the pioneer days of the early part of this century—for Leo Stein's assessment of the "Big Four" is as valid now as it was then—and

1. See Maurice Denis, *Théories, 1890-1910, du symbolisme et de Gauguin vers un nouvel ordre classique*, Paris 1912. Emile Bernard, "Puvis de Chavannes," *L'Occident* IV, no. 25, December 1903, pp. 273-280. Bernard indicates that he visited Puvis prior to 1893 when he left France for Italy and ten years in Egypt. Like Denis, Bernard's prime interest was Cézanne with whom he corresponded and whom he visited in Aix in 1904.

2. Leo and his sister Gertrude were responsible for the formation of the Miss Etta and Dr. Claribel Cone Collection; Leo's ideas had considerable influence on Dr. Albert C. Barnes and many of the paintings collected by him ultimately entered The Barnes Foundation.

3. Leo Stein, *Journey Into the Self, being the letters, papers & journals of Leo Stein*, ed. by Edmund Fuller, New York: Crown Publishers, 1950, pp. 15-18, undated letter (end of 1904 or early 1905). Stein mentions in the letter that Gauguin died two years earlier and refers to the special Toulouse-Lautrec exhibition at the (1904) *Salon d'Automne*. Leo had been at Harvard when Puvis's murals were installed in the Boston Public Library (1896), thus he knew Puvis's work prior to living in France and assumed that his correspondent, who was with Gertrude at Radcliffe, did also.

the public consciousness of today, a great deal has been lost sight of in the popular conception of the ancestry of modern art.

So, it is not insignificant that when Leo Stein began to purchase the major works of Picasso's "Blue," "Harlequin" and "Rose" periods for his and his sister Gertrude's collection, among the first paintings acquired were *Girl with a Basket of Flowers* [1] (fig. 38, p. 175), *Woman with a Fan*,[2] *Young Acrobat on a Ball*[3] (fig. 34, p. 172) and *Boy Leading a Horse*,[4] all of 1905 and all conspicuously influenced by "the grays and pale tones" of Puvis de Chavannes. With Leo Stein's commentary reflecting the general approbation of Puvis among those seriously concerned with modern art as an introduction, it is no wonder that most of the important early collectors of modern art in America, but not exclusively in America, valued Puvis's work and purchased it together with other works by modern rather than academic contemporaries of his.[5] A.E. Gallatin wrote, "[Puvis de Chavannes's] lofty and severe compositions . . . take the highest rank among the world's masterpieces of mural decoration."[6] One of the first purchases Roger Fry made as Curator for the Metropolitan Museum of Art in 1906 was *The Shepherd's Song* (cat. no. 32) by Puvis. He tried very hard to buy two important paintings which John Quinn later purchased and which were ultimately acquired for the museum from the sale of Quinn's paintings after his death in 1925.[7] Included in the S.I. Shchukin collection in Moscow was a version of *The Poor Fisherman*.[8]

John Quinn was the first among the American collectors of modern art to become seriously interested in Puvis de Chavannes. The first painting acquired by Quinn was *The Beheading of Saint John the Baptist* of 1869[9] which he purchased in 1911 together with seven drawings. As a collector, Quinn always relied heavily on advisors, often of literary as well as visual bent. He was advised by the English painter Augustus John and encouraged by his friend James Gibbons Huneker, observant but often erratic art critic whose main interest lay in music and literature.[10] At the Armory Show[11] in 1913, the purpose of which was to introduce or at least to provide a forum for the introduction of modern art to the American public, Puvis de Chavannes was prominent among the painters exhibited; fifteen of his works were included in the show, the paintings hanging opposite those of Matisse.[12] At the

1. Private Collection (Daix and Boudaille, XIII.8). See Leo Stein, *Appreciation: Painting, Poetry and Prose*, New York:Crown Publishers, 1947, p. 173 for a description of the events surrounding his purchase of this work.

2. Harriman Collection, Washington D.C. (Daix and Boudaille, XIII.14).

3. Pushkin Fine Arts Museum, Moscow (Daix and Boudaille, XII.19).

4. Paley Collection, New York (Daix and Boudaille, XIV.7).

5. The Havemeyers, whose Manets are the foundation of the modern collection of the Metropolitan Museum of Art, owned two pictures by Puvis, including the study for the Sorbonne mural, acquired in 1889 (see Sterling and Salinger, pp. 228-230). We are not including discussion of the numerous paintings already in the collections of Americans such as John G. Johnson, P.A.B. Widener, Henry Walters, the Potter Palmers and others whose collecting interests in the main lay outside modern art. All of them owned important canvases by Puvis de Chavannes well before the turn of the century or shortly thereafter.

6. A.E.G.[allatin], *Whistler, Notes and Footnotes and other Memoranda*, New York and London, 1907, p. 58.

7. See *Letters of Roger Fry*, vol. I, ed. by Denys Sutton, London: Chatto & Windus, 1972, letters no. 181, pp. 257-8 and no. 263, pp. 318-9. See Sterling and Salinger, p. 231.

8. Pushkin Fine Arts Museum, Moscow, dated 1879. See J. Tugenhold, *Apollon*, "S.I. Chtchoukine's Collection of French Painting," no. 1-2, 1914, pp. 5-46, who reproduces *Le Pauvre Pêcheur* and *La Commisération* (pastel). The author also wrote a monograph on Puvis. See also *Mir Iscousstva*, no. 6, vol. I, 1899, 50-52 and 91-106, (three paintings exhibited in St. Petersburg at that time—*The River, Cider* and *Winter*); *Mir Iscousstva*, St. Petersburg, vol. 9, 1903, pp. 130-136, "From Poussin to Maurice Denis," J. Meier-Graefe (in Russian); *L'Exposition Centennale de l'Art Français*, 1912, *The River, Cider* and *Epic Poetry*.

9. Collection Barber Institute of Fine Arts, University of Birmingham.

10. Huneker was the preeminent music critic of his day. He began to write an art column for the New York *Sun* in October 1906 and due to his extensive travel in Europe in order to keep up with the concert and opera performances, he was often well informed on continental art events and reported on these regularly in his columns. Huneker had been to the 1904 *Salon d'Automne* and had seen Durand-Ruel's first American exhibition of impressionists in 1886.

11. International Exhibition of Modern Art, New York, February 17—March 15; Art Institute of Chicago, March 24—April 15; and Copley Hall, Boston, April 28—May 18, 1913.

12. Cat. nos. 483, 556-568 inclusive and 1057. This last, entitled in the Armory Show catalogue "Decorative Panel" belonging to Martin A. Ryerson of Chicago, is probably *L'Automne, c.* 1883 (see Pierre Godet, "Puvis de Chavannes et la Peinture d'Aujourd'hui", *L'Art Décoratif*, XXVII, 1912, p. 47.)

first meeting of the Association of American Painters and Sculptors in December, 1911, J. Alden Weir was appointed President. This was the official group that conceived and organized the Armory Show. Although Weir was succeeded almost immediately by Arthur B. Davies, it may be noted that it was Weir who twenty years earlier had convinced Puvis to undertake the Boston Public Library commission. Weir studied in Paris from 1873 to 1877 at the time of the work on the Panthéon murals. Organizers such as Arthur B. Davies held Puvis in high esteem (pp. 193-194) and Quinn himself was a major lender, contributing two paintings, *The Beheading of Saint John the Baptist* and *Nude* (cat. no. 10) and eleven drawings in addition to his many loans of other artists. While the exhibition was still in New York, Quinn on March 2, 1913 acquired *The River* and *Cider* which Roger Fry had tried earlier to buy. Huneker wrote Quinn from Berlin: "I congratulate you on the various Puvises. The one man except Vermeer who will be as scarce in the future as honesty among politicians."[1] Huneker had been the first American critic to publish an article on Cézanne (in 1906) and although, as we have pointed out, he was erratic, he was deeply interested in contemporary developments in art. Quinn who, in addition to lending, was an important organizing force and financial backer of the Armory Show, published an article entitled "Modern Art from a Layman's Point of View" in which he stated:

> The Luxembourg paid 71,500 francs for a painting by Puvis de Chavannes [Rouart Sale, December 1912] that I could perhaps have secured for 500 francs twenty years ago. There were two great artists [Puvis and Degas] whose best work, while they were producing work, could have been bought for a few hundred francs and yet those officials were as blind as bats to the genius of these two great men. The Luxembourg had, I believe, but one example of Puvis de Chavannes [*The Poor Fisherman*, purchased in 1887]; The Louvre, I think, has none. To make up for their official neglect, the Louvre bid up to over $90,000 for a single painting by Degas and lost it, and the Luxembourg succeeded in getting only one painting by the great de Chavannes.[2]

Barely two years later, in January 1915, Quinn, at the request of Bryson Burroughs, placed his three major paintings by Puvis on indefinite loan to the Metropolitan Museum of Art where they remained until his death nine years later.[3] Around this nucleus, Burroughs arranged a small exhibition which included *The Shepherd's Song* (cat. no. 32), *Sleep*,[4] *The Balloon* and *The Carrier Pigeon*[5] (cat. nos. 12 and 13) and *Child Carrying Apples*,[6] a total of eight paintings. In his lecture on Puvis, delivered to art students in front of the group of paintings he had gathered for the exhibition, Burroughs said:

> The lineage of Puvis is clearer than most. His style is the outcome of the consistent and orderly line of French tradition through Chassériau, Ingres and David back to Poussin, but vivified and enlivened in his case by the mixture of the romantic element which came in the work of Delacroix . . . Puvis evolves his works from the standpoint of imagination and then asks from nature continual corroboration and advice . . .

1. March 13, 1913; see *Letters of James Gibbons Huneker*, ed. by Josephine Huneker, New York: Charles Scribner's Sons, 1922, p. 154.

2. *Art and Decoration*, no. 5, Special Exhibition Number, March 1913, pp. 155-158, 176; Degas' *Dancers Practising at the Barre* was purchased by Mrs. Havemeyer at the Rouart Sale for 478,000 francs ($95,700) and is now in the Metropolitan Museum of Art; *Hope* by Puvis was purchased from the same sale and is now in the Louvre. Ironically, in an act of extraordinary generosity—or sympathy—Quinn bequeathed Seurat's *Cirque* to the Louvre upon his death, the very painting that Puvis had passed by at the Independents Salon of 1891 (see p. 19).

3. See Bryson Burroughs, "A Recent Loan of Paintings," *Bulletin of The Metropolitan Museum of Art*, vol. X. no. 4, April 1915, pp. 75-76.

4. Borrowed from Theodore M. Davis, donated that year by the owner (see Sterling and Salinger, pp. 227-228).

5. Burroughs was very much excited by his rediscovery of these paintings, especially poignant because of the parallel significance between 1870-71 and 1915 in French history.

6. On loan from the Coudert Collection.

A precious part of the legacy that Puvis has bequeathed, namely that, as in the old times, the artist is free to create his subject as well as his work. ... To Gauguin and the painters of his group, to Maurice Denis and the others who broke away from the thraldom of impressionism, he was the active inspiration.[1]

Burroughs could see Puvis as a connecting link as well as valuing his work in and of itself. His fixing of the artist in his rightful historic place in the development of the French tradition is precisely the factor which has been neglected by the mainstream of critical thought in relation to modern art, since the time of his talk.

Huneker, also in 1915, revised a piece on Puvis written five years earlier, a typically scatter-shot approach, well researched, in some senses wide of the mark but containing a few *aperçus*, and while he praised Puvis's art he also maintained a certain degree of detachment from all-out approbation.

Although he has been dead since October 24, 1898, critical battles are still fought over the artistic merits of Puvis de Chavannes. Whether you agree with Huysmans and call this mural painter a pasticheur of the Italian Primitives, or else the greatest artist in decoration since Paolo Veronese, depends much on your critical temperament. ... Marius Vachon, despite his excessive admiration for Puvis has rendered a service to his memory in his study, because he has shown us the real, not the legendary man. ... Some idealists were disappointed to find Puvis to be a sane, healthy, solidly built man, a bon vivant in the best sense of the phrase, without a suggestion of the morbid, vapouring pontiff or haughty Olympian ... but a fighter for his ideas; and those ideas have shown not only French artists, but the entire world, the path back to true mural tradition. It is not an exaggeration to say that Puvis created modern decorative art. ...

New York has at the Metropolitan Museum at least one of his works, and in the collection here of John Quinn, Esq., there is the brilliant masterpiece, *The Beheading of John the Baptist,* and the two large mural decorations, *The River* and *The Vintage* [*Cider*]. ... They are magnificent museum pictures.

... He didn't worry much over antique methods, nor can it be said that his work is an attempt to rehabilitate the Italian Primitives. On the contrary, Puvis is distinctly modern, and that is his chief offence in the eyes of official French art; while the fact that his "modernity" was transposed to decorative purposes, and appeared in so strange a guise, caused the younger men to eye him suspiciously. ... Thus in the estimation of rival camps Puvis fell between two stools. ...

His men and women are not precisely pagan, nor are they biblical. But they reveal traits of both strained through a drastic 'modern' intellect. They are not abstractions. ... There is a spirit of humanity not of decadence. Puvis, like Moreau, did not turn his back to the rising sun. He admired Degas, Manet, Monet. ... The ... landscapes of Puvis are not merely scenic backgrounds, but integral parts of the general decorative web, and they are not conceived in No Man's Land, but selected from the vicinity of Paris. ... He is a master harmonist. He sounds oftener the symphonic than the lyric note. He gains his most moving effects without setting in motion the creaking allegorical machinery of the academy. He shows the simple attitudes of life transfigured without rhetoric. He avoids frigid allegory, yet employs symbols. His tonal attenuations, elliptical and

1. See *Lecture to Art Students*, unpublished manuscript in the Metropolitan Museum of Art, 1915.

syncopated rhythms, his atmosphere of the remote, the mysterious—all these give the spectator the sense of serenity, momentary freedom from the feverishness of everyday life, and suggest the lofty wisdom of the classic poets.[1]

It is not surprising to note that both Quinn and Huneker admired the work of Arthur B. Davies, the primary organizer of the European section of the Armory Show, and Quinn also collected the work of Maurice Prendergast and commissioned from him in 1914-1915 two large mural-size paintings, *The Promenade* and *Picnic*. Both of these artists were significantly influenced by the art of Puvis de Chavannes (see pp. 187-194).[2]

Two of the other major collectors of modern art in America around the time of the first World War were Albert C. Barnes and Duncan Phillips.[3] Not only did their collections centre around French painting of the post-impressionist period—Cézanne, Renoir, Degas, Seurat, Matisse and Picasso—but their respective collections of contemporary American art included Maurice Prendergast, Davies, Lawson, Glackens, among many others. Although all of these collections differed in terms of scale and emphasis on various artists, Puvis de Chavannes was not only included in each, but both Barnes and Phillips made public their views on his art—and their views were influential.

Barnes, in his writings, placed Puvis in a context with Degas, both separate from the impressionists, and he elucidated one of the most essential facets of Puvis's individuality when, in a chapter devoted to "color," he wrote: ". . . there are esthetic effects to which dry color is a positive reënforcement; a painter may use very juicy color, like Monticelli, without thereby becoming an artist of the first rank. . . . if Puvis de Chavannes had emulated Renoir in the use of juicy color, his own distinctive form would have suffered rather than gained."[4] This assertion of the importance of the appropriateness of the specific means to the overall pictorial goal envisaged, is but rarely met with in any of the studies of Puvis's art. Frequently he is reproached for lacking this or that, either flabby in drawing or "feeble" especially in colour, when, as Barnes points out, the crucial determinant of his overall form—the pale, fresco-like atmosphere, the compositional harmonies, the subtle substance of his figures—depend on a particular type of colour-relationship, controlled and executed by a mind that knew exactly what was needed to achieve the desired qualities. Barnes states, "Puvis's work is distinctive in pattern, drawing, quality of color and ability to bring the compositional units into harmonious relations. His feeling for space and his suave, smooth, skilful use of paint have rarely been excelled. . . . the individual units partake of a

1. "Puvis de Chavannes", *Ivory, Apes and Peacocks*, New York: Charles Scribner's Sons, 1915, pp. 193-198. Expanded from an article which appeared in the New York Sunday *Sun*, July 24, 1910. The book is dedicated to John Quinn. Huneker continued to encourage Quinn to buy Puvis. (See Huneker, *Letters, op. cit.*, p. 206, letter to John Quinn, March 26, 1916.) At the time of his death, Quinn owned fifty-one works—paintings, pastels and drawings—by Puvis. See *John Quinn, 1870-1925: Collection of Paintings, Water Colors, Drawings and Sculpture*, Huntington, N.Y.: Pigeon Hill Press, 1926, p. 13.

2. *The Promenade*, 83 ¾ x 134 in. Detroit Institute of Art; and *Picnic*, 77 x 106½ in. Museum of Art, Carnegie Institute. It is possible that these works were commissioned by Quinn to fill some of the space left by the loan of his three large canvases by Puvis to the Metropolitan Museum. On May 18, 1915, Prendergast noted in a sketchbook, now in the collection of the Museum of Fine Arts, Boston, that he had received $500 from Quinn and that in the three preceding months he had received $1000. This would indicate that the commission was given shortly after the paintings by Puvis left his home in January. *The Promenade* was exhibited at the Montross Gallery in April 1915.

3. Dikran G. Kélékian, another early twentieth century collector of modern art, owned an oil study for *Concordia*, 23¾ x 31¼ inches which was loaned to an exhibition, *Paintings by Modern French Masters Representing the Post-Impressionists and their Predecessors*, at The Brooklyn Museum in 1921 (no. 179). Kélékian's collection included, among others, important works by Cézanne and was the first major group of modern paintings to be auctioned in America. At the sale (January, 1922), Lillie Bliss, Duncan Phillips and Dr. Barnes purchased paintings for their collections. See Arsène Alexandre, "The Kélékian Collection," *Illustrated Catalogue of the Notable Collection of Modern French Pictures and a Group of the Works of the Noted American Artist Arthur B. Davies Formed by and Belonging to the Widely Known Antiquarian Dikran Khan Kélékian of Paris and New York*, American Art Galleries, January 30 and 31, 1922, no. 143. The owner bought back *Concordia* at the sale, lending it to various exhibitions including "A Selected Group of Modern Paintings belonging to Dikran Khan Kélékian," American Art Association, Anderson Galleries, Inc., November 6-19, 1938, no. 36 (not a sale catalogue). The painting has since disappeared.

4. *The Art in Painting*, 3rd ed., New York: Harcourt, Brace and Company, 1937, p. 84.

static quality. . . . His large mural decorations are usually well-balanced, fluid compositions with a feeling of a processional flow of one group-unit into another."[1] He discusses the specific character of Puvis's colour noting ". . . the color-ensemble is cool and often dominated by a pervasive blue-and-ivory tonality. He makes extensive use of a delicate deep blue in combination with other delicate colors, notably a fluffy white and shades of lilac, that have the fundamental feeling of blue."[2] Puvis's drawing is described as ". . . light, delicate and graceful. . . . His contour, which at a distance may look sharp and incisive is seen upon close inspection to be irregularly defined by color instead of by sharp line as division or contact of areas. His modeling of figures into a light three-dimensional solidity is well adapted to the delicacy of the general design."[3]

To reproach Puvis de Chavannes because he did not possess the qualities found in many of those he influenced, to forget or ignore what he achieved because others have reshuffled the priorities and have emphasized brightness, motion, improvisation and other qualities foreign to his temperament, is to miss the point of Puvis's art and thus to mistake his aims for those of more admired painters who have eclipsed his reputation by their even greater personal innovations. Without careful analysis and because he himself is not a modern, his impact on many modern artists may escape concentrated notice or even detection, as indeed it has. From our discussion and from the various comments of the artists, critics and collectors, we can appreciate the scope of Puvis's influence on the modern tradition. When we see the paintings, positive embodiments of his all-embracing economy of means, and note the muffled resonance of his broad areas of colour, their subtle patterning textures, their refined linear framework, the contrapuntal spatial effects, somewhat screenlike—simplifications in themselves of his renaissance predecessors—we become aware of a variety of plastic ideas that the younger generation drew upon to cushion and assimilate the vivid broken colour and spontaneous naturalism opened up by the impressionists. Those who followed Puvis, for the most part, did not work on large surfaces and chose to anchor their decorative qualities primarily on one single means—colour—which they keyed up to take over nearly all the roles of decorative art, frequently to the exclusion of compositional or other effects. His influence can be objectively demonstrated in numerous instances and, as we have noted, was acknowledged by the first generation of modern artists in their writings. Restoring historical perspective helps us to observe with less encumbered eyes the very qualities which made Puvis de Chavannes's work so stimulating to those men whose primary interests were ostensibly inimical to his own. Largely because the quest of simplifying painting accelerated so rapidly toward the total elimination of illustrative matter within little more than a decade after Puvis's death, the second generation of modern artists found themselves unable to comprehend the original prophetic appeal of Puvis's concepts to those they considered their true ancestors. Their work was so concerned with surface that they failed to search beneath the apparently no longer promising illustrative skeleton of Puvis's art, and so his reputation, among most painters who came of age after World War I, died. Nevertheless, if the study of the evolution of modern art is to be brought into equilibrium, Puvis de Chavannes will have to be considered for the unique role he played. The first step in assessing the proportions of Puvis's appeal to the great artists of the modern tradition is to reacquaint ourselves with the independent vision, conviction and integrity of his art.

1. *Ibid.*, p. 327.
2. *Ibidem.*
3. *Ibidem.*

Selected Texts

Puvis de Chavannes

But I have never done a study of nature for my landscapes. I watch a lot, I register, and then it is all a question of logic. When one knows the logic of someone, one knows how he is going to behave anyway; when one knows nature, the habits and the conformation of a poplar, one never forgets its figurative anatomy.

The cartoon is the libretto . . . the colour is the music.

Take care, he said, be mistrustful of tradition. Tradition is only a guide. You must know how to choose: there is the tradition of errors just as there is the tradition of truths and we know, unhappily for mankind, which of the two is the more hardy.

> Quoted by Léonce Bénédite, "Puvis de Chavannes," *Art et Décoration,* November 1898, pp. 151-153.

Apart from frescoes, or something that resembles them, all painting is to be deplored in a church. These frames hung on stone walls are painful to see. And then, why large pictures? There are only two paintings which make reasonable sense: mural painting, belonging to the monument, or easel paintings which one can examine by holding them in one's hands.

The sky in *Ludus Pro Patria* . . . is taken absolutely from Nature. One day, on my way to Neuilly, I saw this sky and as it was just what I needed, I took a good look. On arriving at the studio, I painted it right away, in a single try.

> Quoted by Arsène Alexandre, "Puvis de Chavannes, sa Vie et son Oeuvre," *Le Figaro Illustré,* no. 107, February 1899, pp. 22-44, p. 28, p. 40.

One must try to paint subjects from real life. But they must have a general application.

It is necessary to cut away from nature everything that is ineffective and accidental, everything that for the moment is without force. Art completes what Nature roughly sketches. How does one succeed when helping Nature in her efforts towards speech? By abbreviation and simplification. Be careful to express the important facts and leave the rest out. This is the secret of composition, of design and even of eloquence and wit.

> Quoted by Arsène Alexandre, *Puvis de Chavannes,* London and New York: n.d. (*c.*1904) p. xviii.

I am more than perplexed about developing an aesthetic of any kind, being someone essentially instinctive and just the opposite of a complicated person. If it happens that I think about what I have been able to do until now, I find I do not need to search but to synthesize. Without ever falling into the episodic, the scenes which I imagine remain nevertheless probable and human . . . I do not think that one can analyse an artist as one can describe the workings of a watch. The artist is elusive; by investing him with a technique and intentions outside of the evidence, one is fairly certain to be mistaken. His technique is no more than his temperament and his intentions, if he is of sound mind, reflect simple good sense—you have only to look at the picture calmly, from the front and never from behind, where the painter has hidden nothing.

> Quoted by Léon Werth, *Puvis de Chavannes,* Paris: Les Editions G. Crès et Cie., 1926, pp. 52-53.

Emile Zola

Puvis de Chavannes is only a precursor . . .

> "Une Exposition de tableaux à Paris," *Le Messager de l'Europe,* June, 1875.

George Moore

Chavannes shares the modern belief—and only in this is he modern—that for the service of thought one instrument is as apt as another, and that, so long as that man's back—he who is pulling at the rope fastened at the tree's top branches [*Winter,* 1891-92, Hôtel de Ville, Paris]—is filled in with two grey tints, it matters not at all how the task is accomplished.

> *Modern Painting,* London: Walter Scott, Limited, 1893, pp. 26-27

Paul Signac

February 15, 1895, reflecting on the Strindberg-Gauguin episode [see pp. 123 ff.], Signac wrote in his diary, "Let us study Delacroix, Corot, Puvis, Manet and leave these humbugs to their own devices."

> "Extraits du Journal inédit de Paul Signac, I, 1894-1895," *Gazette des Beaux-Arts,* Vol. XXXVI, July-September, 1949, pp. 97-128, p. 117.

The great Puvis has gone. Who is now going to decorate the walls?

> "Extraits du Journal inédit de Paul Signac, II, 1897-1898," *Gazette des Beaux-Arts,* Vol. XXXIV, April 1952, pp. 265-284, p. 283 (entry 28 October, 1898).

Fr. Thiébault-Sisson

[Puvis] passes to the work on the sketch which he does from the living model, in the desired dimensions. Once the sketch is finished, he transfers it on to the canvas and the third phase, the definitive execution of the work, begins. For him it is only a game. In the first small model he has determined in advance the harmony in which he will depict his pieces; he has strictly detailed, in the sketch, the relief and the accent of the forms, the most minute particulars of the drawing; he also works with no hesitation, without changing his mind and this work is carried out with surprising swiftness. The five panels exhibited in 1896 at the Champ-de-Mars and which represented the greater part of his Boston decoration, required less than three months for their execution. The conception of them had cost him six.

> "Chez Puvis de Chavannes," *Le Figaro Illustré,* May, 1898, p. 99.

Arsène Alexandre

His expression is always *plastic,* it is not at all *literary*; in a word, it is with forms that he achieves his thoughts and not with intentions. This indication is too important not to be emphasized, after all the mistakes the critics have made in this respect.

> "Puvis de Chavannes, sa Vie et son Oeuvre," *Le Figaro Illustré,* February, 1899, p. 37.

John La Farge

And though it may be the landscape of dreamland, his landscape is perhaps the most astonishing part of his work.

In the small reproductions a sort of tone and appearance of color is given to the spaces that appear monotonous and pale in the full work.

It is true that his paintings are really out of place in the modern architecture of France, and however well they may look, for instance, in the Panthéon, it is only necessary to consider the outrageous architectural framing to his big painting in the Sorbonne to realize how much more architectural his ideas of design were than those of the architects whose buildings he adorned.

Scribner's Magazine, Vol. XXVIII, no. 6, December 1900, pp. 673, 676, 679.

Julius Meier-Graefe

[Puvis de Chavannes] invented a free, half classic, half modern legend, very far removed from the instruction which sometimes compelled the earlier painters to exchange their palettes for archeological text-books. . . . He did not paint this or that myth of the Greeks, but the poetry of their culture.

The Development of Modern Art, London and New York: 1908, Vol. II, pp. 51-52 (translated from *Entwicklungsgeschichte der Modernen Kunst,* 1904).

Kenyon Cox

In [Puvis de Chavannes], to a noble simplicity and a great feeling for composition, rather in spaces than lines, has been added a strong sense of landscape and a mastery of light and values, so that his work, while as "mural" as Giotto's, is as modern as Monet's.

Though he died in 1898, an old man covered with honors, Puvis de Chavannes is still one of the most vital influences of contemporary art, still a leader of the young school, still one of the most discussed and criticised of artists.

Old Masters and New: Essays in Art Criticism, New York: Fox, Duffield and Company, 1905, pp. 143 and 210.

Charles Ricketts

The first time I saw Puvis de Chavannes was in the Louvre. He was standing in front of that admirable antique sometimes called a *Sea Deity,* sometimes *Alexander the Great*: in the crowding or herding out of the visitors leaving the gallery I saw him again, one of the last to leave, before *Le Deluge,* that masterpiece of Poussin. . . . I called upon him two years later with a friend, like myself a youth of twenty, and . . . I remember him as the man of his work, simple, grave and genial, touched and charmed by our raw and uncultivated admiration for his painting. He had just finished his first pastel, a later phase of his practice in which he has passed into the collections of tardy purchasers. He confessed to being still the owner of all his small pictures, for criticism does not allow a variety of range to a man, and "the painter who paints large must not paint small." From time to time his speech became admonitory, and he launched forth into disapproval of current tendencies, the photographic drawing of man, "*la perfection bête qui n'a rien à faire avec le vrai dessin, le dessin expressif!*" [stupid perfection which has nothing to do with real drawing, expressive drawing!] and against "*les pochades d'atelier et de vacance*" [the rapid sketches of the studio or vacation]. I remember the insistence with which he underlined the fact that the cartoon for the Sorbonne was but the skeleton of the design without the colour-scheme which would transform it.

> "Puvis de Chavannes: A Chapter from 'Modern Painters' ," *Burlington Magazine*, XIII, April 1908, p. 12.

Auguste Rodin

As for the greatest artist of our time, Puvis de Chavannes, did he not try his best to spread all around us that sweet serenity to which we all aspire? His sublime landscapes, where holy Nature seems to cradle upon her bosom a humanity at once loving, wise, noble and simple, surely provide us with an admirable lesson. He has expressed everything, this incomparable genius—help for the weak, love of work, self-sacrifice, respect for high thought. It sheds a wonderful light upon our era. It is sufficient to look at one of his masterpieces . . . to feel capable of noble deeds.

What further proves that the masters bring new ideas and inclinations to their generation is that they have often great difficulty in having them accepted. They sometimes spend almost their whole lives in struggling against convention. And the more genius they possess, the more chance they have of being for a long time misunderstood. Corot, Courbet, Millet, Puvis de Chavannes, to only mention a few, did not win unanimous acclamation until the end of their careers.

> *L'Art*, Entretiens réunis par Paul Gsell, Paris: Bernard Grasset, 1911, p. 305, p. 309.

Pierre Godet

I have not laid emphasis here on the properly decorative side of this influence, or on this revival which many others have already pointed out and praised, of an authentic mural art through the simplicity and serenity of the grouping and the brightness of the tone. It is enough that we give thanks for this most propitious chance which has permitted Puvis de Chavannes to submit himself to the needs of the age which has been most hostile to all collaboration between the individual genius and social life, and to become, by dint of sheer energy, a decorator of public buildings for the instruction and the general good of all—in conditions, moreover, insufficient and nearly always unworthy of him. No one, considering the services he has rendered in order to have been such a practical and productive spirit, would reproach him for lack of strictness or for having been disloyal to an absolute. Even his formalism is to some extent a boon in the sense that across the first level of convention, he facilitates the access of the crowd to his personal genius. Puvis de Chavannes represents to the maximum the relations which a genuine artist can maintain with the modern world.

> "Puvis de Chavannes et la peinture d'aujourd'hui," *L'Art Décoratif*, January 20, 1912, p. 52.

Percy Moore Turner

Apart from these movements, impressionist, neo-impressionist, post-impressionist, cubist, futurist, there is but little to be said of the art and artists in the second half of the nineteenth century. . . . The only name of real importance is that of Puvis de Chavannes.

Puvis de Chavannes . . . based his art on the great Umbrian masters, having a special predilection for Piero della Francesca, and attacked problems which, left unsolved by them, had been untouched by others. He also took in hand the revival of the art of decorating great wall spaces . . . he also recognized that any lapse in the general colour scheme or any disturbance of harmony caused by a lack of colour balance was no less fatal. In short, he was a synthetist of no mean order. Blessed with a refined and sensitive temperament, almost immaculate draughtsmanship, full of reticence, an intuitive sense in composition, he emerged triumphant from an ordeal as severe as any painter of the nineteenth century had set himself.

The Appreciation of Painting, New York: Charles Scribner's Sons, 1921, pp. 199-201.

Maurice Denis

Puvis de Chavannes had passed on the lesson of Delacroix by stripping and bleaching it. Systematic and even hieratic, his well-ordered and profoundly logical art translated the great aspects of human thought after the manner of Giotto and Raphael. He was at the same time ancient and Christian with a melancholy and seriousness which were very modern. He forced one's attention towards the supreme goal of painting, namely large mural decoration.

Nouvelles Théories: sur l'art moderne, sur l'art sacré 1914-1921 Paris, n.d. (1922), p. 65.

Gustave Kahn

This enthusiasm for impressionism was not entirely exclusive. Sparing as we were in our praises, we did include Puvis de Chavannes and Gustave Moreau. But was this merely for their legendary colour? Rather we were drawn by the majestic simplicity of the one [Puvis] and the flowery and ostentatious hieraticism of the other [Moreau]. We were not at all contradicting our own judgment by admiring Seurat and Signac at the same time. Apart from the fact that we considered ourselves to be leading the fight for new ideas, there was something engaging about them for us and which seemed to represent a parallel to our efforts: this static element, this search for an absolute disengagement which characterized Seurat's art, as a painter or figure draughtsman.

Les Dessins de Georges Seurat, Paris: Bernheim-Jeune, n.d., (1926).

Maurice Denis

If Puvis de Chavannes has been able, to his credit, to deal with complicated allegories and religious subjects of great breadth, like the Saint Genevieve in the Panthéon, it is that he has escaped from the academic through the application of an art stripped of all rhetoric.

"De l'Esprit franciscain en art," 1927, *Charmes et leçons de l'Italie*, Paris: Armand Colin, 1933, pp. 151-153.

Henri Focillon

The masters of 1863, the impressionists, Puvis de Chavannes represented the active forces in French art. Very varied forces, moreover, from which will be born new aspects of painting and new conflicts.

La Peinture XIXᵉ et XXᵉ Siècles du Réalisme à nos Jours, Paris: H. Laurens, 1928, p. 251.

Walter Pach

The explanation why the big mass of "official" artists in France continued on their course can only be that they stifled the timid voice within them that counselled study as to whether the true line of art did not run through the camp of the "innovators" like Chavannes, Degas, Manet and their successors.

Ananias or the False Artist, New York and London: Harper and Brothers, 1928, p. 103.

Maurice Denis

The first image I recall is of the Café Volpini, in a . . . corner of the great fair of 1889 at the Champ de Mars. . . . Here, from June 10 onwards, were exhibited ninety-six of the first works of the new school of painting, framed in white. . . . The drawing, distorted almost to the point of caricature, and the flat colours, outraged the public. . . .

There were seventeen pictures by Gauguin, painted in Brittany, at Arles and in Martinique. . . . The show was first a dazzlement and then a revelation. Instead of windows opening on to nature, like the paintings of the impressionists, here were heavily decorative surfaces, the forms outlined with a thick black line . . . these unusual paintings reveal the influence of Japanese woodcuts. . . . And we were reminded too, of Pissarro's peasant scenes, and above all of Puvis de Chavannes, the painter of *The Poor Fisherman*, that forgotten great master, whose enormous influence on late nineteenth century painting can never be sufficiently stressed.

"L'Epoque du Symbolisme," *Gazette des Beaux-Arts*, Vol. XI, March, 1934, pp. 165-166.

Germain Bazin

One could say that Gauguin is a barbaric Puvis de Chavannes, or if you wish that Puvis is an academic Gauguin. . . .

Puvis de Chavannes, whose training was entirely classical, will demand of Greek-Latin culture that it separate from the present. But, as different as the two painters' sources of inspiration are, their attitude is the same; the exotic for one, the classical for the other.

. . . the plastic methods of each are comparable.

Puvis was therefore, in his own way, a real precursor.

L'Epoque impressioniste, Paris: Tisné, 1947, pp. 50-51.

Thadée Natanson

[Puvis de Chavannes] was full of good will towards everyone but even more obliging still with young people.

. . . it was solely with pleasure, for he had no need to be consoled, that he thought about the admiration of some young people. He was moved by an emotion which he disguised. It is in fact a little in spite of himself that he was led, late in life, to serve as champion of group movements. But it had also happened that, without ever having exhibited with the impressionists, from most of whom he was separated by quite a number of ideas, he had at least the same dealer.

In everything he was a solitary person, with a busy mind.

Peints à leur tour, Paris: Editions Albin Michel, 1948 p. 67, p. 69.

Meyer Shapiro

In [his] attachment to Puvis, the young Seurat responded to what was best and closest to him in the academic art of his schooldays, anticipating here the taste of the most advanced painters of the late '80s, such as Gauguin. The neo-classic tradition at the Ecole des Beaux-Arts was in complete decline then; in the official painting of the Salon it had become contaminated by romantic and realistic art, adopted without full conviction or understanding, much as academic art today takes over elements of abstract and expressionist style while denying the creative source. Puvis rose above his fellow academicians through his knowledge of past art and his serious desire for a noble, monumental style adequate to the conservative ideas of his time—comprehensive images of a stable community, austere and harmonious. But Puvis's order had too little spontaneity and passion. It was cold idealism with no place in its system for the actualities and conflicts which it surmounts or proposes to resolve. Puvis's caricatures, not intended for exhibition, show the violence of feeling repressed in his greyed and balanced works.

In the late '80s and the '90s, other painters, also admirers of Puvis, impelled by the dream of a harmonious society, were to seek out their goal in an existing but distant primitive world in Brittany or the Pacific.

"New Light on Seurat," *Art News*, Vol. 57, no. 2, April, 1958, pp. 44-45.

Klaus Berger

[Puvis de Chavannes] was able to throw a bridge across into a new era, in which the simplicity and grandeur of his form was hailed as liberating, as a way out of the dead-end of impressionism. . . .

. . . Puvis's importance lies in the fact that in an epoch subservient to the quick impression, without lapsing into literary painting, he found his way back to essentials: meaningful content, wholeness of composition, balance of elements, decorative unity. Out of a classical tradition known of old and long forgotten, he created something living. On the dissolution of impressionism, he was able therewith to make a very relevant contribution to the next phase. The generation of 1890 looked upon him as a precursor. Few were able to escape his influence. Van Gogh, Gauguin, Toulouse-Lautrec, the Nabis, even the young Picasso had to come to terms with him.

> *Odilon Redon: Fantasy and Color,* New York, Toronto and London: McGraw Hill Book Company, 1965, pp. 25-26.

Hilton Kramer

Puvis . . . was once a painter of formidable reputation and influence . . . Enlightened opinion at the turn of the century considered him one of the masters of modern painting.

Subsequently his reputation suffered a serious eclipse. Critics no longer felt obliged to have an opinion of his work, and few artists paid it any attention. His name dropped out of discussion—permanently it seemed—and he looked more and more like another fatal casualty of the history of taste. . . .

Puvis's was a sensibility of extraordinary purity and conviction. . . . For him, the art of painting consisted in filtering out all chromatic contrasts to a point where every tone enjoyed an equal visual weight and the surface of the picture became a flat, continuous, unbroken plane bathed in an unearthly light. What Puvis sought was an intensity—a spiritual intensity for which the subtlest visual equivalents had to be found—without vividness or verisimilitude. No other 19th century painter of comparable ambition so deliberately resisted the temptation to exploit the sensuous appeal of pure color, or made so much of the dry, gray, neutral medium that remained once the more obvious resources of chromatic drama had been eschewed.

> Hilton Kramer, "Rediscovering Puvis de Chavannes," *The New York Times*, vol. CXXI, Sunday July 16, 1972, section 2, p. 17.

Catalogue of the Exhibition

All works in the exhibition are illustrated. Dimensions are given in both inches and centimetres for catalogue entries; height precedes width. Supplementary illustrations of works *not in the exhibition* are denoted by (fig.). A complete list of supplementary illustrations will be found on pages vi-vii.

Pierre Puvis de Chavannes (French, 1824-1898)

Return from the Hunt, circa 1859
Oil on gesso-covered panel; 14½ x 11⅜ in. (36.8 x 28.8 cm.)
Signed lower right: Puvis de Chavannes
Nelson Gallery—Atkins Museum (Nelson Fund)

Catalogue no. 1

42

Ref. *Handbook Nelson Gallery of Art Atkins Museum.* Kansas City, Vol. I, 1973, p. 258 (inventory no. 33-149).

Reduced version of *Un Retour de Chasse* which was exhibited in the Salon of 1859 and which the artist donated to the Musée des Beaux-Arts, Marseilles.

Return from the Hunt is a blue and white monochromatic variant on a *grisaille.* The composition is made up of interlocking figures; a criss-crossing landscape background with high horizon line keeps the space shallow and projects the units, frieze-like, in a forward plane, strongly recalling Poussin's tightly-knit interlocking compositional arrangements.

The texture of the bluish-white flesh is dense and brushed in to give a dry tautness to the figures. Contours are clear-cut and varied rather than uniform and Ingres-esque. The influence of Delacroix and Chassériau is, even at this relatively early stage in Puvis de Chavannes's development, pronouncedly subsidiary to that of Poussin.

There is conspicuous differentiation between textures, some of which are dense and others loose. Details such as the left hand of the man bearing the standard are summary abbreviations. Areas are brushed in over an apparent underpainting which is made a consistent and appealing feature of the surface of the panel. For example, the trees on the left are lightly painted, as are the units in the foreground. This subtle range of varying textures enhances the individuality of Puvis's technique and adds a carefully planned aspect, a control which differs from the fussy calculation of the academic painters. This premeditated organization and corresponding adjustment of pictorial means to it, which is derived from Puvis's study of Poussin, must have appealed greatly to Seurat, who made a positive theme of showing the textural patterns of underpaint in his work. The pervasive use of white and other pale tonalities here does not have a fresco quality, the dusky powdered look that many of the later paintings, especially those produced after 1880, reveal. This clarity and variation on a theme of blues and whites, where shadows are elaborated in deep blue and units such as the horse and rider in the right background are a blue silhouette on blue, clearly foreshadow Picasso's "Blue" period paintings of 1901-1904. Whether or not Picasso ever saw this picture (it is not impossible) is less important than the fact that pictorial ideas abound in the minds of artists who conceive in visual rather than literary terms and that these pretexts serve, in Puvis no less than in Picasso, their visual imaginations. The antiquarianism of the academic painters of Puvis's generation never got beyond technical display and literary fetishism. Puvis here, in 1859, firmly established that he was not of academic bent and we can well understand the hostility to his work from the academic camp as well as the lamentations that such a gifted painter would not commit himself to joining their ranks.

Return from the Hunt is an important landmark in Puvis's work for it announces much that is elaborated upon in the paintings of the four succeeding decades of his development.

Pierre Puvis de Chavannes

Autumn, circa 1864
Oil on canvas; 20¼ x 15¾ in. (51 x 40 cm.)
Unsigned
National Collection of Fine Arts, Smithsonian Institution
Gift of John Gellatly

Catalogue no. 2

Unfinished study for composition of the same title in
the Musée des Beaux-Arts, Lyons.

Pierre Puvis de Chavannes

Autumn, circa 1864
Oil on canvas; 40 x 32 in. (102 x 81 cm.)
Signed lower left: P. Puvis de Chavannes
Museo de Bellas Artes, Caracas

Catalogue no. 3

Version of composition of the same title in the Musée
des Beaux-Arts, Lyons.

Pierre Puvis de Chavannes

The Wine Press, circa 1865
Oil on canvas; 18½ x 13½ in. (47 x 34 cm.)
Signed lower left: P. Puvis de Chavannes
Lent by The Phillips Collection

Catalogue no. 4

Ref. Duncan Phillips, *The Phillips Collection: A Museum of*
  Modern Art and its Sources, Catalogue, Washington,
  D.C.: The Phillips Collection, 1952, p. 83.

Pierre Puvis de Chavannes

Allegory of Sadness (Alegoria del dolor), circa 1865-70
Oil on canvas; 16³/₁₆ x 10⅝ in. (41 x 27 cm.)
Unsigned
Museo de San Carlos, Instituto Nacional de Bellas Artes y Literatura, Mexico, D.F.

Catalogue no. 5

Pierre Puvis de Chavannes

LA GUERRE

War, 1867
Oil on canvas; 43¼ x 59⅛ in. (110 x 149 cm.)
Signed lower left: P. Puvis de Chavannes
John G. Johnson Collection, Philadelphia

Catalogue no. 6

Ref. Mentioned along with the other three compositions, in "The Atelier: Puvis de Chavannes," *The Art Amateur*, December, 1890, p. 5, as belonging to Mr. Johnson. Durand-Ruel Galleries, New York, *Exposition of Paintings, Decorations and Pastels by Mr. Puvis de Chavannes*, December 15-31, 1894, catalogue no. 17. A complete study of the problems of the Amiens murals will be found, together with documentation, in Louise d'Argencourt, *Les Peintures murales de Puvis de Chavannes au Musée de Picardie*, Université de Paris—Sorbonne, 1973 (unpublished).

One of a series of four reduced versions of Puvis's murals for the Musée de Picardie, Amiens, first exhibited at the Salon of 1861 (*Bellum—War* and *Concordia —Peace*). In 1863, two complementary murals, *Work (Le Travail)* and *Rest (Le Repos)* were shown at the Salon. *Peace* was purchased by the state and donated to the city of Amiens. Puvis, not wishing to see the murals separated, donated *War* to the city. In 1863, he donated *Work* and *Rest* to Amiens to be installed together with the other two compositions. The medium for the larger murals is oil mixed with wax (*peinture à la cire*).

Exhibited in the impressionist exhibition of 1888 organized by Durand-Ruel and held at the National Academy of Design, New York. The four reductions were acquired by Mr. Johnson from Durand-Ruel in 1888. Although not intended to be separated from *War* and *Peace, Work* (1867) and *Rest* (1867) are now in the Widener Collection, National Gallery of Art, Washington, D.C.

Pierre Puvis de Chavannes

Peace, 1867
Oil on canvas; 43¼ x 58½ in. (110 x 148 cm.)
Signed lower left: P. Puvis de Chavannes
John G. Johnson Collection, Philadelphia

Catalogue no. 7

(See previous entry)

Ref. Durand-Ruel Galleries, New York, *Exposition of
   Paintings, Decorations and Pastels by Mr. Puvis de Chavannes,* December 15-31, 1894, catalogue no. 16.

Pierre Puvis de Chavannes

Greek Colony, Massilia, 1868
Oil on canvas; 38¾ x 57½ (98.5 x 146 cm.)
Unsigned
Lent by The Phillips Collection

Catalogue no. 8

Ref. *A Collection in the Making,* Cambridge: The River-
side Press, 1926, p. 26; Will Hutchins, "Two
Composition Sketches by Puvis de Chavannes,"
Art and Understanding, Vol. I, no. 2, March, 1930, pp.
230-239; Duncan Phillips, *The Phillips Collection: A
Museum of Modern Art and its Sources, Catalogue,*
Washington, D.C.: The Phillips Collection, 1952,
p. 83.

Duncan Phillips wrote in 1926, three years after having
acquired *Greek Colony, Massilia* and *Marseilles, Port of the
Orient,* "Great master that he was of monumental
design, he devoted most of his time to architectonic
creations. Yet from what we know of his easel paintings
we realise that he would have easily attained to the
front rank had he worked on a smaller scale with a
wider range of pigments. The sketches for Marseilles
with their deep enchanting blues and opalescent tones
reveal what a wonderful colorist Puvis could be. The
exigencies of his fundamental principle for mural
painting required however a sacrifice of the sensuous
appeal and of light and shade."

In this composition there is rich colour and freedom of
brushwork unusual for Puvis. Especially colourful are
the intense blues in the sky and mountains. For example, in the bright oriental orange, pink-red of the standing figure with jar, the colour is added with utmost
internal freedom. The figure itself is drawn in pencil
over the landscape and sea beyond. An enormous degree of colour variety in the background areas and vigorous paint manipulation cause an atypical
atmospheric effect. The composition is roughed in by
colour areas; the foreground centre, representing fire, is
a slab of red and the figure with arms clasped is deep
rosy red. The less worked-up left side is more ethereal in
character, the cave unit reinforced by pink bricks and a
broad horizontal green stripe and the area to its right.
In the small centre group of four figures, the standing
figure to the left is painted in pale blue; that to the
right is greyish yellow-green with free-flowing hair of
the same colour. The group on the right, especially the
rosettes and the horizontal strokes under the rosettes
and on the salmon-orange figure, and the basket of

Pierre Puvis de Chavannes

Marseilles, Port of the Orient, 1868
Oil on canvas; 38¾ x 57½ in. (98.5 x 146 cm.)
Unsigned
Lent by The Phillips Collection

Catalogue no. 9

fruit, recall Maurice Prendergast, as do the red dot necklace and flower basket near the seated figure and the generally mauve-purple hues in various parts of the composition. With colour areas not "finished," spatial relations are remarkably demarcated. The keynote red-orange shirt is vivid and bold. The overall decorative-expressive drama results from a combination of calculated boldness and a fine feeling of colour harmonies.

Ref. *A Collection in the Making*, Duncan Phillips, Cambridge: The Riverside Press, 1926, pp. 26-27; Will Hutchins, "Two Composition Sketches by Puvis de Chavannes," *Art and Understanding*, Vol I, no. 2, March, 1930, pp. 230-239. Duncan Phillips, *The Phillips Collection: A Museum of Modern Art and its Sources, Catalogue*, Washington, D.C.: The Phillips Collection, 1952, pp. 82-83.

The compositional organization is more highly developed in *Marseilles, Port of the Orient* than in *Greek Colony, Massilia* (cat. no. 8) even though internal areas are boldly manipulated. For example, the sailor at the top with red hat, white shirt, blue sack and mauve trousers, is freely worked in. However, patches are unpainted or areas of the canvas are uncovered, such as the mast and rigging in the upper right. The entire lower right quadrant is so broad and freely handled that it is reminiscent of Daumier (as are some of Puvis's caricatures). In several of the figures in this area, rippling muscular accentuation by colour brushstroke defines the value and creates at the same time the mottled colour effect. As in *Greek Colony, Massilia,* the centre right figure with salmon-orange shirt is here not a focal point, because the colour intensity of the vivid Manet-esque green of the sea carries its own weight. The figure in white trousers to his left is also Manet-esque, as is the still life of muskets and flasks on a black blanket in the foreground. It is conceivable that there was some exchange of ideas between Manet and Puvis around this time (cf. Manet's *The Departure of the Folkestone Boat,* 1869, Philadelphia Museum of Art, Tyson Collection). The oriental group on the carpet, the reading sage, the figure at lower left with red dress, the pink-white-blue colour conjunction in the seated and kneeling female figures are reminiscent of Whistler (cf. *Purple and Rose, The Lange Lijzen of the Six Marks,* 1864, John G. Johnson Collection). It is possible that Puvis had been looking at Whistler's work around that time even though his overall result is not intrinsically exotic. The white sails and Château d'If background landmark are also reminiscent of Whistler and presage Albert Marquet's simplifications of the background in his port views. The lower five figures are related to such artists as Moreau (see cat. nos. 41-44), Monticelli, Redon (see cat. nos. 70-72) and Rouault. The painting's decisive colour drama would have made as strong an impression on the artists who saw it at the time it was painted as it does on us today.

Pierre Puvis de Chavannes

Nude, 1868
Oil on canvas; 16 x 10 in. (40.6 x 25.4 cm.)
Signed lower right: Puvis de Chavannes
Nanette Fabray MacDougall

Catalogue no. 10

Ref. Loaned by John Quinn to the Armory Show, 1913
(no. 557). See *1913-1963 Armory Show 50th Anniversary Exhibition,* Utica-New York: 1963, *Femme nue,*
p. 200, ill. p. 180. See also *The John Quinn Collection
of Paintings, Water Colors, Drawings and Sculpture,*
Huntington: Pigeon Hill Press, 1926, p. 13, ill. p.
84 (Quinn sale no. 466).

Pierre Puvis de Chavannes

At the Fountain, 1869
Oil on canvas; 71⅜ x 57 in. (182 x 145 cm.)
Signed lower left: P. Puvis de Chavannes
Museum of Fine Arts, Boston
Bequest of Mrs. Robert Dawson Evans

Catalogue no. 11

54

The composition reunites two figures from *Rest* of 1863. The influence of Ingres's *La Source* is apparent in the drawing of the figures. A smaller version, *La Source*, is in the Musée Saint Denis, Reims. The foreground landscape is very loose, unlike the dense handling of Manet and more in the Courbet tradition which was also adapted by Renoir in his earliest work of the sixties. The smooth flesh contrasts with the foliage and the intense blue sky behind the trees. The white clouds are barely brushed in. The phosphorescent lavender-purple of the toga on the figure at left plays with the blue of the sandal straps. Figures, for instance the woman and child and donkey in the background, are summarily handled. There is a series of interlocking criss-cross patterns in the background to the left: blue modulated to greyish blue and olive green to pale greyish green. The pouring water, staff, branches and trunks of trees at right all provide sinuous curvilinear motifs in contrast to the upper left background of the composition. The trees function as pillars and are much denser than the similar units in Corot even though the influence of Corot on Puvis can be discerned. These trees also compare with those in Frédéric Bazille's *Men Bathing* (*Scène d'été*) of 1869 (fig. 1). The composition also inspired Paul Signac's *Les Femmes au Puits* of 1892 (Cachin, *Signac, op. cit.,* p. 60, pl. 49).

Fig. 1   Frédéric Bazille, *Men Bathing*, 1869

Pierre Puvis de Chavannes

The Balloon, 1870
Oil on canvas; 53½ x 33 in. (136.5 x 84 cm.)
Signed and dated lower left: P. Puvis de Chavannes 1870
Private collection, New York

Catalogue no. 12

56

Pierre Puvis de Chavannes

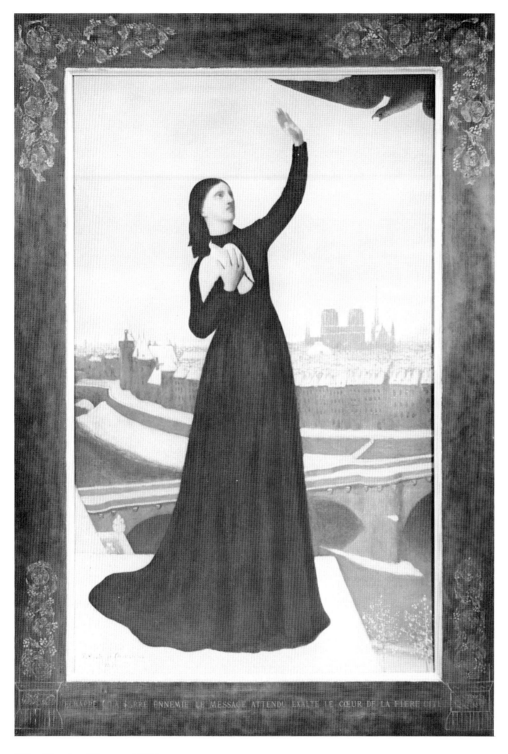

The Carrier Pigeon, 1871
Oil on canvas; 53½ x 33 in. (136.5 x 84 cm.)
Signed and dated lower left: P. Puvis de Chavannes 1871
Private collection, New York

Catalogue no. 13

Catalogue no. 12

Ref. Bryson Burroughs, *Lecture to Art Students*, Metropolitan Museum of Art, 1915 (typescript of unpublished lecture in the library of the museum, pp. 31-33). The paintings were "discovered" by Burroughs and exhibited along with paintings by Puvis in the collection of the Metropolitan Museum as well as those owned by John Quinn (*The Beheading of St. John the Baptist, Cider* and *The River*) in 1915; W. A. Bradley, "Some French Artists during the Siege and Commune," *Print Collectors Quarterly,* VI, 1916, pp. 190-194, (illustrated); Henry Harkness Flagler, *The Story of a Dream*, Dover, 1923; see also Puvis de Chavannes, *"Lettres (1861-1876),"* ed. Conrad de Mandach, *La Revue de Paris,* X, Dec. 15, 1910, pp. 684-688, letters to Léon Belly of June 18, 19, 1871; *The Correspondence of Berthe Morisot,* London: Lund Humphries, 1959, pp. 58-61.

Frame painted and inscribed by the artist: *La Ville de Paris investie confie à l'air son appel à la France* (The besieged city of Paris confides its appeal to France to the air). Small oil sketch for this painting in the collection of the Musée Carnavalet, Paris (see fig. 2). Puvis also made a lithograph of the composition.

This painting, along with *The Carrier Pigeon* (cat. no. 13) was donated *c.* 1873-74 to a lottery to raise money for the victims of the Chicago fire. J. Buisson wrote:

One day in his Place Pigalle studio, Puvis showed me two drawings which he was very fond of and regretted having given to a charity lottery. They represented two female figures, tall and slender, almost bodiless. One was sending her spirit with the balloon to take away news of France; the other reached out with eager hands to greet the carrier pigeon, escaped from the claws of the German eagle to bring news to Paris. The idea, the sentiment, the setting, the snow-covered quais and bridges, the isolation, the entombment, the mourning for the homeland torn asunder, what Frenchman would not find his own emotions reflected in those of the artist? The drawings had been photographed and fifty thousand copies were sold within a few days. The drawing for the Red Cross produced the same sensation; on that day Puvis carried with him the soul of the people; his public was the whole of France.[1]

Photographs of this and of *The Carrier Pigeon* (cat. no. 13) were exhibited at the Durand-Ruel exhibition of 1887 thereby, together with the studies and lithographs, making available the compositions to modern artists.

1. *"Pierre Puvis de Chavannes, Souvenirs Intimes,"* part II, *Gazette des Beaux-Arts,* XXII, September 1899, p. 222.

Fig. 2   Pierre Puvis de Chavannes, *Sketch for "The Balloon,"* 1870

Catalogue no. 13

Ref. See cat. no. 12

Frame painted and inscribed by the artist: *Echappé à la serre ennemie le message attendu exalte le coeur de la fière cité* (Escaped from the enemy's grip, the long-awaited message exalts the heart of the proud city). Small oil sketch for this painting in the collection of the Musée Carnavalet, Paris (see fig. 3).

Puvis also made a lithograph of this composition.

Fig. 3   Pierre Puvis de Chavannes, *Sketch for "The Carrier Pigeon,"* 1871

Pierre Puvis de Chavannes

Daphnis and Chloe, 1872
Oil on canvas; *tondo* 36 in. diameter (91.5 cm.)
Signed and dated lower left: P. Puvis de Chavannes, 1872
University Art Museum, Berkeley, Gift of Mr. and Mrs. Samuel Josefowitz, Lausanne, 1965

Catalogue no. 14

Ref. *Selection 1966 The University Art Collections*, foreword,
   Peter Selz, University of California, Berkeley,
   1966, pp. 65-67 (colour plate).

Pierre Puvis de Chavannes

Hope, 1872
Oil on canvas; 40⅜ x 51 in. (102 x 127.5 cm.)
Signed and dated lower left: 1872   P. Puvis de Chavannes
The Walters Art Gallery

Catalogue no. 15

Ref. Gustave Kahn, reviewing the 1887 exhibition at Durand-Ruel, wrote: "It is curious to consider two *Hopes* at this same exhibition—one nude with her little *English miss* head, the other clothed. The head has become more noble, the curve of the nose more hieratic and religious, the red flowers shaded off in the first picture are clearer in the second where Hope is clothed." ("Exposition Puvis de Chavannes," *La Revue Indépendante,* Vol. VI, no. 15, January 1888, p. 145.)

The painting was mentioned as being in the collection of Erwin Davis by 1890 in "The Atelier: Puvis de Chavannes," *The Art Amateur,* 1890, p. 5 (catalogue no. 1) as one of ten paintings by the artist in the U.S., all coming from Durand-Ruel.

See W.R. Johnston, "*L'Espérance* of Puvis de Chavannes," *Walters Art Gallery Bulletin,* XXI, January 1969, pp. 2-4, acquired in 1902. See Gauguin, *Still Life with 'Hope' by Puvis de Chavannes,* 1901 (cat. no. 55) and J.M. Whistler, *Rose et Vert, L'Iris: Portrait of Miss Kinsella* (cat. no. 67).

Nude version, 1872 in the Louvre. This version exhibited at Salon of 1872.

Pierre Puvis de Chavannes

Hope, 1872
Black chalk on grey paper tinted buff; 8¼ x 10¹/₁₆ in. (20.5 x 25.5 cm.)
Signed and inscribed lower right: *à Leon Bouillon P. Puvis d C*
The Walters Art Gallery

Catalogue no. 16

Ref. See John Quinn, 1870-1925 *Collection of Paintings,
Water Colors, Drawings and Sculpture,* Pigeon Hill
Press, 1926, p. 13. (Purchased by Bryson Burroughs and given by Mrs. Burroughs to the Walters Art Gallery.)

Pierre Puvis de Chavannes

Death and the Maidens (The Reaper), 1872
Oil on canvas; 57½ x 46⅛ in. (146.1 x 117.2 cm.)
Signed and dated lower right: P. Puvis de Chavannes 1872
Lent by the Sterling and Francine Clark Art Institute, Williamstown, Massachusetts

Catalogue no. 17

Ref. *List of Paintings in the Sterling and Francine Clark Art Institute, Williamstown, Massachusetts,* Williamstown: 1972, p. 80 no. 54. Acquired by Robert Sterling Clark in 1918. A preparatory oil sketch for the composition is in the National Gallery, London.

The three standing figures in the left background are similar and possibly influenced by Degas's *Jephthah's Daughter* (Smith College Museum of Art). The figure of *Death* in the lower left foreground recalls the work of George Frederick Watts (for example, *The Sower of the Systems*, 1872, Art Gallery of Ontario).

The leftmost of the two standing figures in the right foreground was adapted by Gauguin in 1899 for his *Maternity* (W582).[1] Gauguin would have known the picture from Puvis's 1887 exhibition at Durand-Ruel and/or subsequent showings.

The kneeling figure in the background recalls similar usages in classical terra cottas of figures attached to bases and was adapted again in *The Bathers* (cat. no. 31). The standing figures recall Mantegna in their drawing and the group in the background are caught in motion in a manner which relates them to Poussin via the above-mentioned Degas. The textural handling of the background is a near Courbet-esque scumble similar to that in *At the Fountain* (cat. no. 11) of 1869. Al- though set in this green landscape of crisp, rugged texture, there is a kind of classical firmness to the figures. Together with this clarity, there is no real atmospheric quality, although the figures themselves are painted in pale tonalities and their three-dimensionality is here more in evidence than in Puvis's later work. For example, there is a gentle use of scumbling in the gown of the standing girl in pink which, together with shadows painted in colour, must have appealed immensely to such men as Gauguin and Maurice Denis. The furrows in the dress of the kneeling figure augment the gentle three-dimensionality by acting as a stabilizing factor (originally the entire dress was pink). Motifs such as these establish a compositional interplay with the horizontals of the clouds which themselves have an early Italian source. The interconnecting flat triangular zones in the background and the irregularly contoured shapes formed by the intersection of figures, all set against the rising plane of the background, is another reason Puvis appealed to modern painters who were interested in this same motif as it was employed to advantage in Japanese woodblock prints. Puvis's colour is dry, never rich or especially appealing in itself. His effects are achieved through calculated relationships and his spontaneity is by way of intellectual conception, not in execution. A restrained boldness and an ordered decorum pervades *Death and the Maidens*. Nonetheless, Puvis was not afraid of loose ends here and there and this lack of "finish" was also an attraction for the younger generation.

1. Observed by Wayne Anderson, *Gauguin's Paradise Lost*, New York: The Viking Press, 1971, p. 248.

Pierre Puvis de Chavannes

The Woodcutters, circa 1870-1875
Oil on canvas; 30 x 44½ in. (76 x 113 cm.)
Unsigned (seal of artist's estate on stretcher)
Lent by Gilbert M. Denman, Jr.

Catalogue no. 18

Ref. *Important European Paintings from Texas Private
Collections*, New York: Marlborough-Gerson Gallery, 1964, catalogue no. 33; *Seven Decades: 1895-
1965, Crosscurrents in Modern Art*, April 26—May 21,
1966, catalogue by Peter Selz, New York: Public
Education Association, catalogue no. 40.

The monumentality of *The Woodcutters* is rare in Puvis's
work. A forest of tree trunks and felled logs forms the
architectonic gridwork of its composition. Relationships
between colour-made units throughout the painting account for the effectiveness of the design. Puvis did not
expand his art in the forceful direction indicated
here—construction, richness, weight—but moved toward flatter, paler and generally lighter, decorative
forms. At times, however, his later work takes into account the type of density found in this composition (see
cat no. 31).

A contrast in textures is evident throughout: a
densely-painted area such as the left background is
played against uncovered patches, such as the limbs of
the two figures in the left foreground or the five at the
right which are merely toned. Space is not deep but
contained and elaborated by means of complex se-
quences of relationships. Silhouettes are suppressed in
the deepest section of the background, causing this area
to rise up in order to project the emphatic colourfulness
of individual units against the screen thus created. The
two figures in the central background leaning on the
greenish-grey tree have a gentler substance and are neither weighty nor wispy in the Whistlerian sense. In the
six figures in the right background, the lilac dress of the
seated woman is dappled and the other dressed figure
on the log is blue with thick white strokes. These summary details contribute to the constructive feeling of the
ensemble. There is an enormous variety of brushwork

employed for different purposes, to model densely as well as to create focal points throughout the composition. Examples of this variety include the figure in the doorway in the right background, mysterious and atmospheric, and the standing classically-posed nude in the left background, heavily textured with pale pink-purple flesh. A contrast is also evident in the dispersal throughout the composition of dappled trees, two on the left, two in the centre and one on the right. Contours are achieved in a correspondingly varied manner—distinct outline such as in the left hand of the semi-nude kneeling figure in the left foreground, direct contrast of adjoining areas of colour such as in the standing woman in the middleground in brick red, and a broad combination of both in the handling of certain of the deep verdant foliage and dappled tree units. The foreground of the painting is painted very freely, sketchily, all the way across, as are selected areas in other parts of the composition. Compositional continuity is achieved by means of a series of horizontal bands running from left to right but not always traversing the entire canvas. These discontinuous linkages, such as the direction of limbs which act as skewers in space, work together with triangular arrangements, diagonals and eye-leading colour focal points of similar hues which are found in units widely distributed throughout the canvas.

There is a subtle and intense experimental use of various sources, especially technical. Puvis's personal vision is a classicism transformed from within the French tradition, but it follows strictly neither the doctrinaire aspects of Ingres and his followers, nor Delacroix, nor the simplified and atmospheric pastoral quality of Corot although adapting aspects from each. In a sense, Puvis sought to extend the direction in which Chassériau was leading by borrowing features from two contrasting visions and blending them.[1] We cannot therefore stereotype Puvis's art so easily as many critics, familiar with

only one type of painting, have done. As Goldwater noted, "Puvis's manner of painting was extremely variable."[1] Only when a variety of paintings—studies, easel paintings, reductions, including important atypical examples such as *The Woodcutters*—are brought together, does this become apparent, whereas isolated observation and formulation of generalizations solely on the basis of the large murals have led to serious misconceptions about the range of values Puvis de Chavannes was seeking to express in his art.

There are a number of preparatory drawings for this composition which, however, was never enlarged. It is possible that the composition was a rejected project for a mural never undertaken. D'Argencourt dates the painting between 1870 and 1880 and states that it is possibly contemporary with *L'Eté*, 1872-73 (Musée des Beaux-Arts, Chartres) and was perhaps planned as a pendant, *Winter*.[2] D'Argencourt also mentions and reproduces a preparatory drawing and a related pastel of *Orpheus* which may date from a later period, since the artist's production in this medium dates from the mid-eighteen eighties. An additional drawing, which I believe is preparatory for this painting and which is squared off for transfer to a larger state, is reproduced in La Plume, thus reinforcing the idea that *The Woodcutters* is a project for a large mural. The painting is one of a group comprising the two large oil sketches for *Ave Picardia Nutrix, Cider* and *The River* of 1864-65 (Metropolitan Museum of Art, New York),[3] *Greek Colony, Massilia* and *Marseilles, Port of the Orient* (cat. nos. 8 and 9) of 1868.

---

1. In terms of synthesizing contrasting traditions—in this case classicism and impressionism—the composition of *The Woodcutters*, especially but not exclusively in the compositional use of trees and the interspersion of figures, provided a dramatic model for Seurat's *La Grande Jatte*.

1. Goldwater, *Some Reasons*, p. 41.

2. *Les Peintures murales de Puvis de Chavannes au Musée de Picardie, op. cit.*, p. 97. Puvis returned to theme of *Summer* and *Winter* in the 1890s in his first group of paintings for the Hôtel de Ville, Paris.

3. See Sterling and Salinger, pp. 225-227. *Cider* and *The River* were exhibited in 1894 in Paris at Durand-Ruel's and again the same year in New York. Reviewing the Paris show Charles Yriarte wrote, "These broad generalizations which M. de Chavannes likes, are in the sketch stage and, such as they are, they tell us all that they are trying to say: but the public, taken aback, will perhaps say that they have been called in too soon . . . " "Six oeuvres de M. Puvis de Chavannes Galerie Durand-Ruel," *Le Figaro*, November 10, 1894, p. 1.

Pierre Puvis de Chavannes

The Meeting of Saint Genevieve and Saint Germain, 1876
Oil on canvas; 20½ x 40 in. (52.1 x 101.6 cm.)
Signed lower right: Puvis de Chavannes
Lent by Maud Hill Schroll

Catalogue no. 19

Ref. *Minneapolis Institute Bulletin*, Vol. XIX, March 1,
    1930, p. 45.

Pierre Puvis de Chavannes

Ludus Pro Patria, circa 1881
Oil on canvas; 37 x 49¼ in. (93.9 x 125 cm.)
Signed lower left: P. Puvis de Chavannes
Toledo Museum of Art, Gift of Edward Drummond Libbey

Catalogue no. 20

Ref. *The Toledo Museum of Art, Museum News*, no. 130, November—December, 1951 (50th anniversary issue).

Study for the right section of the large mural of the same title in the Musée de Picardie, Amiens, which was completed in 1883. A study for another section of the same mural, very similar in tonality, is in the collection of the Walters Art Gallery, Baltimore and a reduction of the entire mural belongs to the Metropolitan Museum of Art, New York (see Sterling and Salinger, p. 228).

The canvas appears to be slightly toned. There is a considerable variety of colours within the overall pale range—pinks, green, mauves, yellows, beiges in the foreground, greyish-green, blue in the thicker textures in the central background area. The trunk of the tree is thick white, beige-grey and the foot of the tree is green and beige. Many areas are overpainted, for example the sail unit at the right. Ideas were adjusted as the composition progressed and little or no attempt is made to provide "finish" to cover these alternatives.

The grouping of eight figures, including three children, is tight; in one group, the body of the child leaning backwards with his arm around the old man with staff is distorted and flattened out in a manner later to be adapted by Gauguin. There is no anatomical articulation. This type of pose is part of Puvis's standard repertoire. Subsidiary figures in the background are simple and their reflections in the water even more so; there is a clear-cut pattern of background units from the trees on the left to the intersecting horizontal patterned layers in the centre to the blue foliage at the right.

Features are blocked in by adjacent colour areas rather than defined exclusively by line—for example, the right hand of the centre figure in blue.

With Puvis de Chavannes, as with perhaps few painters, isolated details of his work reveal unexpected territory to contrast with our former impressions or preconceptions based on a far more generalized knowledge, often secondhand. Puvis does not hide his spontaneity under a bushel; just the contrary, for if we approach a painting such as *Ludus Pro Patria* from the smaller areas or parts to the whole, instead of the other way around, our conception is modified. In a composition such as this, where there is a real variety of patterned shapes and texture, where delicate is played against gently rugged, we find simplifications and distortions which cause us to search more deeply into the intimate pictorial means employed by the artist to achieve his effects. Classical repose and detachment, yes; Ingres, Quattrocento, as well; but with these we also find glimpses of Masaccio and Rembrandt-inspired textures and Delacroix-inspired variety of colour simplifications. These may represent a counterpoint or undercurrent to Puvis's calm, cool exterior but his flexibility also caused him to encompass sources whose effects were atmospheric and, in turn, moderns such as Maurice Denis did not fail to observe Puvis's use of varied textures to enhance atmospheric effects.

Pierre Puvis de Chavannes

The Poor Fisherman, circa 1879-1881
Oil on canvas; 28¾ x 36¼ in. (73 x 92 cm.)
Unsigned
Smith College Museum of Art

Catalogue no. 21

Perhaps the single best known and admired of Puvis's compositions, *The Poor Fisherman* exists in at least four painted versions and a lithograph made for Vollard's *L'Album des Peintres-Graveurs,* 1897 (second series). See Una E. Johnston, *Ambroise Vollard, Editeur: An Appreciation and Catalogue,* New York: Wittenborn and Company, 1944, p. 116; see also Ambroise Vollard, *Recollections of a Picture Dealer,* London: Constable, 1936, p. 61. The definitive version is in the Louvre, of 1881 (61 x 76 in.), a smaller version in the Pushkin Fine Arts Museum, Moscow of 1879 (26 x 36 in.) and an upright version in the Tokyo Museum of Modern Art (39⁷/₁₆ x 26¾ in.). The Smith College example is painted on a toned ground which is uncommon for Puvis. However, Maurice Denis comments on the painting in the

museum at Bourbon-Lancy (*Journal III.* 1938, pp. 205-6), ". . . the beautiful oil sketch done in sienna of the *Famille du Pêcheur*" (*The Fisherman's Family*). This painting, done in the mid-seventies, a few years prior to *The Poor Fisherman,* would seem to be a precedent for such a technique. The definitive version of *Famille du Pêcheur* was formerly in Dresden (destroyed) and a later small replica is in the Art Institute of Chicago.

The baby is wrapped in a pink-mauve blanket tinged ever so slightly with red; the foliage has touches of green, blue and light blue with brownish ground; the water is a densely textured pale green and the sky is a colourful white-blue-pink. The patterns made up of the appendages—anchor, folded arms, leaning mother, baby, shorelines, oars, make a distinct rhythmical sequence which is integrated with that of the sequence of chromatic colour patterns. The Smith College painting possibly dates from between the Moscow and Louvre examples. The painting was copied, or rather interpreted, by Seurat (see fig. 4 p. 102) and copied by Maillol (Musée National d'Art Moderne, Paris).

Pierre Puvis de Chavannes

Tamaris, circa 1880
Oil on canvas; 10 x 15½ in. (25.4 x 39.4 cm.)
Signed lower left: P. Puvis de Chavannes
The Metropolitan Museum of Art, The H.O. Havemeyer Collection, Gift of Mrs. J. Watson Webb, 1930

Catalogue no. 22

Ref. Sterling and Salinger, pp. 228-229.

Gentle angularity in patterns is stressed; the shoreline
and sky are similar to *Pleasant Land* (cat. no. 23) and
this type of composition would have been of interest to
Seurat. Generally reminiscent of Corot, its purple flowers and grey sky also forecast similar textural and colour effects in Maurice Prendergast.

Pierre Puvis de Chavannes

Pleasant Land (Doux Pays), 1882
Oil on canvas; 10⅛ x 18⅝ in. (25.8 x 47.3 cm.)
Signed lower left: P. Puvis de Chavannes
Yale University Art Gallery, The Mary Gertrude Abbey Fund, 1958.64

Catalogue no. 23

Ref. F. Forster-Hahn, *French and School of Paris Paintings in the Yale University Art Gallery: A Catalogue Raisonné*, New Haven: 1968, pp. 22-23 (with complete provenance and bibliography).

Finished study for or contemporary reduction of the large mural painted for the home of the painter Léon Bonnat on the rue Bassano in Paris and now in the Musée Bonnat, Bayonne.

The frame on *Pleasant Land* is original. The canvas inserts were designed and painted by Puvis de Chavannes. Painted borders around the large murals in the Panthéon recalling tapestries and also the painted floral borders surrounding the frescoes by Andrea des Castagno and Paolo Uccello in the Cathedral of Florence (painted by other hands later than the frescoes) occur on the frames or borders of canvases of other works by Puvis. Among these are catalogue nos. 12 and 13.

Puvis's works have frequently been referred to as tapestry-like. It is possible that among the influences exerted by this composition on Seurat, is the interest in painted frames, which harmonize with and set off the pictures in a manner complementary to the artist's work. Frames were of great interest to the neo-impressionist painters as well as to some of the impressionists.

The figures have very delicate, clear brown outlines, loose brushwork and a subtle equipoise which lends not only balance but a certain dignity to the ensemble. There is a rhythmic play on the leaf motif which occurs throughout: the upper left corner, centre, foreground and lower right. The whites are reminiscent of Whistler and the overall delicacy of Picasso *circa* 1905. The influence on Gauguin is most apparent (for example, *Young Breton Boys Wrestling*, of 1888, collection of Mr. and Mrs. Nathan Cummings, W273).

Pierre Puvis de Chavannes

Sacred Grove, circa 1883
Watercolour and pencil on paper; 7½ x 7½ in. (19.05 x 19.05 cm.)
Signed lower right: P. P. Ch.
Lent by The Phillips Collection

Catalogue no. 24

Ref. Duncan Phillips, *The Phillips Collection: A Museum of Modern Art and its Sources, Catalogue*, Washington, D.C.: The Phillips Collection, 1952, p. 83. A similarly treated watercolour, *Bathers*, study for *Ave Picardia Nutrix*, is in the collection of the Metropolitan Museum of Art, New York. See Jacob Bean, *Dessins français du Metropolitan Museum of Art, New York de David à Picasso*, Paris: 1973, pp. 60-61, no. 79, *Baigneuses*.

Figure to right white-grey and those to left blue-red-black. This type of watercolour would appear to be one of the sources of Maurice Prendergast's watercolour style, especially his late loose watercolours (see fig. 46, p. 191).

Pierre Puvis de Chavannes

The Sacred Grove, circa 1884
Oil on canvas; 36½ x 82⅞ in. (92 x 210 cm.)
Signed lower left: P. Puvis de Chavannes
The Art Institute of Chicago, Potter Palmer Collection

Catalogue no. 25

Ref. Mentioned in "The Atelier: Puvis de Chavannes," *The Art Amateur*, December, 1890, p. 5 as belonging to the Potter Palmers. See also John H. Neff, "Puvis de Chavannes: Three Easel Paintings," *Museum Studies*, 4, The Art Institute of Chicago, Chicago: 1969, pp. 66-86. Pissarro wrote his son Lucien from Lyons, July 5, 1898: "There is a fine museum with completely beautiful decorations by Puvis de Chavannes; his famous *Sacred Wood* makes a superb effect in the monumental stairway resembling the one in Rouen" (Pissarro, *Letters*, p. 327).

Reduction of the large mural in the Musée des Beaux-Arts, Palais Saint-Pierre, Lyons which was exhibited at the Salon of 1884. See catalogue no. 24 for watercolour study of this composition. See also Toulouse-Lautrec, *Le Bois Sacré, Parodie du Panneau de Puvis de Chavannes du Salon de 1884* (cat. no. 45).

Pierre Puvis de Chavannes

Au Clair de la Lune, 1885
Oil on canvas; 17½ x 14¾ in. (44.4 x 37.4 cm.)
Signed and dated lower right: Puvis de C. 8[?]5 and signed lower left: P. Puvis de Chavannes
Inscribed on back: *à Madame L[eo] Delibes/au clair de la lune par son ami Pierrot.*
The University of Kansas Museum of Art, Gift of Harold Kaye

Catalogue no. 26

Ref. Martha Barton Robertson, "On the importance of Puvis de Chavannes," *The Register of the Museum of Art*, The University of Kansas, Lawrence, Kansas, Vol. I, no. 9, December 1957, 147-151. (The author does not note signature with date.) The painting was formerly in the J.J.Emery Collection given to the Cincinnati Art Museum in 1924 and deaccessioned and sold at public auction in 1945.

The date of 1885 is indicated by the relationship of the figure to that at the extreme left (Melpomène) in *The Sacred Grove* of 1884. (See reduced replica of *The Sacred Grove*, cat. no. 25.) The motif of the starry blue sky is later employed in *Astronomy*, *c.* 1895-96 for the Boston Public Library.

Textures vary throughout the canvas: treatment is summary in the head and face areas with very sketchy patches on the face, upper right arm and chest. The wheat to the left is more thickly painted and the bands of blue to the right are freer. Overall handling is loose, delicate and rapid with the dress a pale pink-white, yellow flowers, wispy branches and a silvery white painted directly on the raw canvas. This silver area acts as a plane which creates space on the right side of the composition.

74

Pierre Puvis de Chavannes

Euterpe, circa 1885-90
Oil on canvas; 16½ x 9 in. (42 x 23 cm.)
Signed lower right: "*à Madame Philippe Gille très affecteusement P. Puvis de Chavannes*"
Lent by Mr. and Mrs. Richard L. Feigen

Catalogue no. 27

Pierre Puvis de Chavannes

A Vision of Antiquity—Symbol of Form, circa 1887-1890
Oil on canvas; 41½ x 52½ in. (105.4 x 133.3 cm.)
Signed lower left: P. Puvis de Chavannes
Museum of Art, Carnegie Institute, Pittsburgh

Catalogue no. 28

Ref. *Catalogue of the Painting Collection, Museum of Art, Carnegie Institute, Pittsburgh*, 1973, p. 139 (with provenance and bibliography).

Reduction of the large mural of the same title in the Palais des Arts, Lyons of 1885. This painting was exhibited in the Second Annual Exhibition (Pittsburgh International), 1897 (no. 186) and purchased by the museum in 1897.

A Vision of Antiquity is a "classic" Puvis de Chavannes, pale, dainty, serene, with a colour scheme of whitish-pink, blue, mauve and green over a toned ground which is allowed to show through in many areas. The picture is composed of a series of irregular, horizontal shapes fitted together in subtle harmonies, pale but with affirmative highlights and emphases. These include patches of variegated pale pinks, greys and browns in the rocks to the right which are highlighted by denser pinkish-beige accents at the top of each outcropping. The subtle variety of these colour accents within the pale range of tonalities is not at first apparent: yellow flowers over the reclining white goat in the lower foreground; red to the right of the seated shepherd's crook and white over the back of the seated woman in green cloak, who is very reminiscent of Giotto. Many areas are painted over with accentuations in the same colour range, for example the purplish-reds over pinkish-white-purple in the reclining foreground woman with amphora and the similar treatment of the woman in green and the standing woman in blue at the right.

Throughout, there is a varied use of line. In the seated nude at left seen from the back, there is a firm outline from her right hip to her knee. Then a beige colour area adjacent to the right of her lower leg defines the contour down to the foot. Her right arm is defined by a patch of uncovered canvas painted right up to the area of the arm as far as the hand. The upper left shoulder and arm are defined by pencil strokes. This variety of linear elements, joined with colour and colour patterns, is a basic feature of modern painting found for example in Gauguin, Denis and also in such men as Modigliani, whose interests in the old master traditions are well known.

No area is perfunctory; the canvas is organized according to the golden section which lends clarity to the composition without betraying the mechanism of the geometric division. The geometry was not an end in itself even though endless preparations for the transfer of the composition to the wall required precision and repeated studies. Seurat doubtless observed Puvis's approach carefully.

The elongation of trees and figures, the tranquillity and detachment, varied texture and processional sequence of figure alignment by way of rhythmic patterns is a fundamental source for the large figure compositions of Maurice Prendergast. The pale running Pegasus figures on the shore are a major source of Arthur B. Davies's figures.

A Vision of Antiquity and its variant *The Shepherd's Song* (cat. no. 32) are modern reinterpretations of Giovanni Bellini's *Allegory, circa* 1488 (Uffizi Gallery, Florence).

René Gimpel wrote in 1919:

> Carnegie Institute. The best picture is a Puvis de Chavannes: glimpse of antiquity, a celestial epic, with gods and goddesses, herdsmen and goats, Eros, the lute, quasi-winged horses, affectionate dalliance, obliteration of the sky, the earth, and human beings before the dazzle and blue violence of a sea which is no more than a vast lake.[1]

1. *Diary of an Art Dealer, op. cit.*, p. 91, entry February 13, 1919.

Pierre Puvis de Chavannes

Inter Artes et Naturam (Les Bienfaits de la Paix), 1890
Oil on canvas; 25½ x 67½ in. (64.8 x 171.4 cm.)
Signed lower right: P. Puvis de Chavannes
The National Gallery of Canada, Ottawa

Catalogue no. 29

Ref. R.H. Hubbard, *The National Gallery of Canada Catalogue of Painting and Sculpture,* Vol. II, Modern European Schools; Toronto: University of Toronto
Press, 1959, p. 43, no. 6331.

Preparatory oil sketch for the large mural of the same
subject in the Musée des Beaux-Arts, Rouen which was
exhibited at the first *Salon du Champ-de-Mars* in 1890. A
reduced replica of the mural is in the collection of the
Metropolitan Museum of Art, New York (cat. no. 30).

Pierre Puvis de Chavannes

Inter Artes et Naturam, 1890

Oil on canvas; 15⅞ x 44¾ in. (40.3 x 113.7 cm.)
Signed lower right: P. Puvis de Chavannes
Lent by The Metropolitan Museum of Art, Gift of Mrs. Harry Payne Bingham, 1958

Catalogue no. 30

Ref. Sterling and Salinger, pp. 230-231. The authors refer to the picture as possibly a study for the large mural in the Musée des Beaux-Arts, Rouen but it is probably a reduction painted after the mural. Catalogue no. 29 is a study for the mural and the two paintings present an excellent opportunity for firsthand comparison of both the preparatory sketch's rugged spontaneity and the careful, terse finish of the replica. Exhibited in the Third Annual Exhibition (Pittsburgh International) 1898 (no. 210).

This painting was immediately seized upon by the younger painters as confirmation that Puvis de Chavannes could utilize figures in contemporary rather than classical dress, something which they had had to overlook in their admiration for the purely pictorial qualities of his earlier art. In portraying what is not quite an everyday outdoor scene Puvis himself looks to such men as Courbet and Manet for the pose of the seated man in the right foreground.

The figure reclining in the left foreground recalls Whistler (see cat. no. 67). The striding youth to right of centre forecasts Picasso's adaptations of Greek *kouroi* (see *The Two Brothers* of 1905, fig. 39, p. 176). And the overall disposition of figures within a simplified landscape setting and the mother and child of Picasso's *Circus Family* (cat. no. 76), also of 1905, is specifically related to *Inter Artes et Naturam.* Picasso's work of *c.* 1919-1923 includes paintings, drawings and pastels for which the standing woman in the background resting on an architectural fragment could well be a source. Redon adapted features from this composition including the simply clad pale female figures (see cat. no. 70) and he also reworked such motifs as the classical winged Pegasus and figure on the wall in the background in his paintings and pastels of more than a decade later. Vincent van Gogh not only made a drawing of the composition (cat. no. 49), but its horizontal format and elements within affected his work in the final series of paintings done in June and July, 1890. Pissarro, Berthe Morisot and Mary Cassatt, as well as Maurice Denis, painted the theme of the mother and child picking fruit in the early nineties and the mood of Puvis's composition probably had its effect on their choice.

Pierre Puvis de Chavannes

The Bathers, circa 1890
Oil on canvas; 22⅞ x 15 in. (58 x 38 cm.)
Signed lower left: P. Puvis de Chavannes
Art Gallery of Ontario

Catalogue no. 31

The Bathers can be dated *c.* 1890 and possibly as late as 1893. The subdued greenish-browns in the foliage, the subtle gradations of blue in the area behind the standing figure, the firm stress on three-dimensional modelling and the absence of dominating pale, dry colour tonalities all indicate a work of the early nineties. Its tonality and unusually smooth texture relate also to *Winter* of 1891-92 (Hôtel de Ville, Paris). The composition's illustrative resemblance to *Girls by the Seashore* (fig. 11, p. 122) of 1879 (Musée du Louvre) provides a false lead in trying to date the painting.

Collections: Durand-Ruel, Paris (purchased from the artist, July 3, 1893); Durand-Ruel, New York (as of October 24, 1894); Charles H. Senff (*c.* 1895/99-1928): Durand-Ruel, New York (1928); M. Knoedler and Company; Private collection; Art Gallery of Ontario (accession number 74/30).

Exhibitions: Durand-Ruel Galleries, New York, *Exposition of Paintings, Decorations and Pastels by Mr. Puvis de Chavannes*, December 15-31, 1894; Albright-Knox Art Gallery, Buffalo, "The Nineteenth Century: French Art in Retrospect, Eighteen Hundred to Nineteen Hundred," November 1-30, 1932, Number 49, plate XII; Society of the Four Arts, Palm Beach, Florida, "Modern Art Loan Exhibition," January 2-23, 1938, Number 84; The Wadsworth Atheneum, Hartford, Connecticut, "The Nude in Art," January 1—February 3, 1946, Number 11; Joslyn Memorial Art Museum, Omaha, Nebraska, "The Beginnings of Modern Painting," October 4—November 4, 1951; The Corcoran Gallery of Art, Washington, D.C., "Visionaries and Dreamers," April 7—May 27, 1956, Number 22.

References: Arsène Alexandre, *Puvis de Chavannes*, London and New York, n.d. (*c.* 1904), plate 40; Léon Werth, *Puvis de Chavannes*, Paris: Les Editions G. Crès & Cie., 1926, plate 22 (erroneously dated 1894); *Important Paintings by Old and Modern Masters Collected by the late Charles H. Senff*, New York, Anderson Galleries, March 28-29, 1928 (no. 68, reproduced), bought by Durand-Ruel ($6250); reproduced *International Studio*, December, 1929, p. 108; B.L. Reid, *The Man from New York; John Quinn and his Friends*, N.Y.: Oxford University Press, 1968, p. 501, refers to Mrs. Charles H. Senff: "widow of man who bought Manet and Puvis twenty years ago" (John Quinn, 1921); Marie-Thérèse de Forges, "Un Nouveau Tableau de Puvis de Chavannes au Musée du Louvre," *La Revue du Louvre*, 1970, nos. 4-5, pp. 244-245, fig. 4, p. 245 (*Baigneuses*, "collection inconnue") and note 13, p. 244; Paris, Palais Galleria, *Très importants tableaux modernes*, 11 June, 1974, no. 24 (*Les Baigneuses*); *Handbook/Catalogue Illustré*, Art Gallery of Ontario, Toronto, 1974, p. 213; *Gazette des Beaux-Arts*, Vol. LXXXV, March, 1975, "La Chronique des Arts," p. 25, no. 92.

Related drawings: Sanguine drawing of standing figure reproduced in *Les Arts*, June, 1906 (Collection Mme. Esnault-Petterie); *Study for the Bathers* (standing bather), Fogg Art Museum, Harvard University, Grenville L. Winthrop bequest, acc. no. 1943.893; *Two Figures in a Landscape (Study for Bathers)*, pencil, Fogg Art Museum, Harvard University, Grenville L. Winthrop bequest, acc. no. 1943.900.

Pierre Puvis de Chavannes

The Shepherd's Song, 1891
Oil on canvas; 41⅛ x 43¼ in. (104.5 x 109.9 cm.)
Signed and dated lower left: P. Puvis de Chavannes 1891
Lent by The Metropolitan Museum of Art, Rogers Fund, 1906

Catalogue no. 32

Ref. Sterling and Salinger, p. 231. See also *Letters of Roger Fry, op. cit.,* Vol. I, pp. 257-258. Exhibited in the First Annual Exhibition (Pittsburgh International), 1896 (no. 233).

The four figures, goats and landscape are a re-use of the same units in *A Vision of Antiquity* (cat. no. 28) of several years earlier. Among the major differences is the square format which, together with more muscular figures, gives a compact solidity in place of the more delicate and lithe quality of the earlier composition. An exam-

ple of this transformation is the costume of the seated figure with right arm revealed, as opposed to the distinctly Trecento abstract simplification of the corresponding figure in the Pittsburgh painting. The rugged pink-mauve horizontal patches in the foreground help to establish the relatively more massive quality. The overall density in paint texture contrasts with the flatter surfaces found, for example, in such works as *Pastoral Poetry,* 1895-96 (cat. no. 39) and *Inter Artes et Naturam,* 1890 (cat. no. 30). The addition of the mountains in the background tends to give a backdrop effect rather than

Pierre Puvis de Chavannes

Normandy, 1893
Oil on canvas; 36 x 25 in. (91 x 63 cm.)
Signed and dated lower left: P. Puvis de Chavannes 93
Anonymous loan

Catalogue no. 33

depth. There is a distinct contrasting or linking of foreground to back by way of the complementary profiles of the mountain in the left background and the outstretched and partially covered right arm of the standing figure in the right corner foreground. The mountain to the right was painted over water and sky. There appears to have been no hesitation on the artist's part to rough in areas and consider this a finished picture. The greens and flowers recall Whistler and Prendergast and the handling of the upper right corner recalls Vuillard in colour, tonality and application.

Ref. Durand-Ruel Galleries, New York, *Exposition of Paintings, Decorations and Pastels by Mr. Puvis de Chavannes,* December 15-31, 1894, catalogue no. 1. See Aristide Maillol, *Girl Tending Cows, circa* 1890 (cat. no. 63), Paul Gauguin, *Nuit de Noël,* 1896 (cat. no. 54) and Roger de La Fresnaye, *Landscape with Woman, Cow and Dog (Marie Ressort), circa* 1913 (cat. no. 79).

The artist also made a lithograph of the same composition, *La Normandie,* 1893, *L'Estampe Originale* IV, plate 36, edition of 100 printed in brown.

Pierre Puvis de Chavannes

Study for "Charity," circa 1893-94
Oil on paper mounted on canvas; 95 x 138 in. (241 x 350.5 cm.)
Unsigned
Lent by Coe-Kerr Gallery, Inc., New York

Catalogue no. 34

Ref. See Marius Vachon, *Puvis de Chavannes*, Paris,
    1895, p. 146.

Study for one of four *voussures* representing the virtues of
Paris for the ceiling of the *escalier du Préfet*, Hôtel de
Ville.

Pierre Puvis de Chavannes

Charity, 1894
Oil on canvas; 36 x 28 in. (91.4 x 71 cm.)
Signed and dated lower right: 94   P. Puvis de Chavannes
Washington University Gallery of Art, St. Louis

Catalogue no. 35

Ref. Exhibited in 1894, Durand-Ruel Galleries, New York, *Exposition of Paintings, Decorations and Pastels by Mr. Puvis de Chavannes*, December 15-31, 1894, no. 7. This canvas is a reduction, listed in the above-mentioned catalogue as "Variation of the decoration of the Hôtel de Ville of Paris." Exhibited in the First Annual Exhibition (Pittsburgh International), 1896 (no. 234). See Holmes Smith, "The Technique of Puvis de Chavannes," *Bulletin of Washington University*, Series II, Vol. VII, Number III, April, 1909, pp. 16-24.

Holmes Smith, Professor of Drawing and History of Art at Washington University wrote:

> One who saw in the public exhibitions, the pale-tinted canvases of Puvis de Chavannes, so wan and ghost-like amid the turbulent and forceful naturalistic paintings that were popular about the middle of the last century, would hardly have credited such delicate conceptions to the mind of a man whose indomitable will and unswerving struggle towards his ideal gradually and finally changed the attitude of his critics from one of violent hostility to that of enthusiastic admiration. So that the maligned and almost friendless experimenter in pale harmonies, of the sixties, became the fêted and honor-laden master of the nineties. And this change of attitude was not brought about by any concession to popular demand, for by the time of his greatest success, his paintings had become even paler and even more Chavannesque than before.

Smith enumerated the general characteristics of Puvis's art and then described *Charity:*

> Parallelism and rhythm occur in the repeated long lines of the nun's garments, in the stem of the tree that cuts across her figure, in the main lines of the mother and child, and in the vertical termination of the rude wall behind. We see paleness of color and flatness of treatment both in the surfaces of the figures and in the objects that make up the landscape; and a greyness of flesh-tones as seen against the snow-white background. We see a certain uncouthness of form, notably in the exaggerated length of the nun's arms and in the extraordinary size of her hands.

> It is on the blending of delicate colors that the merit of the painting chiefly depends. Observe the skilful superposition of the white of the nun's cloak upon the white of the snow. How far these tones are from actual white will appear by comparing them with a piece of white note-paper. It will then be seen how much tender color there is in these tones which we call white. For the rest, the color scheme ranges by delicate gradations from purplish blue in the figure of Charity to pale amethyst in the clothing of the seated child, these being combined with varying tones of pink-grey and blue-grey and quiet browns and yellows, the whole making a delightful harmony of varying tones of grey. Beyond the figures, the wintry sunset sky glows faintly behind a loose film of rose-grey clouds. . . .

> . . . there is now on the walls of the St. Louis Artists' Guild a large copy in color of one of the most famous of his great series of decorations. The original from which this copy was made is the Hemicycle in the principal lecture theatre at the University of Paris. . . .

> The copy now on daily exhibition at the gallery at Union and Kensington avenues was made by two artists in Paris, one Mr. Charles H. Field, who was formerly a student in the St. Louis School of Fine Arts, and who as a student showed marked ability in decorative composition and color, the other Mr. Casteluccio, a Spaniard. In this painting the copyists have given us a very excellent suggestion of the color scheme and methods of composition as practiced by the master; and in it we see those qualities enumerated above which make it fulfil the canons of decorative art.

He also called attention to the fact that a replica of *Summer* (J.H. Wade Collection, Cleveland Museum of Art) was exhibited in St. Louis several years earlier. Thus we gain an idea of how Puvis's influence was disseminated through university art classes, exhibitions and copies in the early part of the century.

The tall figure recalls somewhat Maurice Denis, the standing child, which is a deep slatey greyish-blue, and the kneeling woman resemble Picasso. Textures throughout are relatively rugged; for example, there is a series of rugged white slashes in the lower left corner. None of this disrupts the basic calm and tranquillity of the composition. See also *Study for Charity* (cat. no. 34).

Pierre Puvis de Chavannes

Study of a Woman (Abundance), 1895
Lithograph, printed in brown; 12⅛ x 6 in. (30.8 x 15.2 cm.)
Signed lower right: 37/P P de C (pencil)
Lent by The Brooklyn Museum, Charles Stewart Smith Memorial Fund

Catalogue no. 36

Ref. *L'Estampe originale*, Plate 88, Album IX. See
    L'Estampe originale: A Catalogue Raisonné, Donna M.
    Stein and Donald H. Karshan, New York: The
    Museum of Graphic Art, 1970, p. 32. See also Ca-
    mille Mauclair, *Puvis de Chavannes*, Paris: Plon,
    1928, pl. XXXII, *Etude pour les vertues de Paris (La
    Charité)*, drawing in the Petit Palais, Paris.

Pierre Puvis de Chavannes

Harvesting (Récolte des Pommes), circa 1895
Oil on canvas; 15¼ x 9¾ in. (38.75 x 24.75 cm.)
Signed lower left: P. Puvis de Chavannes
National Collection of Fine Arts, Smithsonian Institution
Gift of John Gellatly

Catalogue no. 37

Ref. Bryson Burroughs, *Lecture to Art Students*, 1915, un-
    published manuscript in the Metropolitan Mu-
    seum of Art.

Pierre Puvis de Chavannes

Epic Poetry, circa 1895
Oil on canvas; 49½ x 24½ in. (126 x 62 cm.)
Signed lower left: P. Puvis de Chavannes
Museum of Fine Arts, Boston
Bequest of David P. Kimball in memory of his wife, Clara Bertram Kimball, 23.506

Catalogue no. 38

Catalogue no. 38

Finished study or possible reduction of one of the eight upright compositions surrounding the stairway of the Boston Public Library. This composition forms a pendant with *Pastoral Poetry* (cat. no. 39). The complete title is *Epic Poetry: Homer crowned by the Iliad and Odyssey (La Poésie Epique: Homère couronné par l'Iliade et l'Odyssée)*. The finished mural was exhibited at the *Salon du Champ-de-Mars* in 1896 together with *Pastoral Poetry, Dramatic Poetry* (fig. 35, p. 172), *History* and *Astronomy*.

The colour scheme is lavender-blue and pale blue with purplish shadows in the rock areas. Shadows are used as distinct patterns, for example, in the neck of Homer and the pattern to the right on the togas of the two standing figures. There is a paleness resembling fresco throughout the composition and the patterns created by contrast are gentle rather than emphatic. A different texture and direction to brushstrokes is evident in areas of the composition; for example, in the foliage individual strokes resemble those of Seurat (see cat. no. 47); longer strokes with a more pronounced texture are seen in the garments; gentle but vigorous long free horizontal brushstrokes are found in the foreground with an even broader underpaint showing through. This area is a mixture of lavender, pale green-white and grey. Thin glaze-like strokes are found in the purple shadow on the rock. There is a smooth fluidity in the sky and the garments of the attendant figures. Pencil marks, in areas such as the bush under the lyre, to the left of Homer, and the foreground bushes are allowed to show through. The rock outcropping in the left background is similar to that in *The Shepherd's Song* of 1891 (cat. no. 32).

The figures to the right recall early Picasso somewhat in drawing, as does the pale fluidity of the thinly-painted sky area. Maurice Denis is also indebted to pictures such as this for the static quality and simplifications of his figures in landscape.

See Fr. Thiébault-Sisson, "Ateliers d'Artistes: Puvis de Chavannes," *Le Figaro Illustré*, no. 98, May, 1898, pp. xv, 96-99, who reproduces a photograph (p. 96) of Puvis de Chavannes taken in his studio next to a scale model of the Boston Library, cut away in section, with small rough oil sketches for the upright panels, several painted together on one piece of canvas, tacked to the wall, indicating that Puvis intended them as a unified group and shuffled the arrangement of the compositions to achieve the relationship he sought.

Pierre Puvis de Chavannes

Pastoral Poetry, 1896
Oil on canvas; 47¾ x 23¾ in. (121 x 61 cm.)
Signed and dated lower left: P. Puvis de Chavannes 96
Anonymous loan

Catalogue no. 39

Catalogue no. 39

Finished study for one of the eight upright compositions surrounding the stairway of the Boston Public Library. This composition forms a pendant with *Epic Poetry* (cat. no. 38). The complete title is *Pastoral Poetry: Virgil (La Poésie des Champs: Virgile)*.

The finished mural was exhibited at the *Salon du Champ-de-Mars* in 1896 together with *Epic Poetry, Dramatic Poetry* (fig. 35, p. 172), *History* and *Astronomy*. The colour scheme is predominantly pale, chalky and fresco-like throughout, comprising greys, blues, pale lilacs and greens. Within the overall calm atmosphere, brushwork is active in many areas with touches of gently contrasting colours, for example blues and whites over greens in the clump of trees at the right. Upon close examination, areas such as these are simplified to the point of abstraction. The colour intensity is greatest in the foreground lower section in which, as it moves back into space, the greens and blues become progressively paler. Breadth in handling is apparent throughout. There is firmness, control, ease, a suave sense of calculation in the creating of colour relationships and the arrangement of space. A minor theme is the spontaneity which is found only in internal details rather than in the overall working out of ideas. Line and texture vary throughout and the appearance of thin painting is deceptive. For example, within the fresco-like atmosphere occurs a light scumble in the neck areas of the white garment and ragged flecks of gently contrasting pale, chalky colours and ragged outlines which are very similar to those found in certain works by Milton Avery (see cat. no. 86). The flowers in the foreground, white and pink at the foot of Virgil, and the tree at lower left are made up of long brush-strokes. In the immediate foreground, blue water and blue reflection of the trees, the straw beehives which stand teepee-like on a structure resembling a dock are a delicate tan in tonality, all have a slightly more emphatic textural quality made up of these pronounced strokes.

There is an overall zig-zag compositional arrangement of colour areas, broad side-to-side horizontals—water, rock, bands of the background, all fitted together in a manner recalling that of Gauguin. The tree trunk in the left foreground corner is picked up and echoed by the angularly-shaped blue cloak, the crook of the left arm and interlocking broad triangles of the background, so that on the vertical-horizontal framework is superimposed a subtle angularity. The shapes of the beehives and the juncture of tree branches also amplify this theme running through the composition. Another subsidiary theme within the vertical-horizontal composition is the series of curving profiles found in the rock, water and clump of trees in the right background. Other compositional punctuations include the two figures at the right, and the man and oxen in the left background at the juncture of the pale lilac and greyish blue areas.

Analysis of the pictorial constituents of the painting reveals a series of subtly adjusted colour, textural, pattern, linear and light relationships which are very broad and deceptively simple, those features most appealing to the modern artists at the end of the last century. *Pastoral Poetry* is similar in general character to *A Vision of Antiquity* (cat no. 28) and *Epic Poetry* (cat. no. 38) and shows the progressive simplification in every aspect of Puvis's approach, transforming his vision in a creative development of more than forty years.

92

Edouard Manet   (French, 1832-1883)

Moïse sauvé des eaux, circa 1860
Oil on canvas; 14 x 18 in. (35.5 x 46 cm.)
Signed lower right: E Manet (possibly not autograph)
Lent by the Nasjonalgalleriet, Oslo

Catalogue no. 40

Ref. Etienne   Moreau-Nélaton,   *Manet   Raconté   par
lui-même*,   Vol I,   Paris: Henri   Laurens   Editeur,
1926, p. 33 (Fig. 27, *Baigneuse*, 1861).

Gustave Moreau   (French, 1826-1898)

Les Piérides
Oil on canvas; 59 x 37⅜ in. (150 x 95 cm.)
Unsigned
Musée Gustave Moreau, Paris

Catalogue no. 41

Ref. *Catalogue des Peintures, Dessins, Cartons, Aquarelles
     exposés dans les galeries du Musée Gustave Moreau*, Jean
     Paladilhe, Paris, 1974, p. 50, no. 87.

94

Gustave Moreau

Prométhée, circa 1868
Watercolour on paper; 10⅝ x 6⅝ in. (27 x 17 cm.)
Signed lower left: Gustave Moreau
Musée Gustave Moreau, Paris

Catalogue no. 42

Ref. *Catalogue des Peintures, Dessins, Cartons, Aquarelles exposés dans les galeries du Musée Gustave Moreau*, Jean Paladilhe, Paris, 1974 p. 72, no. 313.

Cf. Puvis's Prometheus in the background of *Dramatic Poetry* (fig. 35, p. 172), Boston Public Library, for very similar motif.

Gustave Moreau

Eve
Oil on canvas; 16½ x 8¼ in. (42 x 21 cm.)
Signed lower left: Gustave Moreau
Musée Gustave Moreau, Paris

Catalogue no. 43

Ref. *Catalogue des Peintures, Dessins, Cartons, Aquarelles
exposés dans les galeries du Musée Gustave Moreau*, Jean
Paladilhe, Paris, 1974, p. 56, no. 133.

Gustave Moreau

Pasiphaé
Watercolour on paper; 14½ x 7½ in. (37 x 19 cm.)
Signed lower left: Gustave Moreau
Musée Gustave Moreau, Paris

Catalogue no. 44

Ref. *Catalogue des Peintures, Dessins, Cartons, Aquarelles exposés dans les galeries du Musée Gustave Moreau,* Jean Paladilhe, Paris, 1974, p. 74, no. 353.

Henri de Toulouse-Lautrec   (French, 1864-1901)

"Le Bois Sacré," Parodie du Panneau de Puvis de Chavannes du Salon de 1884, 1884
Oil on canvas; 68 x 150 in. (172 x 380 cm.)
Unsigned
Lent by The Estate of Henry Pearlman

Catalogue no. 45

Ref. *An Exhibition of Paintings, Watercolors, Sculpture and Drawings from the Collection of Mr. and Mrs. Henry Pearlman and Henry and Rose Pearlman Foundation,* The Brooklyn Museum, 1974, no. 13 (with provenance and bibliography).

Toulouse-Lautrec painted the parody in the winter of 1884. It hung in his studio on the rue Tourlaque from 1886 to 1897 and thus would have been seen by a number of his friends and visitors—all the young modern painters.[1] Suzanne Valadon modelled for Lautrec at the same time she modelled for Puvis and Renoir and thus the work is not merely an exotic interlude, a stale joke cast away and forgotten, but rather a reminder of a presence in the world of art which could neither be pigeonholed nor disregarded.

    Toulouse-Lautrec, at twenty, had pointed in a witty parody to the weakness of Puvis's art. Into Puvis's picture of the *Sacred Wood of the Muses,* exhibited in the Salon of 1884—a pallid landscape with white-robed classic figures and Greek columns—Lautrec had introduced a crowd of visitors in modern clothes, his own dwarf body among them—the reality of art as a world of living men with all their grotesque deformities.[1]

    The figure and two pigs to the left of the composition, directly borrowed from *The Prodigal Son,* reveal that Lautrec looked at other paintings by Puvis, including *The Prodigal Son* which was in the Salon of 1879. Lautrec may indeed have been intending more than a passing allusion to himself as the prodigal son as he sits before an easel with a canvas on which is written 'Meissonier' and 'MacKay'.[2] The group of figures is obviously meant to portray a number of out-of-place intruders in the style of Manet; the Japanese figure at the extreme right; the figure with checked blue and white overalls—a contemporary worker thrust into the midst of Puvis's calm classical world; and Lautrec himself who is seen from the back just above one of the seated muses reading a newspaper, appearing to relieve himself. Two of Puvis's figures are omitted and replaced by this procession in which a policeman watches over the

1. See M.G. Dortu, *Toulouse-Lautrec*; Paris: Editions du Chêne, 1952 for photograph of Lautrec at work with painting hanging on wall of studio.

1. Meyer Shapiro, "New Light on Seurat," *Art News,* Vol. 57, no. 2, April 1958, p. 45.
2. This refers to a now obscure incident involving a portrait commissioned by Meissonier which was rejected by the man who commissioned it. The "prodigality" Lautrec alludes to may have been the fact that he did not paint in the accepted style of Meissonier. The proximity of the pigs to Meissonier's canvas is an additional comment by Lautrec.

crowd. Almost no element in the painting is free from Lautrec's wit. The flying angels carry a tube of paint and on the pediment of classical architecture is a clock reading 9:05. The handling of the surface retains Puvis's spontaneity but the drawing is more lithe and supple. The delicate poses, for example the two foreground figures conversing at left of centre, have become only slightly less formal than in Puvis's painting. Puvis's typical floral elements, in this case narcissi, are scattered across the foreground. The colour quality retains Puvis's pale tonalities, here given a slightly golden yellow haze and fluid texture.

Georges Seurat   (French, 1859-1891)

Paysan Travaillant, 1882-1883
Oil on panel; 6¼ x 9⅞ in. (15.8 x 24.8 cm.)
Unsigned
Lent by Wildenstein and Company

Catalogue no. 46

Ref. *Inventaire posthume*, Atelier Seurat, May 3, 1891, no.
    43; (not in Dorra and Rewald or de Hauke).

Georges Seurat

Centre Moyenne Distance, Femme à la jupe rose: étude pour la Grande Jatte, 1884-1885
Oil on panel; 6½ x 9 in.(15.6 x 24.4 cm.)
Unsigned
Private Collection

Catalogue no. 47

Ref. Dorra and Rewald, *Seurat: L'Oeuvre peint biographie et catalogue critique*, Paris: Editions d'études et de documents, 1959, no. 127, p. 137. De Hauke, no. 121 (*Paysage et personnages*), pp. 74-75. Exhibited in the first impressionist exhibition in America, "Works in oil and pastel by the Impressionists of Paris," New York, American Art Galleries, 1886.

Fig. 4   Georges Seurat, *Landscape with "The Poor Fisher-man" by Puvis de Chavannes, c.* 1881

Seurat's connection with Puvis, as we have noted in cit-
ing Alexis (1884), Fénéon (1886) and Kahn (1888) (see
pp. 18-19), has been recognized since the beginning of
serious critical commentary on his work and has continued through the writings of our own day. Several authors have related certain of Seurat's early drawings to
Puvis,[1] and his small landscape with *The Poor Fisherman*
by Puvis (see fig. 4), variously entitled *Hommage à Pierre
Puvis de Chavannes*[2] and *Allusion au Pauvre Pêcheur*[3]
confirms his interest as of *circa* 1881 (the year Puvis's
painting was shown at the Salon). Russell states, "the
fact that he pounced on the picture is indicative of his
preoccupation with Puvis."[4]

"His art grows out of opposites: Puvis and the Impressionists. He had known both almost from the beginning of his career."[5] It is with *Une Baignade, Asnières
(Bathing Place, Asnières)* fig. 5 p. 103, National Gallery,
London, of 1883-84 (retouched *c.* 1887) that the interest
is absorbed into Seurat's own vision, and nearly every
critic since Alexis has commented on that relationship.
Benedict Nicolson, in 1953, observed the relationship
between the picture and Puvis's *Doux Pays* of 1882 (cat.
no. 23):

> It is not impossible that this kind of rather
> nostalgic classicism attracted Seurat when,
> two years after *Le Doux Pays* was painted, he
> himself produced his first masterpiece, *Une*

Baignade, Asnières, which shows the same compositional motifs of an almost unbroken horizon, boats in the water and a foreground
sloping from top to bottom right, peopled by
nude or semi-nude figures. At the same time it
must be stressed that Puvis uses idealized
figures inspired by Poussin and the Antique,
whilst Seurat chooses ordinary human beings
bathing by the banks of the Seine, without
idealizing them.[1]

Shapiro noted the same relationship[2] and William I.
Homer added:

> Seurat's search for a compositional matrix
> that would help him integrate his disparate
> observations led him to ... Puvis de Cha-
> vannes. ... we are not surprised to find the
> uncluttered spaces, solemn figures, and meas-
> ured rhythms of Puvis's *The Happy Land* ...
> echoed in *Une Baignade,* painted two years
> later. The pale and somewhat chalky tonality
> of Seurat's opus, too, recalls the earlier deco-
> rations by his mentor. It is no wonder, then,
> that one critic greeted *Une Baignade* as "a fake
> Puvis."[3]

Following Homer, Herbert writes:

> The chalky architectural colors of *Pleasant
> Land* find an echo in Seurat's first painting of
> mural scale, *Bathing Place, Asnières,* for in spite
> of his quasi-impressionist studies of colour sen-
> sations, he was still close to traditional paint-
> ing in 1883-84. ... Faced with the problem of
> a monumental painting nearly two by three
> meters large, Seurat looked to the greatest liv-
> ing master of mural art, even to the point of
> subduing his cherished color. The colors of
> *Bathing Place* are low-keyed, almost chalky,
> and in contrast to the bright hues of Impres-
> sionist painting which leap from the wall ...
>
> It is Puvis's compositional framework that
> chiefly attracted Seurat. Unwilling to sacrifice
> the classicising structure of the great French
> tradition of the casual compositions of the Im-

1. See John Rewald, *"La Vie et l'oeuvre de Georges Seurat,"* in which he
   compares Seurat's *Le Berger Endormi* (Louvre) (de Hauke, p. 310 of *c.*
   1878) with Puvis; Dorra and Rewald, *op. cit.,* pp. XXXIV-XXXV. *"La
   sérénité et les sujets antiquisants des décorations murales de Puvis de
   Chavannes;"* see also R.L. Herbert, *Seurat's Drawings,* New York:
   Shorewood Publishers Inc. 1962, p. 27.
2. Henri Dorra and John Rewald, *op. cit.,* no. 4 (dated *c.* 1879-1880).
3. De Hauke, no. 6, *c.* 1881.
4. John Russell, *Seurat,* New York and Washington: Frederick A. Praeger, Publishers, 1965, p. 30. Shapiro, "New Light on Seurat," *op. cit.,*
   p. 44, dates the picture "about 1882."
5. Shapiro, *op. cit.,* p. 44.

1. *Burlington Magazine,* XCV, December, 1953, supplement unpaged. The
   painting here referred to is the Yale version. It is also possible that
   Seurat saw Puvis's *Sketch for Summer, c.* 1873 (National Gallery, London) whose foreground bathing figures were suppressed in the
   definitive composition (Musée des Beaux-Arts, Chartres). Both Puvis
   and Seurat were familiar with Bazille's *Men Bathing* (fig. 1, p. 55) of
   1869.
2. *Op. cit.,* p. 44.
3. "Seurat's Formative Period: 1880-1884," *The Connoisseur,* Sept., 1958,
   pp. 61-62. See also Homer, *Seurat and the Science of Painting,* Cambridge: The M.I.T. Press, 1964, p. 97 where the author adds, "In
   painting *Une Baignade* Seurat seems to have wanted to combine
   Puvis's sense of decorative design with a modern divisionist approach
   and contemporary subject matter—all of which was governed by a
   controlled value scheme."

Fig. 5   Georges Seurat, *Une Baignade, Asnières,* 1883-84, reproduced by courtesy of the Trustees, The National Gallery, London

pressionists, Seurat applied his brighter out-of-doors colors to a contemporary scene in a way that justified a later remark, that he was "modernizing Puvis de Chavannes." *Bathing Place* and *Pleasant Land* have in common many major elements: the right-to-left diagonal of the bank; water and land forming nearly equal triangles; distilled, often geometric shapes; placing of major features along linear axes. Underlying both compositions is a mathematical skeleton harking back to the classical tradition; Puvis depends upon the Golden Section, Seurat upon a simpler subdivision of the canvas into thirds and halves.[1]

Whether or not Seurat's approach to framing by setting his paintings off by a series of dots contrasting in tone to his composition and then enclosing that in a white frame—itself painted in his later works—is due to Puvis's enframing borders (of which an example painted by himself surrounds *Pleasant Land*) is a question open to discussion.[2] Although the relationship to *Pleasant*

Land is unmistakable, the painting was still in process when Puvis's *Sacred Grove* was shown at the *Salon* of 1884 and certain motifs, namely the muse reclining by the riverbank and several of the seated muses with hands on their laps, also recall and could have reinforced Seurat's *Baignade* (see fig. 5). A number of the small *croquetons* for the final composition do not include the reclining man in the left foreground.[1] The preparatory Conté crayon drawing[2] for this figure emphasizes strongly the profile contour as does Puvis's corresponding figure.

Daniel Catton Rich, in 1935, in his study of Seurat's *La Grande Jatte*[3] wrote:

> For the recording eye of the impressionists, Seurat substituted the organizing mind of the classical artist. . . . He belongs to that side of the French tradition which has returned from time to time to the tranquilizing elements of

1. Herbert, *op. cit.*, pp. 25-27, *et. seq.*
2. See Robert Goldwater, "Some Aspects of the Development of Seurat's Style," *The Art Bulletin*, XXIII, no. 2, June 1941, p. 118, note 5 and Gustave Kahn, "Peinture; Exposition des Indépendants," *La Revue Indépendante*, VI, April, 1888, pp. 160-164.

1. See de Hauke, no. 91 (William Rockhill Nelson Gallery) and de Hauke, no. 80 (Cleveland Museum of Art), among others.
2. Musée du Louvre (de Hauke, no. 590). This general correspondance might be an indication that Seurat was familiar with Puvis's composition in its working stages and thus a possible confirmation of his aquaintance with him.
3. *Seurat and the Evolution of "La Grande Jatte,"* Chicago: The University of Chicago Press, 1935, pp. 47-49.

Greece and Rome. . . . In the Greek and Roman obeissances of Puvis de Chavannes we find the connecting link between the classic attitude of the past and the artists of the second half of the last century. Few critics have noticed Seurat's dependence on the man who decorated the Panthéon, but it is clearly to be read in both "The Bather" and "La Grande Jatte." Ignoring for a moment the difference in subject, we find in Seurat's two paintings Puvis's typical back-drop of slender trees and river bank. Regardless of their decorous poses imitated from Greek vases or Roman wall paintings, Puvis's figures form part of a calculated pattern and in certain compositions are repeated in a system of vertical poses that almost foretells "La Grande Jatte." Over Puvis's wall decorations there hovers a delicate veil of color, which in its grayed violets and powdery blues likewise left its mark on Seurat. . . . Puvis . . . employed a type of simplified and abbreviated contour that may easily have influenced Seurat's more severe, sensitive draftsmanship.

Shapiro relates *La Grande Jatte* (1884-1886) to Puvis's *Greek Colony, Massilia* (Marseilles) of 1869,[1] and, of course, Fénéon's description of a "modernized Puvis" (see p. 18) has been the original clue since Seurat's own time that the artist was not in the slightest annoyed by the comparison. In *Centre Moyenne Distance, Femme à la jupe rose, Etude pour "La Grande Jatte"* (cat. no. 47) of 1884-1885, the essential compositional elements of the larger picture exist: the profiles and rigid stances; the compositional byplay between figures and setting—a grid of vertical-horizontal elements, modulated by the glowing unctuousness of the paint texture and colour quality itself so that any sense of mechanization is kept in tow. Delicacy and atmosphere are maintained and the miniature scale for presenting an architectonic conception seems not to interfere with our grasp of the monumental scheme. Everything is simplified without a loss of grasp on the presence of the place; simplification is joined with detachment as the vertical units act as guideposts into the depth of the composition. Shadows play an important organizing role as they always do in Seurat, his subtle use of their patterns helping to create the spaciousness within which we feel ourselves able to move. Puvis has been transformed— "modernized" to a contemporary eye—and it aids us in understanding Seurat to comprehend one of his important contemporary sources by which the classical tradition became accessible to the young man and thus also to see how he filtered his perceptions of the Quattrocento masters with whom critics are so fond of linking him, even though he never saw their monumental wall paintings firsthand. Scale was of immense importance to Seurat and the appeal of the size of Puvis's work ought not to be underestimated.

Of *The Models* of 1886-1888,[1] Seurat's compatriot Signac recorded the following comment in his journal: "The back of the woman at the left, among others, and the accessories, are superb pieces [of painting], as beautiful as the most successful of Puvis's and Renoir's works, of whom Seurat in this painting seems to unite the qualities. . . "[2]

Signac even finds Puvis's overriding principles—or at least principles he would like to derive from Puvis's art—in accord with Seurat's latest, large compositions.

Signac, at the end of his life, wrote:

> Sad as the chosen subject might be, cheerless as its component picturesque elements might be, the picture will never give—except to the insensitive—the expression of tragedy if the prevailing lines, tints and tones are not in plastic agreement with the sentiments which the artist wishes to convey. If the mast of the barque in the *Poor Fisherman* by Puvis de Chavannes was not inclined in the direction of inhibition (counter-clockwise) this picture would not be suggestive of sadness. Puvis, pupil of Poussin, knew how to handle the elements of the composition. If the *Chahut* and the *Cirque* of Seurat were not composed of dynamogenous lines, tints and tones, they would not be pictures of movement and joy, despite their titles. These eternal rules, applied by Poussin, Puvis de Chavannes and Seurat, reinforce the fragility of the picturesque through the pictorial.[3]

1. The Barnes Foundation.
2. Paul Signac, "Extraits du Journal inédit de Paul Signac," II, 1897-1898, *Gazette des Beaux-Arts,* April 1952, ed. John Rewald, p. 272 (30 December, 1897). Shapiro also finds a relationship between *The Models* and Puvis, but one of a more theoretical than pictorial nature. See Shapiro, *op. cit.,* p. 44.
3. *Le Sujet en peinture: Le Pittoresque et le Pictural, Encyclopédie Française,* XVI, Paris: 1935, pp. 16, 84-87.

1. *Op. cit.,* p. 44.

Pierre-Auguste Renoir (French, 1841-1919)

Standing Bather, 1887
Oil on canvas; 17 x 10⅜ in. (43 x 26.8 cm.)
Signed lower left: Renoir
Sterling and Francine Clark Art Institute, Williamstown, Massachusetts

Catalogue no. 48

Ref. *Impressionist Paintings: 33 Renoir, 2 Monet*, Exhibit Six, Williamstown: Sterling and Francine Clark Art Institute, n.d. (1956), no. 157 (with provenance).

It is well known that Renoir in the early eighteen eighties began to seek out sources which would aid him in his search for a more solid and monumental form. In the spring of 1881 Renoir spent six weeks in Algeria and in the fall the artist made his first trip to Italy where he visited Venice, Florence, Rome, Naples and Pompeii as well as Sorrento and points further south. Surprisingly, he most admired Raphael's fresco *Galatea* in the Villa Farnesina and those in the Vatican.[1] He was also deeply impressed by the ancient Roman wall paintings.[2] Upon his return early in 1882 he stopped to visit and paint with Cézanne and was taken ill. He remained with Cézanne for some months to convalesce and undoubtedly discussed with him his impressions of the paintings seen in Italy. Considering their relationship, this visit may have been expressly occasioned by a desire to report his observations fresh to Cézanne who had never visited Italy. Indeed, it is interesting to note that Pissarro relates that Renoir told him while looking at Cézanne's paintings at Vollard's exhibition in 1895 that they had a "quality like the things at Pompeii, so crude and so admirable!"[3] Renoir and Cézanne were from the standpoint of their art very open but critical experimenters. They looked at and formulated from nature and the traditions. Theories or esoteric interpretations of art such as interested Gauguin, Seurat, Signac, Denis and their comrades were of no interest to them. Renoir and Cézanne conducted research of an empirical kind into the nature of the visible world. No matter how complex their respective picture ideas, or even technical approaches to their work, their feelings or "sensations" kept these explorations spontaneous.

Speaking of the period from about 1882 through 1887, Renoir related to Vollard, "A sort of break . . . came in my work about 1883. I had wrung Impressionism dry, and I finally came to the conclusion that I knew neither how to paint nor draw. In a word, Impressionism was a blind alley, as far as I was concerned."[4] After his Italian journey, Renoir recalled, he was wary of working out-of-doors: "Out of doors there is a greater variety of light than in the studio, where, to all intents and purposes, it is constant; but, for just that reason, light plays too great a part outdoors; you have no time to work out the composition;

you can't see what you are doing."[1] About the same time, Renoir had read Cennino Cennini's *Treatise on Painting*[2] which impressed him enough that he tried to adapt some of the effects described therein to his work. He later wrote a short foreword to an edition published in 1911.[3] Renoir's work at this time takes on a distinctly classical cast in its fulness and compositional complexity. His reactions to the above cited sources led him to experiment with a paler colour scheme with subdued intensities and with a marked emphasis on linear outline, especially in figures and nude compositions. A conscious striving for simplicity, a return to essentials, supplanted some of the spontaneous naturalism of the previous decade. According to Vollard, Renoir told him: "At this time I also did some paintings on cement, but I was never able to learn from the ancients the secret of the inimitable frescoes."[4] In 1884, Renoir began his major composition of the period, *The Bathers*[5] (fig. 6 p. 107) on which he worked for approximately three years. The sources of the composition are well established— Girardon's relief frieze, *The Bath of Diana* at Versailles and Boucher's *Diana at the Bath*.[6] But these are primarily compositional rather than sources of colour quality. We would propose an additional source of inspiration for *The Bathers* in the decorative murals and paintings of Puvis de Chavannes. Indeed, when Renoir first exhibited his *The Bathers* at the Galerie Georges Petit in 1887, it was under the title "*Baigneuses, essai de peinture décorative.*"

Renoir had been home from Italy for three years when he undertook to paint *The Bathers*. To augment his reading of Cennino Cennini, aimed at achieving a fresco-like colour quality and surface in his work, the artist would have looked to sources at hand to study as models. Apart from Ingres, whose waxen surfaces Renoir did not emulate, his interest in Raphael and early Roman wall paintings would have been served by the readily available murals of Puvis—so often referred to, although mistakenly, as "frescoes"—whose work Renoir undoubtedly saw at their dealer Durand-Ruel as well as in the Panthéon and at the yearly Salons. Renoir travelled a great deal during this period and could well have stopped in Amiens where, among others, he would have seen Puvis's mural *Ave Picardia Nutrix*, especially

1. See Ambroise Vollard, *Renoir: An Intimate Record*, New York, 1925, p. 102. Renoir is reported to have said, "I must confess that my greatest joy was Raphael" (p. 102).

2. "Fresco painting has always interested me . . . they're the most exquisite pictures in the world," *ibid.*, p. 103.

3. Pissarro *Letters*, p. 276 (letter of November 21,1895)

4. Vollard, *op. cit.*, p. 118.

1. *Ibid.* Ironically, Seurat is quoted as having criticized Puvis de Chavannes for working out his ideas in the studio (see p. 19).

2. *Ibid.*, p. 122

3. Auguste Renoir, *Lettre précédant la traduction du Livre d'Art de Cennino Cennini*, Paris: ed. Victor Mottez, 1911.

4. Vollard, *Renoir, op. cit.* p. 123. As late as 1916 Renoir was experimenting with a type of fresco painting (see *Paintings by Renoir*, The Art Institute of Chicago, 1973, cat. no. 83).

5. Philadelphia Museum of Art, The Mr. and Mrs. Carroll S. Tyson Collection (signed and dated 1887).

6. Musée du Louvre (see Vollard, *Renoir, op. cit.*, p. 25). Renoir employed similar poses to those in *The Bathers* at least as early as *c.* 1879 (see *Study for Tannhauser*, Sterling and Francine Clark Art Institute).

Fig. 6   Pierre-Auguste Renoir, *The Bathers,* 1887

the right section, a study for which, entitled *The River,* he might also have seen at his dealer's.[1] There is a general illustrative similarity between the theme of this painting and *The Bathers.* Much more important, however, to Renoir's immediate purposes would have been *The Sacred Grove* which was exhibited at the Salon of 1884 and which has all the basic constituents of Puvis's style—coolness, detachment, simplicity, large scale and fresco-like dryness in the colour.[2] Renoir would have had the opportunity to study this picture carefully in the spring of 1884 when he was either conceiving or actually preparing some of his numerous studies for *The Bathers.*[3] Although static in their composure, Puvis's nudes also gesture and are posed in a manner related to

those of Girardon, a source which, together with Poussin, would have appealed to Puvis. But Girardon's decorative frieze relief was sculpture and clues as to fresco-like colour and pictorial space composition would have to come from another source. Puvis was the living exemplar of the classical tradition and even though both Renoir and Cézanne revered the great Venetians, Rubens, the eighteenth century men and Delacroix, the clear delineation of Puvis's figures, the order of his compositions, carried on another aspect of the French tradition which Renoir could also admire just as Cézanne was devoted to the classicism of Poussin. Although a direct copying of figures would have been contrary to Renoir's nature, what was readily available to him in Puvis's work encouraged him to cross the boundaries of affiliation. If the artist could study Cennini and Girardon he surely looked at Puvis.

In addition to the work itself, circumstances would seem to support the supposition that Puvis was an influence on Renoir at this time; by Christmas of 1882, Suzanne Valadon (1865-1938) came to pose for Puvis de Chavannes; he was fifty and she seventeen and for several years thereafter she was Puvis's mistress. Su-

1. Collection, The Metropolitan Museum of Art (see Sterling and Salinger, pp. 225-227).
2. *Pleasant Land* had been exhibited at the Salon of 1882.
3. For example, the preliminary figure study drawing, *Badende Mädchen,* 1883? with seven major and two subsidiary nudes, Bührle Collection, Zurich (see *Sammlung Emil G. Bührle,* Zurich: Kunsthaus, 1958, pp. 109-110, no. 172, ill. p. 216). The semi-nude seated figure at the right is particularly reminiscent of Puvis's drawing style in *The Sacred Grove.* Suzanne Valadon could have been the model for these figures.

zanne Valadon posed for *The Sacred Grove*[1] and in 1884 and again in 1886 posed for the murals destined for Lyons. These were exhibited as a triptych at the Salon of 1886.[2] Although long since ceasing to be romantically attached, she posed intermittently thereafter for Puvis until 1889 for work including the *Allegory of the Sorbonne.* From 1884-1886 Valadon posed for nudes which Renoir painted at that time, probably including some of those in *The Bathers.* Over the three-year period while he was making preparatory studies for and repainting *The Bathers,* Valadon also posed for such pictures as *Bather Arranging her Hair*[3] (dated 1885) and *Woman Plaiting her Hair*[4] of 1886. *The Bathers* has been described as follows:

> The composite effect of the color-organization is that of a succession of light, delicate, mostly pale tones of green, tan, coral, pink, terra cotta, all more or less permeated with lavender, and all practically equal in light-content, so that the ensemble is relatively uniform in tonality. . . . The surface is mat and dry and the general color has the feeling of extremely delicate pastel . . .
>
> The modeling is done by a gradual transition from lavender shadows to light brownish-coral and tan . . . The difference in color and in drawing and modeling between foreground and background establishes an adequate contrast between the two areas without detracting from the tapestry-effect of the picture as a whole. . . . the composition is one of volumes in space with clean-cut intervals between the different masses, as well as between the component parts of these as they enter into rhythmic arabesque-formations.
>
> . . . the total design is of high decorative value. The rigidly stylistic appearance is a natural result of the studied execution, which extended over a period of several years and involved many preliminary sketches.[5]

Compare this description with *A Vision of Antiquity* (cat. no. 27) which Renoir would have seen at the Salon of 1886 and it becomes plausible that these lavender tonalities, tapestry effects and the like, emanate from Renoir's study of Puvis de Chavannes.

We think it significant that Suzanne Valadon should have posed virtually simultaneously for the two painters at the very moment when Renoir was investigating a more classical orientation in his work and when, indeed, influences such as Raphael and Girardon can be documented in the formulation of *The Bathers* composition. In their shared intimacy, can Valadon and Renoir have failed to have discussed Puvis's approach to painting, leading Renoir to consider it carefully? From what we know of Renoir's inquisitive personality, it would have been out of character for him not to have followed up on this direction. Renoir would not have been at the 1895 banquet for Puvis had he not respect for the alternative the older artist had developed in his classically-inspired art. As if to underscore this fact, along with Monet, Renoir was on the organizing committee for that event.[1]

The strands of Renoir's sources in the eighties, both ancient and contemporary, are varied and difficult to weave together. His objectives are apparent from the later direction of his art. He continued to share his ideas with Cézanne and visited him again in 1885, 1888 and 1889, and they frequently painted the same motif together. It is of value then to draw attention to aspects of Renoir's technique at this time since it differs markedly from the impressionist technique of Monet and Sisley; it corresponds more to the planned and deliberate approach taken by both Cézanne and Puvis de Chavannes. Perhaps from reading Cennini and perhaps from a knowledge of Puvis's preparatory technique, directly or by way of Suzanne Valadon, Renoir began at this time to make careful multiple studies of the model. Berthe Morisot, close friend of both Puvis and Renoir, recorded in her journal for January 11, 1886:

> Visit to Renoir. On a stand, a red pencil and chalk drawing of a young mother nursing her child, charming in subtlety and gracefulness. As I admired it, he showed me a whole series done from the same model and with about the same movement. He is a draftsman of the first order; it would be interesting to show all these preparatory studies for a painting, to the public, which generally imagines that the Impressionists work in a very casual way. I do not think it possible to go further in the rendering of form; two drawings of women going into the water I find as charming as the drawings of Ingres. He said that nudes seemed to him to be one of the essential forms of art.[2]

Witness to Renoir's adaptation of classical techniques and to his planning of compositions also comes from Maurice Denis who recorded in his *Journal* in 1897: "Renoir traces his drawings and modifies his picture by means of successive tracing."[3] In 1897, Renoir was

---

1. Later she came to pose for Toulouse-Lautrec who had painted his parody of the very painting for which she modelled (cat. no. 45).

2. *A Vision of Antiquity, Christian Inspiration, Le Rhône* and *La Saône.* (Thirty years later Renoir himself painted the theme of *Le Rhône* and *La Saône.*)

3. Sterling and Francine Clark Art Institute.

4. Private Collection, Switzerland. Both Puvis and Renoir have been variously said to have been the father of Maurice Utrillo (born 1883).

5. Albert C. Barnes and Violette de Mazia, *The Art of Renoir*, New York: Minton, Balch and Co., 1935, pp. 96-98.

1. See Philippe Auquier, *Le Figaro*, December 12, 1894, p. 5.

2. *The Correspondence of Berthe Morisot, op. cit.*, p. 130. Morisot was in close contact with Puvis over art matters at this time.

3. *Journal* I, p. 121.

painting his *Bathers in Forest* [1] which was the successor to *The Bathers* of 1884-1887.

The general qualities of Renoir's work of the period 1885-1887 have been described thus:

> Sculptural one-piece modelling, light coral-toned flesh with lavender in shadows, extreme diminution of highlights, unaccented shadows . . . pale and light tonality, hard and smooth surface, sharp contour, abundance of linear rhythms and a distinctive type of color. This color is in general dry, arid and of fresco-quality, occasionally acid and harsh, and sometimes associated with terra cotta tones. [2]

In *Standing Bather* (cat. no. 48) of 1887 we find an example of the one-piece modelling, unaccentuated shadows, pale tonality, sharp contour, linear rhythms, use of lavender tones and dry textural quality—all of which find parallels in the work of Puvis de Chavannes. In addition to drawing and colour handling, the simplified background planes recall such works by Puvis as *Girls by the Seashore* (fig. 11 p. 122) of 1879, *The Bathers* (cat. no. 31), *The Sacred Grove* (cat. no. 25) and *A Vision of Antiquity* (cat. no. 28). [3]

Renoir had connections with Puvis's circle of friends other than Morisot, Valadon and Durand-Ruel. Degas, Rodin and Marcellin Desboutin were also friendly with Puvis. Téodor de Wyzewa, passionate Wagnerite who held both Puvis and Renoir in high esteem, wrote in 1890:

> M. Renoir had become famous: of all the impressionists he was the most delicate, the most feminine. . . . And it was this . . . feminine aspect of his work which displeased him at this time. For several years he was anxious and at moments desperate, studying the old masters of whom he remained a fervent and fearful admirer. He was searching for a more solid, classical art . . . outside of the sensual charm which he knew how to add. *The Bathers* which he exhibited . . . in 1887, and which he found some malicious people made fun of, will remain as the witness to these years of research and hesitation. I cannot forget the extraordinary emotion which this painting aroused in me, so gentle and yet so strong, a delightful blend of precise vision and dreamlike music. The effort of so many years culminated in triumph. M. Renoir at last grasped, not to lose it again, this pure and skilful beauty of form of which he is henceforth the only one, along with M. Puvis de Chavannes, to know the se-

cret. Portraits, nude studies and the children's heads which he painted two years ago are as lively and decisive in execution as the great works of the masters. Now it is a matter of recapturing external grace, ennobled and raised to the level of this art which from now on is wholly classical. And it is with this reconciliation of the power of life and grace of expression that M. Renoir concerns himself since that time. Today, each of the pictures he paints represents for him a distinct manner; for he has not spent ten years in patient and varied study, to which none of our young fashionable painters has the time or inclination to devote themselves, nor has he ceased being a master for ten years in order to become a pupil again, without having gained an abundant and flexible vision capable of adapting to various subjects the various forms which can fit them. . . .

> M. Renoir is a classical painter and one of the most French; this is what endears him to us most deeply. He concerns himself with formal perfection, has a horror of exaggeration, proceeds further and further towards an art of discreet and simple harmony. In that respect he is linked to Poussin and Watteau, who along with Rubens are his real masters. [1]

In sum, we think that Renoir turned for inspiration to Puvis's work of the 1880s for an indication of how to proceed with his own experiments. Having learned what he sought, Renoir moved on to the fuller, richer, weightier art of his post-1890 period. His presence at the dinner for Puvis was an indication of his respect for the man whose work helped Renoir through his "crisis."

---

1. The Barnes Foundation.
2. Barnes and de Mazia, *op. cit.*, p. 93.
3. See also Renoir's *Girls Playing Shuttlecock*, 1887, Minneapolis Institute of Arts and *Le Retour du Champs*, c. 1887 (Sykes Collection), *La Femme, la vache et la brebis*, 1887 (Private Collection, Switzerland).

1. "Pierre-Auguste Renoir," *L'Art dans les Deux Mondes*, no. 3, December 6, 1890, pp. 27, 28. The author was close to Renoir during this period. He secured a commission for Renoir to paint the portrait of Mme. de Bonnieres (de Bonnieres owned a small version of *Girls by the Seashore* by Puvis de Chavannes). Renoir stayed with de Wyzewa in February and March of 1891. It is possible that the critic was attracted to Renoir in part because he knew that Renoir had painted a portrait of Wagner in Palermo in 1881. Renoir admired the composer's work at that period in his life.

Vincent van Gogh (Dutch, 1853-1890)

Drawing after Puvis de Chavannes's Inter Artes et Naturam, early June 1890
Pen and ink on paper; detail from a letter to his sister Wilhelmina (see below).
Rijksmuseum Vincent van Gogh, Amsterdam

Catalogue no. 49

Ref. van Gogh, *Letters,* no. W22, p. 471.

Catalogue no. 49, page from letter to van Gogh's sister
Wilhelmina, June 1890, 8½ x 6¾ in. (21.5 x 17 cm.)

Vincent van Gogh

Women walking along in the fields, July 1890
Oil on paper on canvas; 11¹⁵/₁₆ x 23½ in. (32 x 61 cm.)
Unsigned
Collection Marion Koogler McNay Art Institute, San Antonio

Catalogue no. 50

Ref. de la Faille, *op. cit.*, no. F. 819, *Jeunes filles longeant les champs* (incorrectly listed as oil on canvas).

In June, 1888, Vincent van Gogh had written from Arles to Emile Bernard, "Do you remember 'John the Baptist' by Puvis? I myself think it amazing and as magical as Eugène Delacroix."[1] In August he wrote:

> You see, my dear comrade Bernard—that Giotto and Cimabue, as well as Holbein and Van Dyck, lived in an obeliscal—excuse the word—solidly framed society, architecturally constructed, in which each individual was stone, and all the stones clung together, forming a monumental society. When the socialists construct their logical social edifice—which they are still pretty far from doing—I am sure mankind will see a reincarnation of this society. But, you know, we are in the midst of downright laisser-aller and anarchy. We artists, who love order and symmetry, isolate ourselves and are working to define *only one thing*.
>
> Puvis knows this all right, and when he, so just and wise—forgetting his Elysian fields

—was so good as to descend amiably into the intimacy of our time, he painted a fine portrait indeed: the serene old man in the clear light of his blue interior, reading a novel with a yellow cover—beside him a glass of water with a water-color brush and a rose in it. Also a fashionable lady, as the de Goncourts have depicted them.[1]

The "fashionable lady" could be Puvis's portrait of Princess Cantacuzène and the entire passage, with its detailed recollection of the paintings, strongly indicates that van Gogh had visited the exhibition of Puvis's work at Durand-Ruel's Gallery in November-December, 1887, even perhaps together with Bernard.

In May, 1890, van Gogh journeyed from Arles to Paris where he stayed three days (May 17-20) with his brother Theo and sister-in-law Jo before continuing to Auvers-sur-Oise where he had been invited by his friend Dr. Gachet. During the brief stopover in Paris, which was filled with visits from his old acquaintances and charged with the excitement of meeting Theo's wife and seeing his newly born nephew, van Gogh went to the *Salon du Champ-de-Mars* where he saw and was deeply impressed by Puvis de Chavannes's *Inter Artes et*

1. van Gogh *Letters* III, B8 (11), p. 497 (late June, 1888). The painting referred to could be the version in the National Gallery, London.

1. van Gogh *Letters* III, B 14 (9), p. 508 (early August, 1888).

Naturam, destined for Rouen. The image of tranquillity and pastoral grace which pervades the composition seemed to harmonize with and in some way exemplify aspects of nature which Vincent was attempting to express in his work and to resolve in his life. A long-standing admirer of Puvis, as we can glean from his earlier correspondence with his brother,[1] Vincent not only refers to Puvis's painting and his experience before it in the letters of his last months, but at least one concrete effect on his work itself can be determined. At Auvers Vincent painted a succession of horizontal format compositions which are also referred to in his letters and which signify an exploration of an aspect of his reaction to *Inter Artes et Naturam*.[2]

Shortly after Vincent's arrival at Auvers on May 21, he wrote to Theo and Jo:

> This is an almost lush country, just at the moment when a new society is developing in the old, is not at all unpleasing; there is so much well-being in the air. I see, or think I see in it a quiet like a Puvis de Chavannes, no factories, but lovely well-kept greenery in abundance.[3]

A short time after, van Gogh wrote a long letter to J. J. Isaacson (1859-1943), a Dutch journalist-art critic and painter:

> Back in Paris I read the continuation of your articles on impressionism.[4] . . . I believe in the possibility that a later generation will be, and will go on being, concerned with the interesting research on the subject of colors and modern sentiment along the same lines as, and of equal value to, those of Delacroix, of Puvis de Chavannes —and that impressionism will be their source . . .
>
> I begin to feel more and more that one may look upon Puvis de Chavannes as having the same importance as Delacroix, at least that he is on a par with the fellows whose style constitutes a "hitherto, but no further," comforting for evermore.
>
> Among other pictures his canvas, now at the Champ de Mars, seems to contain an allu-

sion to an equivalence, strange and providential meeting of *very* far-off antiquities and *crude* modernity. His canvases of the last few years are vaguer, more prophetic if possible than even Delacroix, before them one feels an emotion as if one were present at the continuation of all kinds of things, a benevolent renaissance ordained by fate. . . . he would know how to do the olive trees of the South, he *the Seer*. . . . I feel impotent when confronted with such nature, for my Northern brains were oppressed by a nightmare in those peaceful spots, as I felt that one ought to do better things with the foliage. Yet I did not want to leave things alone *entirely*, without making an effort, but it is restricted to the expression of two things—the cypresses—the olive trees—let others who are better and more powerful than I reveal their symbolic language. . . . Therefore I assure you that I cannot think of Puvis de Chavannes without having a presentiment that one day he or someone else will explain the olive tree to us. For myself I can see from afar the possibility of a new art of painting, but it was too much for me, and it is with pleasure that I return to the North.

> . . . until now no one has painted the real Southern Frenchman for us. But when Chavannes or someone else shows us that human being, we shall be reminded of those words, ancient but with a blissfully new significance, Blessed are the poor in spirit, blessed are the pure of heart . . . However deeply convinced we may be of Rembrandt's vision, yet we must ask ourselves: And did Raphael have this in mind, and Michelangelo and da Vinci? This I do not know, but I believe that Giotto, who was less of a heathen, felt it more deeply—that great sufferer, who remains as familiar to us as a contemporary.[1]

Speaking of his attempts in southern France to penetrate the nature in which he absorbs himself, van Gogh reflects on his painting *vis à vis* Puvis's, the essence of whose work he compares with Giotto's. At the same time he felt that Puvis's art would lead the way to the future. Vincent had written to Theo in November, 1889, "Lately I have seen the women picking and gathering the olives, but as I had no chance of getting a model, I have done nothing with it."[2] "This month I have been working in the olive groves . . . I have been

1. On May 3, 1889, van Gogh wrote to his brother from Arles: "Ah! what you say about Puvis and Delacroix is damn true, those two have indeed demonstrated what painting could be, but don't let's confuse things that are worlds apart. Now I, as a painter, shall never amount to anything important, I am absolutely sure of it." van Gogh *Letters* III, no. 590, p. 163.

2. See p. 23 for list. Only one of these compositions conforms to a standard French size (no. F. 809, a 40 *marine*) which means that Vincent especially stretched his canvases in order to explore the frieze motif. (See letter to Theo, van Gogh *Letters* III, no. 640, p. 283, June 17, 1890, in which he acknowledges receiving canvas and paints from Paris.)

3. van Gogh *Letters* III, no. 637, p. 275.

4. Referring to article in *De Portefeuille*, August 17, 1889.

1. van Gogh *Letters* III, no. 614a, pp. 231-233. Van Gogh had corresponded with Isaacson earlier and had sent a copy of one of his letters to Theo in November, 1889. (See letter no. 614.) This subsequent letter to him is mistakenly included by the editors after letter 614 but it cannot date from that time.

2. van Gogh *Letters* III, no. 614, p. 229.

knocking about in the orchards." [1] Perhaps this is one of the reasons *Inter Artes et Naturam* struck him so forcibly and also that in it Puvis had forgotten his Elysian fields and had descended amiably into the intimacy of our time.

Van Gogh was not content to let the image of Puvis's work pass and he followed this letter with another written to his younger sister, Wilhelmina, in which he dwells at length on *Inter Artes et Naturam*:

> There is a superb picture by Puvis de Chavannes at the exhibition. The figures of the persons are dressed in bright colors, and one cannot tell whether they are costumes of to-day or on the other hand clothing of antiquity.
>
> On one side, two women, dressed in simple long robes, are talking together, and on the other side men with the air of artists; in the middle of the picture, a woman with her child on her arm is picking a flower off an apple tree in bloom. One figure is forget-me-not blue, another bright citron yellow, another of a delicate pink color, another white, another violet. Underneath their feet, a meadow dotted with little white and yellow flowers. A blue distance with a white town and a river. All humanity, all nature simplified, but as they *might* be if they are not like that.
>
> This description does not tell you anything—but when one sees the picture, when one looks at it for a long time, one gets the feeling of being present at a rebirth, total but benevolent, of all the things one should have believed in, should have wished for—a strange and happy meeting of very distant antiquities and crude modernity. [2]

The impact of the Puvis was so strong that van Gogh repeated several phrases from his letter to Isaacson. He also included a sketch of the painting from memory which is a general reconstruction of Puvis's composition (cat. no. 49). Van Gogh includes eleven of the eighteen figures, combining by memory such groupings as the mother and child picking fruit and the striding boy seen in profile to their right into one unit and transforming the "men with the air of artists" into a figure seated at his easel being observed by another standing figure. The lounging woman in the left foreground of Puvis's composition is turned around, but the general sense of the composition with the river and town in the background and the panoramic view contained in the long horizontal format is preserved and conveyed in van Gogh's drawing.

Van Gogh's observations of Puvis's work cannot be interpreted as being sympathetic to symbolist ideas. He

had written to Theo in November, 1889 from Arles:

> I have written to Bernard and Gauguin too that I considered that our duty is thinking, not dreaming, so that when looking at their work I was astonished at their letting themselves go like that. For Bernard has sent me photos of his canvases. The trouble with them is that they are a sort of dream or nightmare—that they are erudite enough—you can see that it is someone who is gone on the primitives—but frankly the English Pre-Raphaelites did it much better, and then again Puvis and Delacroix much more healthily than the Pre-Raphaelites.
>
> It is not that it leaves me cold, but it gives me a painful feeling of collapse instead of progress. Well, to shake that off, morning and evening these bright cold days . . . I have been knocking about in the orchards . . . . What I have done is a rather hard and coarse reality beside their abstraction, but it will have a rustic quality and will smell of the earth. I should like to see Gauguin's and Bernard's studies from nature . . . [1]

Picking up the thread of van Gogh's correspondence of June-July 1890, we find him referring on the 24th of June to horizontal formats [2] and in the following letter he wrote his brother:

> I have painted Mlle Gachet's portrait . . .
>
> I have noticed that this canvas goes very well with another horizontal one of wheat, as one canvas is vertical and in pink tones, the other pale green and greenish yellow, the complementary of pink; but we are still far from the time when people will understand the curious relation between one fragment of nature and another, which all the same explain each other and enhance each other. But some certainly feel it, and that's something.
>
> And then there is this improvement, that in clothes you see combinations of very pretty light colors; if you could make the people you see walking past pose and do their portraits, it would be as pretty as any period whatever in the past, and I even think that often in nature there is actually all the grace of a picture by Puvis, between art and nature. [3]

"Between art and nature" sums up van Gogh's feeling that somehow in *Inter Artes et Naturam* Puvis had begun to accomplish the task of stopping people in the normal course of their activity and making of them a new artis-

1. van Gogh *Letters* III, no. 615, p. 233.
2. van Gogh *Letters* III, no. W22, p. 471 (early June, 1890).

1. van Gogh *Letters* III, no. 615, p. 233. Ironically, when Gauguin was together with van Gogh at Arles in 1888, exactly one year earlier, it was rather than Vincent, who thought of Puvis de Chavannes. (See letter from Gauguin to E. Bernard quoted on p. 120.)
2. van Gogh *Letters* III, no. 644, p. 288.
3. van Gogh *Letters* III, no. 645, pp. 288-289.

tic entity—retaining the direct impression of nature but imbuing it with a new and personal vision.

On June 30th, Vincent sent his brother and sister-in-law a sketch of a "horizontal landscape with fields . . . the undergrowth around poplars, violet trunks running across the landscape, perpendicular like columns . . ."[1] On July 23rd he wrote Theo, "I apply myself to my canvases with all my mind, I am trying to do as well as certain painters whom I have greatly loved and admired."[2] And in the last letter sent to his mother and sister, the artist wrote:

> I myself am quite absorbed in the immense plain with wheatfields against the hills, boundless as the sea, delicate yellow, delicate soft green, the delicate violet of a dug-up and weeded piece of soil, checkered at regular intervals with the green of flowering potato plants, everything under a sky of delicate blue, white, pink, violet tones.[3]

All of this emphasis on the delicacy of tones, especially in white, pink, violet, blue and yellow, is precisely the type of colour scheme Vincent found to admire in Puvis. In one of his very last paintings, *Women walking along in the fields* (cat. no. 50) done at the end of July, 1890, when the above letter was written, we can observe the pale green grass, the simplified drawing of the white and very pale violet dresses, the blue furrows, the pale blue background recalling that of *Inter Artes et Naturam* (a particular kind of relatively dry opacity on the cardboard). Also, the two figures recall closely the two at the extreme right of his drawing reconstruction of Puvis's painting (see cat. no. 49). In works such as these we can understand the attempts to absorb effects observed by van Gogh in Puvis and which in their embryonic state were being worked out at the time of his death.

1. van Gogh *Letters* III, no. 646, p. 291. The painting referred to is *Undergrowth with Two Figures* (Cincinnati Art Museum).
2. van Gogh *Letters* III, no. 651, p. 297.
3. van Gogh *Letters* III, no. 650, p. 296.

Paul Gauguin   (French, 1848-1903)

The Yellow Christ, 1889
Oil on canvas; 36¼ x 28⅞ in. (92 x 73 cm.)
Signed lower right: P. Gauguin
Albright-Knox Art Gallery, Buffalo, New York

Catalogue no. 51

Ref. W 327

Paul Gauguin

La Perte du Pucelage (The Loss of Virginity), 1890-91
Oil on canvas; 35¼ x 51¼ in. (90 x 130 cm.)
Unsigned
On loan from The Chrysler Museum at Norfolk, Gift of Walter P. Chrysler, Jr.

Catalogue no. 52

Ref. W 412; Denys Sutton, "*La Perte du Pucelage* by Paul
    Gauguin," *Burlington Magazine*, April 1949, 103-
    105; Wayne Anderson, *Gauguin's Paradise Lost*, New
    York: The Viking Press, 1971, 99-111.

Catalogue no. 53, *verso*

116

Paul Gauguin

Tahitian Landscape, circa 1894

Monotype heightened with watercolour, on wove paper; 8⅜ x 11⅜ in. (21 x 28.5 cm.)
Unsigned
Verso: pencil drawing of *recto*
From a Toronto Private Collection

Catalogue no. 53

Ref. Unpublished.

> See Richard Field, *Paul Gauguin: Monotypes*, Philadelphia Museum of Art, 1973. The seated figure in the foreground recalls somewhat that reproduced in Field, *op. cit.*, p. 71, no. 32, *Seated Figure* (variation on Puvis de Chavannes's *Hope*) which Field dates *c.* 1894-95. A letter from Field, June 28, 1974, confirms the attribution to Gauguin.

The motif of figures in landscape, both foreground and right background, is adapted from *Femmes au bord de la rivière* (W574) and *Nave Nave Moe (Joie de se reposer)*, 1894 (W512). In our monotype there are six figures—two in foreground, three in back and one seated in middleground. The figures on the *verso* appear to be tracings, slightly augmented, of those on the *recto* monotype side of the sheet. That side corresponds to the compositional placement of the figures in W574 whereas on the *verso* they are reversed. Further evidence for the date of *circa* 1894 can be found in Gauguin's woodcut, *Manao Tupapau* (*The Spirit of the Dead Watches*) of *circa* 1893, in which the three figures in the right background correspond in their poses (although not in their order) with the three background figures in *Tahitian Landscape*.

The sheet has several holes which are filled in, thus accounting for a number of "uncovered" areas throughout the composition. The surface is abraded and this in turn gives the impression of the monotype having been done on Japan paper which microscopic examination reveals is not the case. The *verso* has been reinforced along the length of the top of the sheet, probably in the same restoration as the repairing of the holes.

117

Paul Gauguin

Nuit de Noël, 1896
Oil on canvas; 28¼ x 32⅝ in. (72 x 83 cm.)
Signed lower right: P. Gauguin
Private Collection

Catalogue no. 54

Ref. W 519; *Gauguin and The Pont-Aven Group,* The Tate
    Gallery (Arts Council), 1966, p. 26, no. 42.

118

Paul Gauguin

Still Life with 'Hope' by Puvis de Chavannes, 1901
Oil on canvas; 25¾ x 30¼ in. (65 x 77 cm.)
Signed and dated lower right: Paul Gauguin 1901
Lent by Mr. and Mrs. Nathan Cummings

Catalogue no. 55

Ref. W 604

Gauguin wrote to André Fontainas in 1899 that he knew Puvis de Chavannes (see p. 127). In addition to being familiar with Puvis's work from the Salons, the Panthéon and the Sorbonne, he would also have seen exhibitions at Durand-Ruel's including Puvis's one-man shows of 1887 and 1894,[1] and he was present at the banquet in 1895 honouring Puvis. References to Puvis de Chavannes in Gauguin's letters begin to occur during the period of his stay with Vincent van Gogh from October through December, 1888, when he wrote from Arles to Emile Bernard, "Vincent looks to Daumier here, whereas I on the other hand see the influence of colourful Puvis and Japanese art. The women are elegantly coiffured, their beauty reminiscent of Greece. Their shawls pleated around them like the primitives, recall for me Greek friezes."[2] Bernard shared with Gauguin an interest in Puvis de Chavannes and some of his paintings of this period reveal strong influences of Puvis's art.[3] Gauguin had no doubt saturated himself in the paintings of Puvis which he had seen up till that time and the fundamental decorative flatness of Gauguin's shapes, their clean-cut outlines and allover simplicity which he was developing into the primary expressive means of his art were based in part upon his adaptations from the older man. As has been noted by Robert Goldwater:

> There is a more generally significant connection with the work of Puvis de Chavannes than the occasional borrowing of single figures. The similarities, both of pictorial arrangement and iconographical ideals ... are important to note, similarities which become strikingly apparent in the romantic transformation of Gauguin's effort at pictorial simplifications by members of the "school" of Pont-Aven, particularly in the art of Maurice Denis and Emile Bernard.[4]

1. Gauguin implies that he visited these shows and he was living in Paris when each of them was held. See *Paul Gauguin's Intimate Journals* translated by Van Wyck Brooks, New York: Boni and Liveright, 1921. Gauguin completed this manuscript shortly before his death and sent it to André Fontainas to be published.

2. Malingue, no. LXXV.

3. See for example, *Baigneuses*, 1888 (collection Williame), ill. p. 22, *Exposition les Amis de van Gogh*, Institut Néerlandais, Paris, 1960 (cat. no. 14). *Baigneuses* was shown in the Café Volpini exhibition in 1889 and is said to have been catalogue no. 75 in that show. However, it could also have been no. 77 (*Nues*).

4. *Primitivism in Modern Art*, revised ed. New York: Vintage Books, 1967, p. 80. The author points out several paintings by Gauguin in which the influence of Puvis can be traced. "The sideways sitting posture, with, however, the full width of the shoulders shown, that Puvis uses in his *Normandy* (1893) [cat. no. 33] and his *Magdelene* (1897) is used by Gauguin in *The Queen of the Aréois* [W451] and *Ta Matete* [W476] (*ibid.* p. 85, note 34)." It is doubtful whether Gauguin could have seen such a late work by Puvis as *Magdelene*. *The Queen of the Aréois* would also have been influenced by *Hope* (see cat. nos. 15 and 16).

Fig. 7   Paul Gauguin, *The Green Calvary*, 1889

In *The Yellow Christ* (cat. no. 51) of 1889, painted in Brittany, we find these basic pictorial features: distinctly drawn patterns, relatively shallow space which is comprised of a series of horizontal bands, subsidiary figures in the middle ground very much in the manner of Puvis and a generally calm atmosphere which pervades the scene. The major differences are, of course, in the colour which, although subdued in areas, is generally high key and emphatically decorative. The angular jutting out of the foreground figure at the right stems from Gauguin's interest in Japanese wood-block prints. But motifs such as these are reinforced by such works of Puvis de Chavannes as *Saint Genevieve in Prayer* of 1877 (fig. 36 p. 173) in the Panthéon. The pale pink-bluish-white tonality of the foreground figures, especially the one at lower left with the bib, is very Puvis-esque. The localization and lack of idealized illustrative handling of the figures are foreign to Puvis. Gauguin wavers between the Cézanne-esque treatment of volumes in such works as *Marie Derrien* of 1890[1] and the flatter disposition of colour areas which rapidly become a dominant characteristic of his work.[2] What is perhaps even closer to Puvis is *The Green Calvary* (see fig. 7) of 1889 (Royal Museum of Fine Arts, Brussels) which, although linked to a sculpted Breton Calvary at Nizon,[3] shows a distinct

1. Art Institute of Chicago (W387).

2. See also Robert Goldwater, "Some Aspects of the Development of Seurat's Style," *The Art Bulletin*, Vol. XXIII, no. 2, June 1941, p. 129, who compares *The Yellow Christ* to Seurat's *La Baignade, Asnières*.

3. Illustrated in Wayne Anderson, *Gauguin's Paradise Lost, op. cit.*, p. 302.

Fig. 8 Pierre Puvis de Chavannes, *Childhood of Saint Genevieve* (left section), 1877

affinity with Puvis's *The Childhood of Saint Genevieve* (see fig. 8), also in the Panthéon, and which may indeed be an alternate source of the grouping and background motif which comprises Gauguin's picture. Another composition adapted from this source is *Nude Breton Boy* (see fig. 9), Wallraf-Richartz-Museum, Cologne, of 1889.[1] It is plausible that in moving away from his impressionist stage, Gauguin sought established models for his compositional formats, just as had Seurat, and Puvis was a ready source of unlimited motifs. This characteristic remains with Gauguin throughout his development for although he borrows repeatedly from Egyptian, Greek, Javanese as well as local Breton sources for many of his compositions, sculpture sources do not have the same specific suggestive impact on the pictorial rendering of visual ideas as do other paintings.[2] No matter how exotic Gauguin's sources, he kept a photograph of

1. W339.
2. See B. Dorival, "Sources of the art of Gauguin from Java, Egypt and ancient Greece," *The Burlington Magazine*, Vol. XCIII, no. 557, April 1951, pp. 118-122.

Fig. 9 Paul Gauguin, *Nude Breton Boy,* 1889

Puvis's *Hope* with him from the time he left France in 1895.

In the period from 1888 to 1891 Gauguin was very close to Sérusier and Bernard; the standard biblical thematic content, augmented by the bland simplicity—even naivety— exerted on all of them by the mysterious Breton environment and which is found in *The Yellow Christ* (Gauguin was fiercely anti-clerical, yet often quoted scripture and portrayed himself as Christ) is in a work such as *The Loss of Virginity* (cat. no. 52) given a more immediately subjective and therefore arcane meaning by way of the flower held by the girl and the fact that the title probably refers to Gauguin's young mistress, pregnant with his child which was born after his departure in June, 1891, for Tahiti. That Gauguin was subject to the type of symbolic content in his work of this period, and which he apparently came to despise, links him temporarily in matters of style to the younger men who were essentially his followers.[1] Gauguin wrote to de Monfreid in November, 1901:

1. In July 1898, Gauguin wrote to his closest confidant, Daniel de Monfreid, cautioning him not to send invitations to his prospective exhibition at Vollard's to "Sérusier, Denis and company" since he had long been out of sympathy with their aims (see *Lettres de Gauguin à Daniel de Monfreid*, ed. by Mme. Joly-Segalen, Paris: Georges Falaize, 1950, letter no. XLV). He directed his friend to invite, among others, Puvis de Chavannes. As if to reinforce this distinction in his mature work and deny the affinity which once existed between them, Gauguin wrote in June, 1889 to Denis, replying in a bitterly sarcastic

Fig. 10   Paul Gauguin, *Tahitian Women on the Beach,*
1891-92, Robert Lehman Collection, The
Metropolitan Museum of Art, New York

Fig. 11   Pierre Puvis de Chavannes, *Girls by the Seashore,*
1879

You know what I think of all these false ideas
about symbolist or other literature in painting; no point in repeating it and besides we
agree on that point—as does posterity
also—since healthy works of art remain all
the same and all the lucubrations of literary
critics [*élucubrations critico-littéraires*] have been
able to make no difference. [1]

Apart from whatever symbolic meanings *The Loss of
Virginity* may have, there are basic qualities in the picture which are strikingly Puvis-esque. The reference to
Puvis de Chavannes's *Hope* (see cat. nos. 15 and 16) is
unmistakable in the rigidity of the pose of the figure as
well as the iris held by the girl. Perhaps the most obvious reference is the band of blue water and the island
and cloud motifs, which compositional as well as simplified colour effect is derived directly from Puvis. The
use of "lost and found" linear contours throughout and
the simplified long horizontal bands all recall similar

usages in Chavannes's *The Poor Fisherman* (cat. no. 21).[1]
Several writers have called attention to the unmistaka-
ble similarity between Gauguin's *Tahitian Women on the
Beach*[2] (fig. 10) of 1891-92 and Puvis's *Girls by the
Seashore* (fig. 11) of 1879.

Gauguin wrote to his wife in April, 1893, "Puvis de
Chavannes, who is a member of the Institute (and it is
the Institute who nominates the inspectors) is quite
well disposed towards me."[3] Gauguin had hoped to get
a post as a drawings inspector and imagined that Puvis
would help him secure it. This was probably fantasizing
on Gauguin's part but we cannot exclude the possibility
of his having talked to Puvis. Puvis's actual reaction to
Gauguin's art is not known but he had surely seen examples of it from time to time. Degas had been instrumental in arranging a show for Gauguin at Durand-
Ruel's in November, 1893 which Puvis probably vis-

tone to a request for works to be exhibited in a recreation of the
group that had exhibited together in 1889 at the Café Volpini (Bernard, Sérusier, Laval, Schuffenecker): "It would be quite unjustified
to place my Papuan art beside that of the symbolists, the idealists . . .
Art has nothing to do with this house of Péladan." (See Malingue,
no. CLXXI.) As we have noted earlier (p. 3), Puvis himself in 1891 had
emphatically rejected any connection with Péladan.

1. Joly-Segalen, *op. cit.*, letter no. LXXVIII.

1. See Denys Sutton, " 'La Perte du Pucelage' by Paul Gauguin," *The
Burlington Magazine,* XCI, 1949, pp. 102-105 for a detailed discussion of
this painting. The author points out the "chalky effect of the body,"
one of the features which appears to stem from Puvis. See also Wayne
Anderson, "Gauguin's Calvary of the Maiden," *The Art Quarterly,* Vol
XXXIV, no. 1, 1971, p. 95 where he relates the pose to Puvis's *Tamaris*
(cat. no. 22).

2. Robert Lehman Collection, The Metropolitan Museum of Art, New
York (W462).

3. Malingue, no. CXXXV.

122

ited. At any rate, Puvis was very much in Gauguin's mind as we can see from both the paintings and the extended references to him in his letters and in the comments of various observers in the artist's last years. After Gauguin's second sale in February, 1895, he left for Tahiti in the latter part of the Spring. Two events of this time link him again with Puvis: first, Gauguin was in attendance at the Puvis de Chavannes banquet on January 16, 1895 which publicly affirmed his respect for the man's work; the second is the Strindberg letter episode. Gauguin had asked the Swedish playwright, who was a painter as well as a dramatist, to write the introduction for the catalogue of his auction sale at the Hôtel Drouot.[1] Strindberg wrote to Gauguin:

> You have set your heart on having the preface to your catalogue written by me, in memory of the winter of 1894-95, when we lived here behind the Institute . . .
>
> I should gladly have given you this souvenir to take away with you to that island in Oceania, where you are going to seek for space and a scenery in harmony with your powerful stature, but from the very beginning I feel myself in an equivocal position and I am replying at once to your request with an "I cannot" or, more brutally still, with an "I do not wish to."
>
> At the same time, I owe you an explanation of my refusal, which does not spring from a lack of friendly feeling, or from a lazy pen . . .
>
> Here it is: I cannot understand your art and I cannot like it. I have no grasp of your art, which is now exclusively Tahitian. But I know that this confession will neither astonish nor wound you, for you always seem to me fortified especially by the hatred of others: your personality delights in the antipathy it arouses, anxious as it is to keep its own integrity. And perhaps this is a good thing, for the moment you were approved and admired and had supporters, they would classify you, put you in your place and give your art a name which, five years later, the younger generation would be using as a tag for designating a superannuated art, an art they would do everything to render still more out of date.
>
> I myself have made many serious attempts to classify you, to introduce you like a link into the chain, so that I might understand the history of your development, but in vain.
>
> I remember my first stay in Paris, in 1876. . . . something was fermenting.
>
> . . .my young artists had dragged me over to Durand-Ruel's to see something quite new in

Fig. 12   Henri Matisse, *Le Luxe, study for "Le Luxe I,"* 1907

painting . . . . we saw some marvellous canvases, most of them signed Monet and Manet. . . . I looked at this new painting with calm indifference. But the next day I returned I did not know just why, and I discovered that there was 'something' in these bizarre manifestations. . . . Very much struck by these canvases, I sent to a paper in my own country a letter in which I tried to explain the sensation I thought the Impressionists had tried to render, and my article had a certain success as a piece of incomprehensibility.

When, in 1883, I returned to Paris a second time, Manet was dead, but his spirit lived in a whole school that struggled for hegemony with Bastien-Lepage. During my third stay in Paris, in 1885, I saw the Manet exhibition. This movement had now forced itself to the front; it had produced its effect and it was now classified. At the triennial exposition, which occurred that very year, there was an

Fig. 13   Paul Gauguin, *Where do we come from? What are we? Where are we going?* 1897

utter anarchy—all styles, all colours, all subjects, historical, mythological and naturalistic. People no longer wished to hear of schools or tendencies. Liberty was now the rallying-cry. Taine had said that the beautiful was not the pretty, and Zola that art was a fragment of nature seen through a temperament.

Nevertheless, in the midst of the last spasms of naturalism, one name was pronounced by all with admiration, that of Puvis de Chavannes. He stood quite alone, like a contradiction, painting with a believing soul, even while he took a passing notice of the taste of his contemporaries for allusion. (We did not yet possess the term symbolism, a very unfortunate name for so old a thing as allegory.)

It was towards Puvis de Chavannes that my thoughts turned yesterday evening when, to the tropical sounds of the mandolin and the guitar, I saw on the walls of your studio that confused mass of pictures, flooded with sunshine, which pursued me last night in my dreams. I saw trees such as no botanist could ever discover, animals the existence of which had never been suspected by Cuvier, and men whom you alone could have created, a sea that might have flowed out of a volcano, a sky which no God could inhabit.

"Monsieur," I said in my dream, "you have created a new heaven and a new earth, but I do not enjoy myself in the midst of your creation. It is too sun-drenched for me, who enjoys the play of light and shade. And in your paradise there dwells an Eve who is not my ideal—for I, myself, really have an ideal of a woman or two!" This morning I went to the Luxembourg to have a look at Chavannes, who kept coming to my mind. I contemplated

with profound sympathy the poor fisherman, so attentively occupied with watching for the catch that will bring him the faithful love of his wife, who is gathering flowers, and his idle child. That is beautiful! . . .

No, Gauguin is not formed from the side of Chavannes, any more than from Manet's or Bastien-Lepage's!

What is he then? He is Gauguin, the savage, who hates a whimpering civilization, a sort of Titan who, jealous of the Creator, makes in his leisure hours his own little creation, the child who takes his toys to pieces so as to make others from them, who abjures and defies, preferring to see the heavens red rather than blue with the crowd.

Really, it seems to me that since I have warmed up as I write I am beginning to have a certain understanding of the art of Gauguin.

A modern author has been reproached for not depicting real beings, but for quite simply creating his personages himself. Quite simply!

Bon voyage, Master; but come back to us and come and see me. By then, perhaps, I shall have learned to understand your art better, which will enable me to write a real preface for a new catalogue in the Hôtel Drouot. For I, too, am beginning to feel an immense need to become a savage and create a new world.[1]

Gauguin, unabashed by the rebuff, published the letter as the introduction! He answered Strindberg,[2] apprising him of his intentions, and wrote to Arsène Alexandre five days later, "I am enclosing two letters

1. *Paul Gauguin's Intimate Journals, op.cit.,* pp. 35, 36, 39. Letter written February 1 or 2, 1895.
2. Malingue, no. CLIV. February 5, 1895.

124

Fig. 14   Paul Gauguin, *Faa Iheihe*, 1898

which will be printed in the *Revue Blanche* of February 15th and in the catalogue of my sale which takes place on the 18th of this month. I am sure you will find them interesting."[1] Gauguin obviously did not mind having his name linked to that of Puvis, even though it was clear that Strindberg did not understand what Gauguin was trying to achieve that set his work apart from that of Puvis.

Departing with the fresh memory of the events of January-February, it is not surprising that throughout the last years of Gauguin's life numerous visual and written references appear which link his art to that of Puvis de Chavannes. Goldwater pointed out that in *Nave Nave Mahana* of 1896 "The idylls of Puvis de Chavannes have been evoked."[2] In *Nuit de Noël* (cat. no. 54) of *c.* 1896 we find elements which can be traced to Puvis's work. *Normandy* (cat. no. 33) was exhibited at the *Salon* of 1893 and the conspicuously flattened shapes of the bulls in the Gauguin probably owe their placement in the composition to Puvis's work. They also recall the bulls in the background of Puvis's *Saint Genevieve in Prayer* (fig. 36 p. 173). Moreover, the figures in the shrine to the right look back to Puvis in their allover blue tonality, intensified though it may be, as well as to Javanese sculptures, and forward to both Picasso's "Blue" period (see cat. no. 74) and Roger de La Fresnaye (see cat. no. 79). Wayne Anderson has identified the source of *Three Tahitians in Conversation*[3] of 1897-1899 in Puvis. He points out the derivation of the figure in the centre seen from the back as being from the standing nude male figure in *Saint Genevieve in Prayer* in the Panthéon and the relationship of the figure to the right holding flowers to a similar motif in *Death and the Maidens* (cat. no. 17).[4]

It is however, in *Where do we come from? What are we? Where are we going?*[1] (fig. 13 p. 124) painted in 1897 that Puvis's influence is least concealed. In February, 1898, in a letter which contains a detailed watercolour-drawing of the composition to illustrate its points, Gauguin wrote to Daniel de Monfreid:

> Before I die I want to paint a large canvas that I have been thinking about and so for a month I worked day and night in an absolute fever. It is certainly not a canvas like one of Puvis de Chavannes's, with a study from nature then preparatory cartoon etc. It is done skilfully, from the tip of the brush, on to a sackcloth full of knots and wrinkles, so it has a very unpolished appearance.
>
> . . . I feel not only that this canvas surpasses all my previous ones but also that I will never do a better or even similar one. . . . It does not stink of models, or craftsmanship or alleged rules—which I have always shaken off, although sometimes fearfully.
>
> . . . the two upper corners are chrome yellow with an inscription to the left and my signature to the right like a fresco damaged at the corners and laid on to a golden wall.[2]

We know, despite Gauguin's disclaimer, that he did indeed prepare for the painting with a detailed squared-off drawing, following precisely Puvis's technical procedure.[3] The derivations of motifs in this canvas are numerous: the horizontal frieze format itself; the pair-

1. Malingue, no. CLV. Alexandre, it will be noted, wrote extensively on Puvis. (See "Puvis de Chavannes, sa vie et son oeuvre," *Le Figaro Illustré*, no. 107, February, 1899, pp. 21-44).

2. Musée des Beaux-Arts, Lyons (W 548); Goldwater, *Gauguin, op. cit.*, p. 130.

3. National Gallery of Scotland, Edinburgh (W 573).

4. See Anderson, *op. cit.*, p. 248, 346-347.

1. Museum of Fine Arts, Boston (W 561). This painting must have been a conduit for Puvis's ideas to the young Picasso who must have seen it at Vollard's where he had a show in June, 1901. Picasso's "Blue" period begins later that year and at the same time he was probably led to look at Puvis's murals after one of which he made a drawing (see fig. no. 29, p. 169).

2. *Lettres de Gauguin à Daniel de Monfreid, op. cit.*, no. XL.

3. Musée des Arts Africains et Océaniens, Paris (illustrated in Ronald Pickvance, *The Drawings of Gauguin*, London: Hamlyn, 1970, plate 100). The drawing, 20 x 37 cm. was signed and dedicated after the painting itself was completed, hence the date 1898 rather than 1897.

ings and groups of figures in the foreground and their relationship to those in the background; the general re-working of the pictorial ideas expressed by Puvis in *Pleasant Land* (cat. no. 23); the baby in the right foreground so reminiscent of *The Poor Fisherman* (cat. no. 21); the interspersion of vertical and horizontal motifs with static poses; and the similarity between the sequence of simultaneous illustrative incidents and those in *Inter Artes et Naturam* (cat. no. 30). And as if to reinforce the Puvis-esque treatment of horizontal compositions Gauguin painted in 1898 *Faa Iheihe* [1] (fig. 14 p. 125) about which Goldwater has written:

> Gauguin, for all that he was a revolutionary in both rhetorical pose and inner feeling, was very aware of tradition. There is here both the Parthenon and Borobudur . . . but the spirit is that of Puvis de Chavannes. This is Puvis's mild and tenuous golden age—in which Poussin's positive force and activity are replaced by a suspended animation—transplanted into an exotic world. Only now the spiritual, disembodied mildness has become physical languor. Through the painting itself, its warm harmonies, its continuous, closely locked design, its rough texture, this paradise has once more been brought back to earth, and made immediate and sensuous.[2]

Where do we come from? What are we? Where are we going? was exhibited at Vollard's in January, 1899. André Fontainas, carefully reviewing the paintings in the January issue of *Mercure de France*, wrote:

> Gauguin . . . presents ceremonial dancers moving slowly across a landscape thick with undergrowth, or nude bathers amid glorious vegetation strangely lit, but, all too often, the figures of his dreams, dry, colourless and stiff, represent in an imprecise way the badly conceived forms of a clumsily metaphysical imagination whose direction is perilous and whose expression arbitrary. Nothing remains from such canvases except the evidence of deplorable errors, for abstraction is not communicated through concrete images unless it has first, in the artist's own thoughts, taken shape in some physical allegory which through its life gives it meaning. This is the value gained from the high example of Puvis de Chavannes's art. To represent a philosophical ideal he conceived of harmonious groupings whose attitudes were able to convey to us a dream like his own. In the large panel which M. Gauguin is exhibiting, nothing—not even the two supple and pensive figures in their calm and beautiful pose nor the skilful evoca-

tion of a mysterious idol—would reveal for us the sense of the allegory if he had not taken care to write in the top corner of the canvas: "Where do we come from? What are we? Where are we going?". . .

> Besides, I do not wish to appear insistent if I point out . . . on the other panels where is demonstrated the tenacious craftsmanship of a stubborn innovator, in all the somewhat brutal enthusiasm of his efforts.

> All the same, M. Gauguin is without a doubt a rare artist who has for too long been refused the chance to display the full fire of his temperament through some large, decorative composition on the walls of a public building. There we could see just what he can be and, if he were to guard against his abstract tendencies, we would see born of his efforts, I am certain, a powerful and naturally harmonious work of art.[1]

In March 1899, Gauguin responded to Fontainas' misinterpretation of his intentions. Fontainas, like Strindberg four years earlier, sensed some of the salient features of his art and related to it in terms of Puvis, while not being able to comprehend the originality of the paintings. Gauguin is unusually gentle in his reply to Fontainas, as he was with Strindberg, sensing, correctly in this case, a potential friend and ally.

> Despite your aversion, you have tried to study the art or rather the work of a painter who does not move you emotionally, and speak of it honestly. A rare thing among most critics.

> . . . this is not really a reply . . . but rather a simple chat about art . . .

> . . . my dream cannot be fully grasped, it contains no allegory; as a musical poem it needs no libretto, to quote Mallarmé.

> . . . painting and dreaming at the same time, with no perceptible allegory within my reach—perhaps lacking in literary education.

> On waking, my work completed, I repeat to myself: where have we come from? what are we? where are we going? A reflection which

1. "Art Moderne," *Mercure de France*, vol. 29, January 1899, pp. 237-238. It is not surprising that Fontainas invoked Puvis's name in discussing Gauguin's painting for in the same article he reviews Puvis's last mural cycle in the Panthéon, saying "It is the most knowledgeable, original and simple composition that the painter has created." (*Ibid.* pp. 241-242.) Fontainas was not the first to suggest publicly that Gauguin should be given a public wall to paint—like Puvis. Albert Aurier, in 1891, had written: "What! In the dying years of our century we have only one great decorator, two perhaps counting Puvis de Chavannes, and our imbecile society of bankers and polytechnicians refuses to give this rare artist [Gauguin] the least palace, the meanest national hovel where he can drape the sumptuous cloak of his dreams!" ("Paul Gauguin," Feb. 7, 1891, *Mercure de France, Oeuvres posthumes,* Paris: Editions du Mercure de France, 1893, p. 219.)

1. The Tate Gallery, London (W 569).
2. Goldwater, *Gauguin, op. cit.*, p. 150.

no longer forms part of the canvas, expressed in the spoken word quite separately, on the surrounding wall, not a title but a signature.

You see, although I might well understand the value of words—whether abstract or concrete—in the dictionary, I no longer grasp them in painting. I have attempted to transpose my dream into a suggestive decor without recourse to literary means, in the simplest possible manner, a difficult task. You may accuse me of not having been successful there, but not of having tried, advising me to change my aims in order to linger over other ideas which have already been accepted and consecrated. Puvis de Chavannes is the best example. Of course, Puvis's talent and his experience, which I do not have, overwhelm me; I admire him as much if not more than you do but for different reasons. (And, do not be upset, with fuller knowledge.) To each of us his own era.

The State is right not to commission me to decorate a public edifice, a decoration which would offend the ideas of most people and I would be wrong to accept it, having no alternative but to cheat or lie to myself in so doing.

At my Durand-Ruel exhibition a young man asked Degas to explain to him my pictures as he did not understand them. Degas, smiling, told him one of La Fontaine's fables—"You see," he said, "Gauguin is the thin Wolf, without a collar."

Fifteen years of struggle is now succeeding in freeing us from the School, from this whole clash of formulas outside of which there could be no salvation, honour or wealth. Drawing, colour, composition, honest depiction of nature, and what else: even yesterday some mathematician was imposing on us light and immoveable colour (a discovery of Charles Henry).

The danger is past. Yes, we are free and yet I still see peril flickering on the horizon; I want to talk to you about it. This long and boring letter was really only written for this reason. Today's serious criticism, well-read and full of good intentions, tends to impose on us a method of thinking and dreaming which would be yet another form of slavery. Preoccupied with its own particular sphere, literature, it loses sight of what concerns us, namely painting. It this is so, I would, somewhat haughtily, be led to quote Mallarmé's saying, "A critic! Someone who meddles with what does not concern him."[1]

If ever an artist made a forthright statement rejecting literary theory in art, it is that. Gauguin speaks of colour, drawing, composition—the plastic constituents of painting—and nature, as well as his dreams, i.e. the imaginative force or vision of the artist. He resolutely denies symbolist intentions, literary or programmatic content in his work, just as Puvis had done. As Strindberg said in his letter to Gauguin, "Symbolism, a very unfortunate name for so old a thing as allegory."

Gauguin followed the above-cited letter with another to Fontainas, dated August 1899, in which he said:

Puvis de Chavannes, very distressed at reading an unfavourable criticism, said to me one day, "But what is it they do not understand?" The picture—it was his 'Poor Fisherman'—is very simple. I replied:

"To others it will be spoken in parables so that seeing they may not see and hearing they may not understand."

You give me pleasure, very great pleasure, in confessing that you were wrong to think that my compositions, like those of Puvis de Chavannes, were deduced from an abstract idea which I tried to bring to life through plastic representation ... and that my letter clarified this a little for you.

Not wrongly, since I act according to my intellectual nature, but I act a little like the Bible whose doctrine (especially where Christ is concerned) is expressed in symbolic form, under a double aspect; this form first materializes the pure Idea in order to render it more perceptible, affecting the manner of the supernatural; this is the literal, superficial, figurative, mysterious sense of a parable; and then the second aspect gives the Spirit of the first. This sense is no longer figurative; but in its representation makes this parable explicit.

Never having explained my art except through the pictures themselves, I have been misunderstood up until now.[1]

Gauguin wrote to Charles Morice two years later, in July, 1901:

Fontainas, who has always been well-meaning towards me, has reproached me for having been powerless to convey the understanding of my idea, as the abstract title is never expressed in a concrete manner in the canvas, etc. ... ; and he mentioned Puvis de Chavannes, always comprehensible, as being able to explain his idea.

Yes, Puvis explains his idea but he does not depict it. He is Greek while I am a savage, an untamed wolf in the woods [see letter of March, 1899, to Fontainas]. Puvis will entitle

1. Malingue, no. CLXX.

1. Malingue, no. CLXXII.

a picture *Purity [Hope]* and to explain it will depict a young virgin with a lily in her hand—a well-known symbol which will be understood. Gauguin, with the title *Purity*, will paint a landscape of clear waters; with no blemish of civilized man, perhaps one figure.

Without going into detail, there is a whole world between Puvis and me. Puvis, the artist, is a scholar and not a man of letters whereas I am not a scholar but perhaps a man of letters.

Why does the critic, in front of a work of art, seek for points of comparison with the ancient ideas or with other authors. Not finding what he thinks should be there, he no longer understands and is not moved. Emotion first! Understanding comes afterwards. . . .

Explanatory attributes—well-known symbols—would congeal this canvas *[Where are we going?]* into a sad reality and the problem which is posed would no longer be a poem.[1]

Gauguin was doing a great deal of writing at this point and there are contradictions in what he says about being a man of letters when he stated to Fontainas that he lacked a literary education. More noticeable is the fact that it was Gauguin who painted *The Loss of Virginity* (cat. no. 52) as a girl holding a flower; Puvis painted *Hope* (cat. no. 15) holding a small tree in her hand—a reference not to purity but to the hope of recovery from the devastation of the war with Prussia. Nevertheless, Gauguin's final statement comes not in written but in visual form, in *Still Life with 'Hope' by Puvis de Chavannes* (cat. no. 55). Gauguin had copied *Hope* in 1895, when a drawing of the painting by Puvis de Chavannes appeared with a poem by Charles Morice entitled "To Puvis de Chavannes."[2]

The artist also kept a reproduction of *Hope* on the wall of his house in Atuana.[3] In *Still Life with 'Hope' by*

Fig. 15   Catalogue no. 55, detail

Puvis de Chavannes Gauguin uses Puvis's composition as a window device as well as making it play a decorative role totally removed from any literary references. He was able to recreate, from a reproduction, a very suggestive replica of those qualities of paint texture and colour found in Puvis even though it is not an exact duplicate. The actual paint quality is closer to a work such as *Tamaris* (cat. no. 22) than to *Hope* itself. Indeed, this small replica is much less transformed into Gauguin's own style than his drawing of 1894-95. The browns in the landscape, the white cloth and touches of green, the blue outline of the figure, the greyish-white flesh, the lavender flowers at lower left and the pale blue Puvis-esque mountain in the upper right section all attest to Gauguin's powers of evocation in paying homage to the man from whom he had learned so much.

1. Malingue, no. CLXXIV.

2. *Mercure de France*, February, 1895, "Dessin d'après Puvis de Chavannes," *hors texte*. The drawing was undoubtedly a form of homage paid by Gauguin to Puvis on the occasion of the banquet. See also Richard Field, *Paul Gauguin: Monotypes, op. cit.*, p. 71, no. 32 for reproduction of another (possibly monotype) version (whereabouts unknown).

3. See Goldwater, *Gauguin, op. cit.*, p. 40 for a photograph of 1901 showing the reproduction of *Hope* on the wall.

Maurice Denis   (French, 1870-1943)

April, 1892
Oil on canvas; 14¾ x 24 in. (37.5 x 61 cm.)
Signed and dated lower left: M/A/D/ 92
Rijksmuseum Kröller-Müller, Otterlo

Catalogue no. 56

Ref. *Maurice Denis,* Orangerie des Tuileries, June
    3—August 31, 1970, no. 46.

The relationship between the art of Maurice Denis and
that of Puvis de Chavannes was a long-standing and
pervasive one. Throughout his life Denis also wrote
extensively—and perceptively—on the art of Puvis de
Chavannes, beginning with the description of his visit
to the Durand-Ruel Puvis de Chavannes exhibition in
December, 1887 (see p. 15) until the very last entry in
his *Journal* in October, 1943, only a few weeks before his
death (see p. 12) which describes a last visit to see
Puvis's murals in Lyons. His insight was the result not
only of sympathetic artistic and psychological predisposition but of repeated trips to study the murals in Amiens, Rouen, Lyons and Marseilles as well as visits to
the Sorbonne, Panthéon and Hôtel de Ville in Paris,
the impressions of which are all recorded in the *Journal.*
Denis affirms not only his conviction that Puvis's conception of decorative mural painting was an essential
component of the continuing tradition of the visual arts,
but also that it was Puvis's profound understanding of

the early Italian and French traditions, as well as of his
nineteenth century contemporaries, that allowed him to
simplify and give new life to religious and allegorical
subject themes without losing touch with nature. Denis
became the chief exponent in France of Puvis's approach to decoration; his paintings attest to his fundamental adherence to and expansion of ideas first
formulated by Puvis de Chavannes.[1] As early as 1904,
Julius Meier-Graefe wrote: "Denis is . . . a rejuvenated
Puvis."[2] Denis was also a staunch supporter of Cézanne
and the reconciliation of these two strands in his work
was a constant challenge of which the artist was keenly
aware. His natural predilection for the decorative exerted a kind of gravitational pull towards Puvis; at the

1. For a complete list of Maurice Denis's decorative commissions
   —stage decors, murals, stained glass windows and book illustrations—see *Maurice Denis,* Orangerie des Tuileries, 1970, pp. 89-107.
2. *The Development of Modern Art,* Vol II, London and New York: 1908, p.
   53 (translated from *Entwicklungsgeschichte der Modernen Kunst,* 1904). In
   1900 Denis had painted *Les Nymphes aux Jacinthes,* a large mural decoration for Count Kessler's house in Weimar, and Meier-Graefe also
   knew Denis's work from visits to Paris.

Maurice Denis

Décoration pour la chambre à coucher: L'Amour et la Vie d'une Femme d'après Schumann: L'Enfance ou la Cueillette des pommes, 1896
Tempera on canvas; 20 x 78¾ in. (0.51 x 1.00 cm.)
Unsigned
Private collection, Saint Germain-en-Laye

Catalogue no. 57

Ref. *Maurice Denis,* Orangerie des Tuileries, June 3—August 31, 1970, no. 99 (as 1895, see p. 93); S. Barazzetti, *Maurice Denis,* Paris: Grasset, 1945, pp. 147-148. Part of a decorative ensemble comprising seven paintings for the artist's bedroom.

same time, Denis recognized the broad applicability of fundamental tenets of Cézanne's approach and this led him to attempt colour and volume experiments not wholly in tune with his nature. After visiting the *Salon d'Automne* in 1904 where forty-three works were on display (thirty-three Cézannes hung in a room nearby), Denis recorded in his *Journal*:

> It is the fruits of Chavannes's work that strike me most forcibly, with some remorse in confessing that my path was in that direction but that I have recently neglected it. I have a desire to do something large, with broad shades, ringed around a sturdy design. The large panels of Vuillard, the statues of Maillol, that which I perhaps like the best, everything urges me to return to my former art.[1]

Denis's affinities with Puvis de Chavannes were recognized by the critics. Commenting on the acquisition of Denis's paintings by the National Gallery at Helsingfors (Helsinki), Roger Fry observed:

> The *Ulysses and Calypso* of Maurice Denis is certainly among the best recent creations of this sympathetic and scholarly artist. If his work lacks the spontaneity of the earlier pioneers in the movement, it shows none the less

the advantages of scholarship and taste. It is not a little surprising indeed to find that one of the chief exponents of a movement which is generally accused of being revolutionary should be among the most learned of all modern artists. How many reminiscences we find here of the great classic tradition of France, the tradition of Poussin, Ingres and Puvis de Chavannes, a tradition which no movement in France, however revolutionary it may appear, ever loses sight of for long.[1]

Denis himself recognized his place in this tradition and was in the forefront of those modern artists who saw themselves not as revolutionaries turning their backs on the past, but rather as assimilators building upon the innovations of artists such as Poussin, Delacroix, Corot, Puvis and Cézanne, who were in varying degrees "revolutionary" in their day. Upon the completion of his series of large decorative murals for the *Théâtre des Champs-Elysées* in Paris in 1912, Maillol wrote to Denis: "I am happy that you have finished your work. I know that it is a fine achievement and work which no one—since Chavannes—has been able to undertake and carry through so resolutely."[2]

1. *The Burlington Magazine,* Vol. XVIII, October 1910-March 1911, p. 293.
2. Letter of January, 1913 (undated), published in Maurice Denis, *Journal II,* p. 147.

1. *Journal I,* pp. 223-224 (entry, October, 1904).

Maurice Denis

Maternity, circa 1896
Oil on canvas; 32 x 25 in. (80 x 64 cm.)
Signed lower right: MD
Private Collection

Catalogue no. 58

Ref. *Maurice Denis,* Orangerie des Tuileries, June
      3—August 31, 1970, no. 97.

Maurice Denis

Afternoon in the Woods, 1900
Oil on canvas; 28¾ x 39½ in. (73 x 92 cm.)
Signed and dated lower right: M/A/U/D/1900
The Museum of Modern Art, New York, Gift of Mr. and Mrs. Arthur G. Altschul, 1971

Catalogue no. 59

Ref. *Maurice Denis,* Orangerie des Tuileries, June
3—August 31, 1970, no. 158.

Early in 1924, Denis had a major retrospective at the
Union Centrale des Arts Décoratifs which included 464
works of which 329 were paintings. Reviewing the
show, Marc Lafargue wrote:

> One cannot doubt . . . that the painter felt an
> emotion, which remained a guiding force
> throughout his career, when standing before
> the *Poor Fisherman* of Puvis. There is moreover
> a clear filiation between them. Denis often re-
> peated to himself, "For all clear ideas, there
> exists a plastic thought which translates
> them" and also this reflection, "I love order
> because I love beauty passionately." The art-

ist applied this axiom of Puvis by grouping in
a hundred ways his virgins, his family scenes,
his groups of children, this daily life which for
him mingled with another, supernatural life,
evoked by the painter through a selection of
earthly forms, and in images, in the manner of
illuminators, miniaturists and the creators of
stained glass windows.[1]

Later that same year, in honour of the centenary of
Puvis's birth, Denis wrote a long article, full of insight,
on the artist, from which we quote a portion:

1. "L'Oeuvre de Maurice Denis," *L'Amour de l'Art,* Vol. v, no. 1, March,
   1924, p. 86.

132

I did not know Puvis de Chavannes, something I have always been sorry about. I am told nowadays that he would have welcomed me kindly; on the juries he was sympathetic towards my first pictures, which moreover were derived from him. Once I found myself near him on a bus platform; I watched him with ardent curiosity and was dying to speak to him of my admiration. He was rather awe-inspiring. . . .

I am grateful to Puvis for having, at the height of the impressionist period, tried to 'industrialize' painting. To industrialize painting is, in short, to substitute the method understood by the ancients for individual fantasy, for self-taught experimentation. It is to revive tradition. It is to institute a line of conduct according to reason and experience. . . . Puvis's salutary example is at the origin of the modern decorative movement. . . .

The current attitude of the young to painting: cubists and post-cubists, has so upset old viewpoints that Puvis de Chavannes now cuts the figure of a *pompier*. Adept at *la peinture plate* and at painting using the subject, he is for them only a cold continuator of the pupils of Ingres, whereas he is in reality the renewer of the tradition of Poussin and the initiator of the whole great French decorative movement. In a word, he is old-fashioned: like Degas, like Gauguin. In my time he passed for a revolutionary and the watchword of the Academy was that he had ideas but that he did not know how to draw. Today he is despised, because of the painting of ideas, of which he was in fact a superior representative, and also because of his drawing, too purified, too classical—a simple eclipse, which will not last any longer than Delacroix's lapse from favour did. . . .

. . . between the end of academism and the dawn of impressionism, with a deep knowledge of the necessities of mural painting, Puvis de Chavannes has renewed decoration in France.[1]

In 1939, Denis published his *Histoire de l'Art Religieux*[2] in which he discussed Puvis's art and its place in the development of French painting. Two years later, in an essay written for the catalogue of an exhibition of drawings and paintings by Puvis de Chavannes, he once again affirmed his conviction that Puvis was among the most important and influential artists of the latter part of the nineteenth century. Because it so succinctly sums up Denis's thoughts over a lifetime of consideration of Pu-

vis's art, we may quote a significant portion of this little-known statement:

The name of Puvis de Chavannes is passed over in silence by most recent modern art historians: an eclipse similar to that suffered by Delacroix in the last years of the 19th century, a whim of fashion that only lasts a moment. Without him, no more than without Manet or Cézanne, one cannot explain the evolution of painting during the last fifty years.

He is at the origin of the various movements which, after impressionism, introduced into the arts a preoccupation with style and gave subjectivity a prime role, in reaction to the monotony and limitation of naturalism. . . .

A stubborn but cautious innovator, submissive to the instruction which he chose to follow from both the past and his own time, he has created for his own use, stage by stage, a plastic language of logical harmony and of an incomparable purity: an ever clear and intelligible expression of his sensibility, of his vision of things, of the nobility of his soul.

. . . he naturally reconciled the tradition of the classic Masters and the innovations of modern painting. . . .

Vuillard valued him highly and confessed to having worshipped him from an early age. We often used to deplore together the fact that he was so little known . . .

Does this exhibition organized by M. Jacques Blot herald a happy return to Puvis de Chavannes? If this were so, it would also represent a return to the use of the subject, and the prelude to a rebirth of the spirit in French painting, of poetry and of reason.[1]

It is ironic that only five years before Goldwater's above-referred-to article (see page 9), Maurice Denis, whose devotion to the art of Puvis de Chavannes had never lapsed, should call attention to the neglect and near total eclipse of Puvis's reputation by art critics and historians. Little did Denis realize that within a short time, the curve of Puvis's reputation would begin a slow but inevitable upswing, brought on in the main by way of those artists, such as himself, whose work reflects and thus encourages critics to recognize the crucial importance and widespread influence of Puvis de Chavannes.

In *April* (cat. no. 56) of 1892, Denis transforms Puvis's idyllic view of Rouen in *Inter Artes et Naturam* (cat. no. 30) into a simplified sequence of silhouetted figures seen from Saint Germain-en-Laye, with the Seine in the background winding in rhythmic continuation of the paths and outlines of the figures in the foreground. Although the colour of *April* resembles the sunlit impres-

1. *La Revue Hebdomadaire*, no. 49, December, 1924.
2. Paris: Flammarion, 1939 (Chapter XII).

1. Galerie Jacques Blot, "Quelques dessins et peintures de Puvis de Chavannes, présentés par Maurice Denis," March 4-29, 1941.

sionist-inspired tonalities of Maillol's *Girl Tending Cows* (cat. no. 63) of *c.* 1890, the pale whites of the figures, their elongated and crouching simplified poses all recall both Puvis's *Inter Artes et Naturam* and the kneeling woman in the right background of *The Poor Fisherman* (cat. no. 21). The distortions in drawing seen in the figures emanate from Puvis's *The Balloon* and *The Carrier Pigeon* (cat. no. 12 and 13) which compositions Denis undoubtedly knew. The division of the composition into two zones, foreground and background, spread laterally across the horizontal surface of the canvas and divided by the crisp zig-zag of the geometric patterns of the railing, show that Denis, while depending upon Puvis for inspiration, sought to simplify the motif taken over from the older artist. Nevertheless, in the weight of the figures and its delicate gracefulness, *April* represents a conscious and creative application of the basic pictorial constituents of Puvis's art.

In *L'Enfance ou la Cueillette des pommes* (cat. no. 57) of 1896, which forms part of an ensemble of seven horizontal compositions of varying length painted by the artist to decorate his bedroom, we find the format of Puvis's *Inter Artes et Naturam* once again conspicuously brought into play and the theme of that picture itself being adapted for use by the younger man. The actual motif of the women picking fruit from a tree, the woman holding the child, and the column-like interspersion of trees and elongated figures as vertical dividers for the oblong composition, are all borrowed from Puvis's painting. The decorative purpose to which the frieze is put as well as the gentle, harmonious atmosphere are direct outgrowths of Puvis.

One of the characteristic subjects employed by Maurice Denis is the theme of mother and child, of which numerous variations from the 1890s exist. In *Maternity* (cat. no. 58) of *c.* 1896, the flattening of pale patterns, the intimacy which is conveyed by means of decorative simplifications, links Denis to Puvis. However, his informal adaptations of Puvis's more impersonal uses of similar illustrative situations lends a human feeling which is frequently lacking in Puvis's work. The pale white-grey-blue of the baby's dress, the chalky textures which

are almost effaced into a flat two-dimensional pattern, are played against the cool, restrained modelling of the faces. Denis looks beyond Puvis to the Italian renaissance, to Leonardo and the Quattrocento painters of Madonna and child compositions, as did Puvis himself who in certain works owes a debt to the frescoes of Leonardo's Milanese follower Bernardino Luini. Denis, aware of the doubly classical origins of his work—in subject the early Italians and in quality Puvis—makes the theme personal by capturing just that degree of natural intimacy that avoids the cloying sentimentality so dominating in his Italian ancestors.

In *Afternoon in the Woods* (cat. no. 59) of 1900 there is a one-piece tapestry effect: the foreground is subdued in colour while the background bands of pink-blue-green hatchings and ochre and blue bands in the water reinforce rather than negate this one-piece effect, which is so emphatic that it diminishes the sense of foreground-background recession into space. Space is shallow with the vertical trees reaching to the top in a procession against the patterns of the background and the subtly created platform for the foreground figures. The oil technique is employed in a distinctively dry manner and to the feeling of a calm pastoral so typical of Puvis de Chavannes is added a quiet luminosity and spirituality. The kneeling figure in the grey-green dress with criss-cross hatchings and circles recalls Puvis's *Au Clair de la lune* (cat. no. 26). The baby derives from that in *The Poor Fisherman* (cat. no. 21); the two figures in grey and black, one holding a baby, in the background right of centre are flattened as in many of Puvis's; the varied patterns of the leaves, shadows, water and dresses and held within a horizontal-vertical framework grip reminiscent of such compositions as Puvis's *Inter Artes et Naturam* (cat. no. 30) and the two figures standing at the left, pale grey-pink-blue, consciously hark back to Piero della Francesca by way of Puvis.

These are by no means isolated examples of the relationship between the work of Maurice Denis and Puvis de Chavannes but they are a representative selection in which the adaptations of drawing, colour, texture, mood and format can all be traced and objectified.

Edouard Vuillard (French, 1868-1940)

Two Women at a Closet, 1890-1892
Oil on cardboard; 11⅜ x 9¼ in. (29.4 x 23.5 cm.)
Signed lower left: E. Vuillard
Anonymous loan

Catalogue no. 60

Fig. 16 Edouard Vuillard, *The Dressmaker's Shop, c.* 1893

From the outset of his career, Vuillard had a deep and abiding interest in the work of Puvis de Chavannes and was disposed to adapt both technical as well as expressive means from the older man. By extraordinary coincidence his family came from the same village in the Jura as did Puvis's. Vuillard was a schoolmate of Maurice Denis and K.-X. Roussel, both of whom early shared his admiration for Puvis's murals and easel paintings. Jacques Salomon, Roussel's son-in-law and intimate friend of Vuillard, who was to become his most important biographer, has written:

> The names of the painters who most often cropped up in Vuillard's conversation were perhaps those of Puvis de Chavannes, Corot and Delacroix. Some people might wonder at his admiration for Puvis. Consider, however, how close are the subtle colours, almost *grisaille*, dear to the painter of *The Life of Saint Genevieve*, to the spare harmonies which Vuillard enjoyed creating. Puvis's working methods were also a perpetual and precious source of learning for Vuillard.

> To these can be added another, sentimental, reason. When Vuillard was recollecting his childhood memories, he liked to recall the striking impression made on him by 'Monsieur Puvis de Chavannes' who lived near Cuiseaux, when he stepped down from his carriage to come and discharge his contribution to the receiver's office.[1]

> One morning, about 1930, I went to Vuillard's home before lunch. His maid told me that "Monsieur had left early that morning

and would not be back until late evening." Intrigued, I discreetly questioned the faithful Marie, so attached to her master but who had to put up with his long silences. "Monsieur knows very well," she said resignedly, "that Monsieur never tells me what he is doing"—then, after a moment —"all the same, he could very well have gone to Amiens . . . like the last time." This last time was several years before. And, in fact, Vuillard, seized with a sudden desire to see *Ludus Pro Patria* again, had departed to spend the day alone at Amiens. At the top of the staircase of the museum, where these paintings are placed, facing one another, all the preparatory drawings which Puvis had done for the paintings are exhibited in groups, allowing one to follow clearly how the artist worked in transposing his notes and sketches.

> It was to demonstrate their common origin as natives of the Jura that Vuillard one day playfully drew his own portrait, with a hint of resemblance to Puvis.[1]

In a painting such as *Two Women at a Closet* (cat. no. 60) of 1890-92, the pale tonalities of the figures are flattened to patterns which nearly merge into the patterns of the illustrative units of the setting with an intentional ambiguity which is at the heart of Vuillard's decorative vision. A subtle, almost implied atmosphere with weightless, almost intentionally effaced figures, pervades this small picture. It expresses that restraint and overall gentleness so characteristic of Puvis which appealed to Denis and in particular to Roussel, as well as to Vuillard. "It was Vuillard's admiration of Puvis de

1. As Puvis lived in Paris, Vuillard must have recalled Puvis on his visits to his parents or brother during the 1870s when he was already famous enough to be pointed out as a celebrity. Vuillard's father was the tax collector in Cuiseaux.

1. Jacques Salomon, *Auprès de Vuillard,* Paris: 1953, pp. 109-110. The drawing referred to is reproduced on page 109.

136

Chavannes's quiet harmonious compositions and the simplicity of Japanese art that shaped his style."[1]

When Vuillard began to undertake more ambitious projects, such as his series of six horizontal frieze mural decorations for Paul Desmarais (see discussion p. 137) in 1892 and the upright format series of nine panels for Alexandre Natanson in 1894,[2] he fully elaborated on the compositional, tonal and technical repertoire he so carefully observed in Puvis's work. Closely related to the Desmarais series is a large frieze, *The Dressmaker's Shop* (see fig. 16) of *c.* 1893 in which Vuillard's adaptations from Puvis's frieze formats are made explicit. The patterns of the figures rise nearly to the top of the composition in a sequence of horizontal patterns in shallow space. This flat procession has not yet taken on the interior spatial definition in which Vuillard begins to set his *intime* groupings a short time later. Compression of space is one of his subtle adaptations from Puvis, although in *The Dressmaker's Shop* the vivid glazes of bright colours show that he has not as yet determined his characteristic subdued colour scheme and chooses to retain colour qualities borrowed from Toulouse-Lautrec and the impressionists in general.[3]

In *Out Walking* (see fig. 17) of 1894,[4] one of the Natanson panels, the dry quality of the medium, together with the pale, flat colour harmonies—mauve, rose and grey—is deployed in order to set the gentle substance of the figures within the expanse of delicately dappled pathway in the lower half of the composition. The movement in space is neither emphatic nor dramatic. Just as Puvis experimented with *peinture à la cire* in order to achieve greater control over his medium, Vuillard employs the technique of *peinture à la colle*. The artist's application of this technique has been described by Jacques Salomon as follows:

> The technique of painting *à la colle* (powdered pigments mixed with warm glue-water), . . . is a sort of distemper painting and akin to fresco. In fresco . . . the artist paints with powdered colours diluted in water . . . But not only did Vuillard prize the matt tones obtained by this method of painting: he consid-

Fig. 17   Edouard Vuillard, *Out Walking,* 1894

1. Elizabeth Gilmore Holt, *From the Classicists to the Impressionists: A Documentary History of Art,* Vol. III, New York: New York University Press, 1960, p. 518.

2. Illustrated in John Russell, *Vuillard: 1868-1940,* London: Thames and Hudson, Ltd., 1971, pp. 36-39. These explore the compositional possibilities of the two upright panels by Puvis for Rouen, *Pottery* and *Ceramic* which, together with the horizontal *Inter Artes et Naturam,* were among the pictures most closely studied by the younger generation because of their qualities and also because of the use of contemporary illustrative content.

3. (Private collection) This is the type of painting by Vuillard which would have appealed to Maurice Prendergast (see pp. 187-192).

4. (*La Promenade*) The Museum of Fine Arts, Houston, Robert Lee Blaffer Collection, *peinture à la colle* on canvas, 83½ x 37¾ in. (212 x 96 cm.).

ered that this refractory process helped him to keep his excessive facility under control and allowed him to deliberate more fully over his work, if only during the pauses while his colours were drying. It provided him with many an unforeseen discovery: and above all, it allowed him to go on experimenting, transforming and retouching almost *ad infinitum*.[1]

This fresco-like quality is essential to Vuillard's expression and stems directly from Puvis. Others have commented on the relationship of this series of paintings to Puvis. Andrew C. Ritchie, in discussing *Under the Trees*[2] states:

> In Vuillard's case it is not hard to see . . . how much he owes to Puvis and to Botticelli for his decorative schemes . . . Compare Puvis's *Sacred Grove* . . . and Botticelli's *Spring* with *Under the Trees*. Vuillard has drawn from both his tree-defined intervals of space, the arabesque of figure and branch set off against the verticals of tree trunks and the blocking out of the horizon . . . Each of these spatial devices

Vuillard uses to achieve an all-over flatness of effect in order not to destroy or penetrate the wall he is decorating. And for the same reason, whether he paints in oil on canvas or distemper on millboard, his object, like Puvis's and the Japanese print, or the flower decorated wall-paper that was the fashion in the nineties, is to achieve a juxtaposition of flat areas of matt colors which will deploy themselves evenly over a two-dimensional wall surface.[1]

It is no wonder, since so much of his art is pervaded with aspects of Puvis's, that Vuillard said of him: "The spirit of Puvis de Chavannes is a constant influence on our best decorators . . . I consider him . . . as one of the greatest intellects of his time," and "Puvis de Chavannes was in advance of his time. The researches into stylization and expressive synthesis which characterize the painting of today, are clearly noticeable in his art."[2]

Perhaps when the contents of Vuillard's diaries are revealed fifteen years from now, the full extent of his derivations from Puvis shall be made even more explicit.

1. Jacques Salomon, *Vuillard, témoignage,* Paris: 1945 (translated in Russell, *Vuillard, op. cit.* pp. 137-140, here quoted).
2. Cleveland Museum of Art. A companion piece of exactly the same size as *Out Walking* and similar in paint quality.

1. Andrew C. Ritchie, *Edouard Vuillard*, New York: The Museum of Modern Art, 1954, pp. 19-20.
2. Vuillard, *Entretien.*

K.-X. Roussel (French, 1867-1944)

Two Bathers, 1892
Oil on canvas; 9¾ x 16½ in. (25 x 42 cm.)
Unsigned
Private Collection

Catalogue no. 61

The lives and work of Roussel and Vuillard have from the beginning of their respective careers been inextricably linked.[1] Their friendship dated from 1878 when both were students, together with Maurice Denis, at the Lycée Condorcet in Paris. In 1893 Roussel married Vuillard's sister. With Bonnard, they formed a homogeneous group within the Nabis and Roussel remained faithful throughout his life to the decorative orientation which was paramount among the entire group during the nineties. Roussel was also friendly with Maurice Denis with whom he visited Cézanne in Aix in 1906. Roussel executed many large decorative schemes during his career including those done together with Vuillard in 1913 for the *Théâtre de la Comédie des Champs-Elysées,* for the Hahnlosers in Wintertur in 1915, together with Vuillard and Denis for the *Palais des Nations* in Geneva in 1936 and the following year with Bonnard and Vuillard for the *Palais de Chaillot,* Paris.

Roussel was interested in Puvis de Chavannes from the beginning of his career and in *Two Bathers* (cat. no. 61) of 1892 the pale, dry tonalities and the pastoral theme are evidence of his adaptations from Puvis. In *Panneau décoratif: Conversation dans un jardin* (cat. no. 62) of *circa* 1892 which is part of a preparatory study for a mural project, Roussel's approach is very close to that of Vuillard (see fig. 16, p. 136). Pierre Georgel has written:

> In fact, it is evident that *Réunion des Dames* and *Conversation dans un jardin* form part of the same ensemble and correspond to a precise architectural plan, traces of which are clearly visible in the projects. . . . Contemporary with the Desmarais panels, these four paintings are obviously part of the same aesthetic. But Vuillard, while adapting the style of his small pictures to his decorative panels, remains faithful to a picturesque vision of reality. He gives his figures surroundings, which are recognizable despite the decorative simplifications. Roussel, on the other hand, renders them pure and simple, reduced to schematic silhouettes, whose printed dresses begin to vaguely resemble antique costumes, and who serve to link

1. See Jacques Salomon, "Propos sur l'Amitié de K.-X. Roussel et Edouard Vuillard," *Vuillard-Roussel,* pp. 13-21.

K.-X. Roussel

Panneau décoratif: Conversation dans un jardin, circa 1892
Oil on canvas; 15 x 23½ in. (39.5 x 60 cm.)
Signed lower right: **K.-X. Roussel**
Private Collection

Catalogue no. 62

Ref. *Vuillard-Roussel*, cat. no. 212, p. 289.

the creations of Puvis and of Maurice Denis
with the realm of allegory and idealism.
[*Conversation dans un jardin*] is less dominated
by this hieratic strictness.[1]
By the latter part of the nineties, Roussel developed a
colour technique which was adapted from Renoir, Redon, Cézanne and the impressionists in general. However, from time to time he continued to make use of
thematic material derived from Puvis, as well as from
the classical French seventeenth century sources such as
Poussin and Claude Lorrain. (See, for example, *Femmes
dans la Campagne*, 1897, pastel, *Vuillard-Roussel*, cat. no.
221, p. 337.)

1. *Vuillard-Roussel*, p. 288. *Réunion des Dames* is cat. no. 211 and the other
   two of the four paintings referred to are *Les Saisons de la Vie*, cat. nos.
   209 and 210.

140

Aristide Maillol (French, 1861-1944)

Girl Tending Cows, circa 1890
Oil on canvas; 18⅞ x 25¼ in. (47.75 x 64 cm.)
Signed lower right: A. Maillol
The University of Kansas Museum of Art, Gift of Dr. and Mrs. Harold Gershinowitz

Catalogue no. 63

Ref. Jeanne Stump, "Maillol in the 1890's," *The Register
    of the Museum of Art,* The University of Kansas,
    Lawrence, Kansas, Vol. IV, nos. 4-5, March 1971,
    pp. 34-47.

Aristide Maillol

Woman without a Necklace, circa 1918-33
Bronze; 69 in. (175 cm.)
Signed on base: M
Private Collection

Catalogue no. 64

Ref. John Rewald, *Maillol*, London, Paris, New York:
    The Hyperion Press, 1939, pl. 63.

Aristide Maillol was one of the younger generation of painters (he did not devote himself to sculpture until after 1900) who during the 1880s and 1890s felt very close to the work of Puvis de Chavannes. Indeed, during this period, *c.* 1885-1890, Maillol painted a copy of *The Poor Fisherman*[1] (Paris, Musée d'Art Moderne) as well as an interpretation of the theme presented in Puvis's *Prodigal Son* (Collection Dominique Denis, St. Germain-en-Laye). Maillol painted backdrops for the puppet shows of Maurice Bouchor which Puvis attended. The older artist invited Maillol to visit his studio but Maillol was too reticent to take up the invitation.[2]

In *Girl Tending Cows* Maillol looks both to Puvis and also to Monet and Gauguin for inspiration. The pale golden and green tonalities are reminiscent of the impressionist and impressionist-derived Nabi style of Gauguin. The overall gentleness also recalls the mood of both Puvis de Chavannes and Maurice Denis. The drawing of the figure, its pose, the lilac in the skirt, the flat planes and the use of flowers to the right of the girl all are adaptations by Maillol of Puvis's usages. Making the bottom of the skirt a kind of platform is not only Puvis-esque (cf. *Death and the Maidens*, cat. no. 17, *The Sacred Grove*, cat. no. 25 and *The Bathers*, cat. no. 31), but this pose is a feature which becomes prominent in Maillol's sculpture throughout his development (see *La Méditerranée*[3] of *circa* 1902, fig. 18). Indeed, Maillol was able to transfer much of what he learned from Puvis—in drawing, in the proportions of his sculpted figures and their poses—to his mature work.

In a large scale sculpture such as *Woman without a Necklace* (cat. no. 64) the sources in Puvis are plentiful but similar in their essentials. The static poise and amplitude of the figure "Land" holding a rock crystal, to the right of centre in Puvis's *Allegory of the Sorbonne* and that of *Chemistry* (1895-96) for the Boston Public Library, are forerunners of Maillol's sculpture; some of Maillol's wood engravings in such books as *Publius Vergilius Maro, Eclogae;*[4] and the figure of *Abundance* of 1895 (cat. no. 36) provide evidence of the basic debt owed Puvis by Maillol. As we have seen (pp. 15, 17) Maillol was not reticent in acknowledging this debt and he related many instances of his admiration of Puvis de Chavannes to his biographer.[5]

Fig. 18   Aristide Maillol, *La Méditerranée, c.* 1902

1. "Maillol had copied Puvis de Chavannes's *Poor Fisherman* in the Luxembourg and perhaps this had set him in the right direction." (Waldemar George, *Aristide Maillol*, Greenwich: New York Graphic Society, 1965, p. 17.)

2. See Cladel, *op. cit.*, pp. 42-43 and Harry Kessler, *In the Twenties: The Diaries of Harry Kessler*, New York, Chicago and San Francisco: Holt, Rinehart and Winston, pp. 326-327.

3. Collection Dina Vierny, Paris.

4. Made in 1912-14, Published by Count Harry Kessler, Cranach Press, Weimar, 1926. See especially nos. 13, 19, 43 and 50, all saturated with the spirit of Puvis's figures; the kneeling figure to the left of *Chemistry*'s feet is the source of Maillol's *Girl Kneeling, c.* 1900 (see Rewald, *Maillol, op. cit.*, plate 103).

5. See Cladel, *op. cit.*, pp. 34-43.

Ferdinand Hodler (Swiss, 1853-1918)

The Disillusioned One, 1892
Oil on canvas; 21¾ x 17½ in. (55 x 44.4 cm.)
Signed and dated lower right: F. Hodler 1892
On loan from B. Gerald Cantor, Beverly Hills, California

Catalogue no. 65

Ref. Selz, *Hodler*, pp. 32-35, ill. p. 35 (catalogue no. 18).

Hodler's style of the 1870s and 1880s reflects a variety of influences, primarily those related to the clear, stolid, mid-nineteenth century illustrative style of Wilhelm Trübner (1851-1917) and Wilhelm Liebl (1844-1900) in Germany, which was reinforced by Holbein whose work he had studied on a visit to Basle in 1875. It is also possible that Hodler had seen some of Courbet's art which was admired in Germany and known in Switzerland at that time.[1] His extended visit to Madrid in 1878-79 familiarized him with the old masters and monumental painting in general. In 1883 he went to Munich where he was intensely impressed with Dürer, whose clarity of linear outline, general density of volume and often bold juxtapositions of bright and sombre colours was adapted by Hodler in much of his subsequent large scale work.

A self-portrait, *The Angry One* (Kunstmuseum, Bern) of 1881 which displays many of these qualities, was exhibited at the Salon that year in Paris. The same year he travelled to Lyons but Puvis's murals there were not painted until several years later. Geneva and Lyons are not far apart, but no subsequent journey by Hodler has been documented. It would be of considerable interest

1. Courbet was in Frankfurt in 1858-1859. In late 1869 he was in Munich and after June, 1873, Courbet lived in Switzerland.

Fig. 19   Ferdinand Hodler, *Nature*, 1884

to know whether a visit by Hodler to Lyons took place between 1885 and 1891 when the artist is initially known to have seen Puvis's paintings firsthand in Paris. However, photographs or engravings of Puvis's work —especially that in Amiens and the Panthéon —would have been available to the artist. Hodler had contacts in Switzerland with people who knew Puvis and were acquainted with his work; among these was the symbolist poet Louis Duchosal,[1] a great admirer of Puvis.

In the latter part of the 1880s Hodler became very friendly with the French engraver and playwright Marcellin Desboutin (1823-1902) whose portrait he painted. Desboutin, friend of Degas,[2] Renoir, Morisot and especially Puvis de Chavannes, had moved to Geneva more than a decade earlier but maintained his close links with the Parisian art world and he was, no doubt, the primary source by which Hodler learned what was going on there and who were the various important artistic personalities. Indeed it is by way of Desboutin that we can be certain Hodler knew of Puvis's work in detail since the former's biographer describes their close relationship at length, stating that Puvis was "his dearest friend."[3] In 1886, Desboutin wrote to a friend after visiting the museum in Marseilles:

> I was in rapture over the two Puvis de Chavannes: the *Marseilles, Port of the Orient* and *Greek Colony, Massilia*. The latter, especially, has for background and sky the most poetic piece of painting that I have ever seen or dreamed about, even in the masterpieces of the great Venetians and the primitive Tuscans. This devilish Chavannes is decidedly as great a poet as a painter. We can be proud of such an artist.[4]

On June 8, 1895, six months after the banquet for Puvis, Puvis himself helped to organize and was president of a banquet which included two hundred admirers of Desboutin on the occasion of his nomination for the Legion of Honour. Puvis made a speech in which he said, " . . . my old friend, I drink your health with a senti-

1. Duchosal was one of the group of poets who contributed to the *Album des Poètes*, presented to Puvis at the time of the banquet in his honour January 16, 1895. "A Puvis de Chavannes," "Je suis un pauvre oiseau de Genève . . . " See La Plume, p. 56. Hodler painted *Portrait of Louise-Delphine Duchosal*, the poet's sister, in 1885 (Kunsthaus, Zurich).

2. Desboutin posed for two paintings by Degas, *L'Absinthe* (Louvre) of 1876 and *Desboutin gravant avec le comte Lepic* (Musée Municipal, Nice) of *c.* 1876-77.

3. Clement-Janin, *La Curieuse Vie de Marcellin Desboutin*, Paris: H. Floury, 1922, p. 114. Desboutin had known Puvis since their days in Couture's studio. He made three drypoint engravings of Puvis, the first in 1876 and two in 1895.

4. *Ibid.*, pp. 116-117. Their closeness is also confirmed by Paul Baudouin, *op. cit.* pp. 298, 313-314, who relates an incident he witnessed as an example of Puvis's fondness for Desboutin.

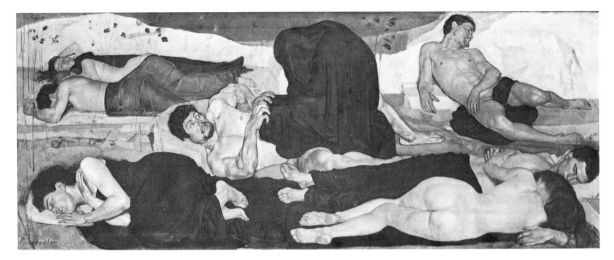

Fig. 20   Ferdinand Hodler, *Night,* 1890

ment of deep and lively affection . . . for everyone, you are held in the most friendly regard, I would almost say a legendary figure."[1] Desboutin responded, " . . . At the height of this esteemed group our homage must first go to our illustrious president Puvis de Chavannes, the great artist who, throughout all time, in all countries, in all schools, has, in his immortal work and to the highest degree, endowed painting with poetry and the plastic form with intellect."[2]

Hodler, by the mid-1880s, manifests a tendency toward theorizing which crystallized in his writings on his approach to painting which he called "parallelism." In such a work as *Nature* (Kunstmuseum Bern, Gottfried Keller-Foundation, fig. 19, p. 145) of 1884, he shows a definite inclination toward the type of detached, clearly delineated work by Puvis such as *The Prodigal Son* (fig. 28, p. 160) of 1879 and *The Poor Fisherman* (cat. no. 21) of 1879-1881.

Paul Klee, after visiting the Luxembourg Museum in Paris in 1905, recorded in his diary "The earlier Hodler stems from 'The Poor Fisherman' by Puvis de Chavannes. The color gray with a mild color scheme."[3]

1. See La Plume, no. 148, June 15, 1895, p. 286 which includes the entire text of the speech.

2. *Ibid.*, p. 287.

3. *The Diaries of Paul Klee 1898-1918*, ed. with an introduction by Felix Klee, Berkeley and Los Angeles: University of California Press, 1964, p. 180, entry no. 645/49. Klee also noted having seen the murals by Puvis in the Sorbonne and Hôtel de Ville as well as the Panthéon on the same trip, proving that Puvis was a major objective for young artists visiting Paris. In 1911 Klee wrote in his diary regarding an exhibition of Hodler's work: "Such things are very stimulating, even though I am not altogether for Hodler. For his significance does not rest in the purely pictorial, toward which I am striving more and more. He knows well how to characterize gesturing people, this I grant him. But I am worried by all these figures which look as if they can't find peace. Hodler is interested only in spiritually hyperintense beings; or

Hodler sent a painting, *Procession of Wrestlers*, to the Paris World's Fair in 1889, where it received an honourable mention and where he first came to the attention of Puvis.[1] In 1891, Hodler exhibited his composition *Night* (Kunstmuseum Bern; fig. 20) of 1890 at the *Salon du Champ-de-Mars* (May-July) where it was admired by the older artist.[2] Hodler came to Paris and was made a member of the *Société nationale des beaux-arts* of which Puvis was president. In 1892 Hodler exhibited *The Disillusioned* (Kunstmuseum Bern; fig. 21) in the first *Salon de la Rose + Croix* exhibition at Durand-Ruel—the same exhibition in which Puvis had refused to participate. However, the organizers had sent a special emissary[3] to Geneva to urge him to exhibit and not a great deal of importance should be attached to the fact that he agreed. *The Disillusioned* (see fig. 21) has distinct affinities with Puvis's art which by now Hodler had had ample opportunity to see and his tendencies toward isolation of figures as well as a mood of detachment become marked. In *The Disillusioned One* (cat. no. 65) of 1892 which represents the left-most figure in the five-figure composition and is probably a study for the larger canvas, we find the same contemplative isolation of the figure, the simplicity of drawing and setting and the intensity of focus on the gestures which we can observe in many of Puvis's easel paintings such as *The*

more exactly, only in their image: spiritually hyperintense painting is neglected rather than put to use. These *Dinge-an-sich* [things per se] become wearisome, especially when there are many of them together, and get on one's nerves. This is my repudiation of the man. But the repudiation by the numerous people who sought to connect him with modern developments remains ridiculous." *Ibid.* p. 265, entry 904.

1. See Bender, *op. cit.* p. 19.

2. *Ibid.* p. 21.

3. Count Antoine de La Rochefoucauld.

146

Fig. 21   Ferdinand Hodler, *The Disillusioned,* 1892

Poor Fisherman (cat. no. 21). This and other related paintings would appear to be the spiritual if not the actual progenitor of Hodler's painting.¹ The landscape and flowers in the foreground, the simplicity of the background and the loose treatment of the entire area surrounding the seated man and focusing our attention on him, is Hodler's adaptation of Puvis's methodology. However, the crisp linear outline and the greater emphasis on contrast are features alien to Puvis and stem from sources in the old masters which interested Hodler. Hodler has left some written commentary about his various works of this period, including *Night* and *The Disillusioned,* in an article entitled *My Present Tendencies—Night*² in which he states:

> . . . art on a small scale is unreal.
>
> . . . Characteristics of my painting from the point of view of the visibility of the bodies represented: (1) the outline of the figures stands out clearly. The outside character of the figures stands out as a whole. A whole group of figures is treated in that way. (2) The figures are clearly visible through their outline and take on an architectonic character: They are monuments of expressive architecture.

In 1893 Hodler exhibited *Communion with Infinite* at the *Salon du Champ-de-Mars* and from this time his large multi-figure compositions showed traces of Puvis's ideas. Whatever natural inclinations toward these psychologically explicit renderings Hodler had prior to his contact with Puvis, these were more than confirmed—they were provided with a conceptual and schematic base by Puvis's body of work. In 1894, *The Chosen One* (Kunstmuseum Bern, Gottfried Keller-Foundation; fig. 22, p. 148) was exhibited at the Salon and the following year *Eurythmy* (Kunstmuseum Bern) of 1894-95. This last mentioned, in addition to conscious borrowings from Dürer's *Four Apostles* in Munich, recalls the processions of saints in the friezes painted by Puvis for the Panthéon in 1877. Hodler appears to have ceased entering his pictures in the Paris exhibitions after 1895. However, the impression made by this crucial interlude in his formation was to last throughout his career. He himself noted "Up to now, my most important painting in which I reveal myself in a new light, is *Night.*"¹ In January 1895, Hodler was one of the Swiss artists who, not being able to attend, sent their greetings to Puvis on the occasion of the dinner given in his honour.²

In perhaps his most important written statement on the aims of his art, a lecture entitled *The Mission of the Artist,*³ written in late 1896 and early 1897, Hodler comments, "The deeper we penetrate into the spirit of nature, the more completely we can express her; the better our means of expression, the better we can delineate her image."⁴ Hodler goes on to state his theory of parallelism as the guiding principle of his art:

1. Van Gogh's *Sorrow,* 1882 and Gauguin's *Agony in the Garden,* 1889, Norton Gallery and School of Art, West Palm Beach, (W 326) also show this type of Puvis-inspired motif. See Bernard Dorival, "Hodler et les Maîtres Français," *Art de France,* no. 1, Paris 1961, pp. 377-380 for a discussion of Hodler's derivations from both Rodin and Puvis.
2. Selz, *Hodler,* pp. 115-116 for selections translated from Hodler's original manuscripts.

1. *Ibid.,* p. 115.
2. La Plume, p. 54, "A group of Swiss artists in Geneva join wholeheartedly in the French artists' demonstration of feeling toward M. Puvis de Chavannes and send to the master the homage of their deep admiration."
3. See Selz, *Hodler,* pp. 119-125. The lecture, delivered March 12, 1897 before the *Société des Amis des Beaux-Arts* in Fribourg, was published in *La Liberté,* Fribourg, March 18, 19 and 20, 1897. See Selz for notes.
4. *Ibid.* p. 119.

Fig. 22   Ferdinand Hodler, *The Chosen One,* 1893-94

If in my mind I compare the main characteristics of things which have made a strong and lasting impression on me, things whose ensemble has struck me most by its strong unity, I must acknowledge in every case the same element of beauty: parallelism. . . .

Parallelism, whether it is the main feature of the picture or whether it is used to set off an element of variety, always produced a feeling of unity. If I go for a walk in a forest of very high fir trees, I can see ahead of me, to the right and to the left, the innumerable columns formed by the tree trunks. I am surrounded by the same vertical line repeated an infinite number of times. Whether those tree trunks stand out clear against a darker background or whether they are silhouetted against a deep blue sky, the main note, causing that impression of unity, is the parallelism of the trunks. . . .

When it is not the main note, parallelism is an element of order. The symmetry of left and right in the human body, the symmetrical opposition which Michelangelo first used, then Raphael—that too is an instance of parallelism. . . .

If we compare these decorative instances with occurrences from our daily life, we again find the principle of parallelism. . . . In all the examples given, it is easy to see a common principle and to understand that the parallelism of the events is at the same time a decorative parallelism.

To aim at unity, at a strong and powerful unity, is to stress one thing above all others, to express it strongly, whether it is a graceful or a powerful subject. There is a general mad rush toward diversity, except a few, who like Puvis de Chavannes, introduce this harmonious note.[1]

So we can see that at the heart of Hodler's concept of art, Puvis is the one contemporary exemplification he

1. *Ibid.* pp. 123-124.

148

selects to convey his meaning. Puvis was obviously in Hodler's mind as a model, or at least point of reference or departure, for his approach to large architectural decorations—he uses the term "decorative parallelism"—as well as for the interpretation of the old masters.

Julius Meier-Graefe commented on Hodler's influence in Vienna where he had close contacts since 1900 and where he visited in 1903 and 1904: "Hodler found a second home in Vienna and was good enough to share with his Viennese friends his discoveries in parallelism which enabled one to see far beyond Puvis de Chavannes."[1] Evidently, the author of these remarks (written in 1903) interpreted Hodler's aims as attempting to carry Puvis to a further state of advance. Yet this contemporary observation underscores the fact that Hodler's theoretical ideas, however simplistic and subjective, were formulated with Puvis in mind. Hodler himself, in an interview published in Vienna in January 1904, entitled "Interview: Ferdinand Hodler on his principles of art and on Klimt,"[2] stated:

> I love clarity in a painting and this is why I love Parallelism. In many of my paintings I have chosen four or five figures in order to express this feeling because I know that impressionism is enhanced by the repetition of one and the same object. . . .
>
> When I began painting, I turned toward Impressionism. But slowly, with many years of study and observation, I came to my current procedure: clear form, simple representation, repetition of motifs.
>
> . . . Among the moderns, I value Klimt very highly. . . .
>
> Klinger I like less; he always wants to say too much. Böcklin is very important, but a little too literary for my taste.

Although differing from Puvis in his strong emphasis on contrast, Hodler insists on seeking ideas in nature and it is ironic to hear him criticize Arnold Böcklin for what the symbolists would consider a positive trait. Perhaps this gives a hint of why Hodler stopped associating with Paris art circles in the nineties.

Hodler is not well-known outside his native Switzerland and only one museum in North America, the Art Institute of Chicago, has constantly displayed his work. Yet, attempts to classify him—as a precursor of expressionism, a participant in the symbolist movement or even as an innovator somehow parallel to Cézanne (an attitude which seems patently untenable)—have never clearly defined his place. Perhaps this is due to his provincial background and also to the confused aims of his grand scale illustrative schemes with their mystical programmatic themes which, as Selz observes, "seem to be done by a painter different from Hodler the landscapist."[1] These landscapes, barren and garish, share in common with Munch—and later Nolde—a rawness of colour quality, yet they attempt to incorporate the very same mystical identification with nature as the figure compositions. Hodler makes no distinction between the two in his writings on parallelism. In Hodler's large compositions, the spectator is always aware of the stark gesticulations and anatomy of the studio drawing, not fully submerged or transformed when the separate pieces were combined into a group. In this respect, the influence of Signorelli and Michelangelo's *Last Judgement* are hardly concealed beneath the surface of bright paint.

Perhaps it is just what he shares with Puvis in terms of large scale programmatic decorations which prevents us from seeing him as a thoroughly "modern" artist, as Klee felt he was not. Thus, it is impossible to concur with a statement that "with Puvis de Chavannes, he was the most important innovator of modern monumental painting."[2] Despite his reliance on Puvis and the early Italians for a considerable amount of his inspiration, Hodler somehow remains a distinctly nineteenth-century figure, a spiritual descendant of the German transcendentalism of Otto Philipp Runge in his attempt to "penetrate into the spirit of nature" and "delineate her image." His attitude toward nature—his mystical identification with it—is conceptually very different from either Puvis or Cézanne and can only be classified with the approach of his northern predecessors. Hodler's means are those of a painter touched by impressionism but the ultimate goals of his art make us aware that he stands clear of the mediterranean tradition and help us to understand why, when we reduce his painting to basics, Dürer and Holbein were, among the old masters, the alpha and omega of his art.[3]

1. *The Development of Modern Art, op. cit.,*, Vol. II, p. 306. In later years the critic felt less enthusiastic about both Hodler and Puvis.

2. Selz, *Hodler*, pp. 117-118.

1. Selz, *Hodler*, p. 42.

2. Eva Wyler, "Introduction: A Look at Hodler," in Selz, *Hodler*, p. 13.

3. For further reading see Selz, *Hodler*, which incorporates a number of short articles and documents on and by the artist as well as a comprehensive biography of the basic studies of Hodler's life, work and development.

Félix Vallotton (Swiss, 1865-1925)

Gossip (Papotage), 1899
Gouache on millboard; 15 x 20³/₁₆ in. (38.1 x 51.3 cm.)
Signed and dated lower right: F. Vallotton 99
Collection of Arthur G. Altschul

Catalogue no. 66

Ref. *Neo-Impressionists and Nabis in the Collection of Arthur G. Altschul*, Yale University Art Gallery, January 20—March 14, 1965, catalogue no. 45, p. 102.

Born in Lausanne in 1865, Vallotton was the Swiss member of the Nabi group. He came to study in Paris at the Academy Julian under Gustave Boulanger and Jules Lefêbvre. He admired Courbet and saw the Manet memorial show in 1884. He visited Austria and Italy in 1889. Vallotton was friendly with Roussel and Vuillard and exhibited with Roussel, Denis, Bonnard, Vuillard, Maillol, Ranson and Sérusier at the gallery Barc de Boutteville in 1893. He showed at the *Salon des Indépendants* from 1891-1894. Vallotton is especially known for his black and white illustrations, woodcuts and lithographs which appeared in magazines and newspapers, and for his posters. In his graphic style he was allied with the French illustrator Hermann Paul

(1864-1940). Vallotton made a woodcut, *Portrait of Puvis de Chavannes*, for *The Studio* which was published in January, 1899, to mark the artist's death (Vol. xv, p. 207).

In *Gossip*, the overall greyish tonality and simplification almost to the point of reticence, as well as the reminiscence of the post of *The Prodigal Son* (see fig. 28, p. 160), underscore the fact that the group of painters of whom Vuillard, Roussel and Vallotton were a part all retained vestiges of Puvis's ideas in their work. Vallotton's later painting reflects deep interest in the old masters, especially Holbein, in its high degree of surface finish. Cf. *La Visite* by Vuillard (see J. Salomon, *Vuillard*, Paris: Gallimard, 1968, p. 43). Vuillard painted portraits of Vallotton and interiors with Vallotton and Misia Godebska in 1899. *La Visite* is very close in composition to *Gossip*, as is Vuillard's *La Veuve en visite* of 1899 (Art Gallery of Ontario).

150

James McNeill Whistler (American, 1834-1903)

Rose et Vert, L'Iris: Portrait of Miss Kinsella, 1893-1902
Oil on canvas; 75 x 35 in. (190.5 x 88.9 cm.)
Unsigned
Signed and inscribed on the back: *Rose et Vert, L'Iris, J. McNeill Whistler*
Original frame designed by Whistler
Lent by Davis and Long Company, New York

Catalogue no. 67

Ref. *American Painting*, October 15— November 2, 1974, New York, Davis and Long Company, no. 34 (with complete provenance).

Whistler lived mainly in Paris between 1892 and 1901 and exhibited three paintings at the *Salon du Champ-de-Mars* in 1897.[1] When Whistler became the first president of the newly founded International Society of Sculptors, Painters, Gravers in April, 1898, Puvis was one of the first artists invited to become an honorary member. Whistler had known Puvis's work since the 1860s and some of his early compositions suggest that he knew such paintings by Puvis as *The Balloon* and *The Carrier Pigeon* (see cat. nos. 12 and 13) or at least the prints made of the compositions. Puvis himself probably looked at Whistler's paintings as well (e.g. *Variations in Flesh Color and Green: The Balcony*, 1868, Freer Gallery of Art and *Cremorne Gardens, no. 2, c.* 1875, Metropolitan Museum of Art, New York).

By 1895, when Puvis exhibited the completed *Les Muses inspiratrices acclamant le Génie messager de lumière*, destined for the Boston Public Library, at the *Salon du Champ-de-Mars*, Whistler could not have failed to take note of the picture, both in itself and also as an indication of what type of painting was going across the ocean where so many of Whistler's patrons lived. Also, Whistler was enjoying great popularity among young American artists, men such as Prendergast and Glackens, who had been to France and who had imbibed Whistler's influence in Paris. Among the younger men in France, Whistler knew both Maillol and Josef Rippl-Ronai (1861-1927), a Hungarian member of the Nabi group who was influenced by Puvis.

The flower in Miss Kinsella's hand recalls Puvis's *Hope* (cat. no. 15). The ethereality of her dress, its billowing vaporous weight derives from the floating-flying muses in Puvis's Boston mural. That Whistler adapted his lighter-in-weight density, as well as the wan delicacy of the characterization, from Puvis is evident if we compare this picture with an illustratively similar portrait, *The White Girl (Symphony in White, No. 1)* of 1862 (The National Gallery of Art, Washington), with its denser, Manet-esque and still even somewhat Courbet-esque handling. We know Whistler was at work on the painting in 1896 when he wrote to the subject that he had shown it to Sargent in his Paris studio. In 1894 Charles Conder (1868-1909) had a love affair with Miss Kinsella and also painted her portrait, *A Summer Afternoon: "The Green Apple"* (Tate Gallery).

Although Whistler certainly adapted features borrowed from Japanese prints, Fantin-Latour and the Pre-Raphaelite painters, which make it impossible to assert that Puvis was an exclusive or even dominant source, there are moments such as this, when Puvis's influence seems to be in the ascendant. Puvis, like Whistler, was extremely fond of grey as a pervasive tonality, and Whistler must have paid close attention to his use of that colour in conjunction with the pale roses and blues and lavenders which so dominated Puvis's work from the later part of the 1880s until his death.

1. In an unpublished letter *c.* 1894 to Marcus B. Huish Whistler wrote from Paris that he had Puvis de Chavannes to dinner. "Our President, Monsieur Puvis de Chavannes, whom with much circumstance we had as guest . . ." (Glasgow University Library, Birnie Philip Bequest, B.P.II, C/11, discoverd and communicated to the author by Katharine Jordan). Whistler was a member of the *Société nationale des beaux-arts* of which Puvis de Chavannes was President. Through J.S. Sargent, Whistler was involved with the project to decorate the Boston Public Library at the same time as Puvis but his work was never completed. This doubtlessly accounted for Whistler's having paid close attention to Puvis's Boston murals exhibited in 1895 and 1896 at the *Salon du Champ-de-Mars.*

Hippolyte Petitjean (French, 1854-1929)

Mythological Scene (En Arcadie), 1895
Oil on canvas; 45 x 57½ in. (114 x 146 cm.)
Signed and dated lower left: Hip. Petitjean 1895
Lent by M. Knoedler and Company, Inc.

Catalogue no. 68

Ref. Robert L. Herbert, *Neo-Impressionism*, New York:
      The Solomon R. Guggenheim Museum, 1968, p.
      79.

Fig. 23   Paul Signac, *Au temps d'Harmonie,* 1894-95

Fig. 24   Henri Matisse, *Luxe, calme et volupté,* 1904-05

There existed a custom, if not a tradition, of neo-impressionist artists looking at the work of Puvis de Chavannes. Indeed, their active critical supporters Félix Fénéon, Paul Alexis and especially Gustave Kahn were solidly in the ranks of Puvis's admirers. Conservative neo-impressionist painters, such as Petitjean, derived some of their compositions directly from Puvis in virtually undigested form; *Mythological Scene* is an example. However, in the nineties artists such as Signac produced compositions which, despite their greater degree of individuality, also closely adhered to Puvis's compositional formats. Such works as *Au temps*

d'Harmonie (Mairie de Montreuil, fig. 23) make conspicuous use of Puvis's programmatic as well as compositional ideas. It is interesting to note that a progressive artist such as Matisse derived important compositional ideas directly from Signac (see *Luxe, calme et volupté,* 1904-05, fig. 24) and thus absorbed Puvis's ideas, while conservative painters such as the American Childe Hassam (1859-1935) borrowed from men such as Petitjean and painted works such as *The Bathers* of 1904 (fig. 25) which arrive at Puvis-esque compositions where one would least expect to find them.

Fig. 25   Childe Hassam, *The Bathers,* 1904

By the late 1880s and early 1890s, Puvis also exerted an influence on the decorative arts in France, not on the techniques of glassmaking but on the nature of the subjects to which some of these innovations were applied. The most notable was the *pâte de verre* technique developed by Henri Cros (1840-1907) as early as 1882. The frosty, pale, delicate colours and surface texture of his small compositions were inspired directly by Puvis. *Incantation* (fig. 26) of 1892 is a clear example of Puvis's influence. As late as 1905, Cros made a relief entitled *The Apotheosis of Victor Hugo*, adopting the subject of Puvis's ceiling mural in the Hôtel de Ville, Paris, of 1893. Cros was influenced in the development of his technique by Pompeiian encaustic painting techniques and by the writings of Charles Henry, who also had an impact on the theoretical writings of the neo-impressionist painters. Cros was in attendance at the banquet in honour of Puvis in January, 1895.[1]

Fig. 26   Henri Cros, *Incantation,* 1892

1. See A.M. Belfort, "Les Pâtes de verre d'Henri Cros," *Cahiers de la Céramique et du Feu,* no. 40, Sèvres, 1967, 167-187 and Janine Bloch-Dermant, *L'Art du Verre en France 1860-1914,* Lausanne: Edita Denoel, 1974, 166-173.

Paul Sérusier (French, 1863-1927)

Legend of Butterflies, circa 1902-1905
Oil on canvas; 19 x 59 in. (48.2 x 149.8 cm.)
Signed lower right: monogram PS
Anonymous loan

Catalogue no. 69

Odilon Redon (French, 1840-1916)

Les Deux Grâces, 1900
Oil on canvas; 16 x 11 in. (40.6 x 30 cm.)
Unsigned
Collection of Dr. and Mrs. Howard D. Sirak, Columbus, Ohio

Catalogue no. 70

Odilon Redon

The Crown, after 1900
Pastel on paper; 22½ x 18¼ in. (22.5 x 46.3 cm.)
Signed lower right: Odilon Redon
Ian Woodner Family Collection

Catalogue no. 71

Ref. Museum of Modern Art, Tenth Loan Exhibition,
      Lautrec and Redon, February 1 — March 2, 1931,
      no. 77 (Coll. Mrs. C.J. Martin, Minneapolis).

Odilon Redon

Red Tree not Reddened by the Sun, 1905
Oil on canvas; 18 x 14 in. (45.7 x 35.5 cm.)
Signed lower right: Odilon Redon
Lent by Arthur Tooth and Sons, London, U.K.

Catalogue no. 72

Ref. Klaus Berger, *Odilon Redon: Fantasy and Color*, New
      York, Toronto and London: McGraw Hill Book
      Company, 1965, cat. no. 96.

Fig. 28   Pierre Puvis de Chavannes, *The Prodigal Son,*
1879

Fig. 27   Odilon Redon, *Sketch after "The Prodigal Son"*
by Puvis de Chavannes, 1880

Redon's admiration for the work of Puvis de Chavannes.
lasted throughout his career as a graphic artist, painter
and pastellist. We have already pointed to his having
been warned against studying Puvis's work by Bresdin
in 1873 and also his having made a drawing in 1880 after *The Prodigal Son* (see figs. 27 and 28). In 1910, Redon
recorded in his journal:

> What a curious question: there is talk of
> bringing the remains of Puvis de Chavannes
> to the Panthéon.
>
> But, having in the past heard the laughter
> of the crowd which thronged in amusement in
> front of his pictures (notably *The Poor
> Fisherman* and *Hope*), I can only greet this idea
> with a sad smile.
>
> ... those who were indifferent before are
> indifferent still and today's demonstration to
> the contrary must hide from us many uncer-
> tain things. ...

What does not change, what is living and
present forever, is the permanent life of a master through the works he has left behind. The
voice of Puvis de Chavannes is still heard in
the Panthéon through the frescoes [sic] of
Saint Genevieve. Why add the ashes, whose
silence, after all, belongs to the unknown.

The glorification and deification of a great
man lie in the homage we pay him by the
high value we place on his works, in his lifetime or after it.

It would be strange to see Parliament concerning itself with art other than for a
community! What? One would be concerned
with an artist, a poet! The great mural
painter Puvis de Chavannes is worth it; he
was worth it.[1]

1. Redon, *A soi-même*, p. 109 (entry of May, 1910).

160

It is clear from this statement that Redon placed "high value" on Puvis's works and this is clearly manifest in a number of colour, textural and figural adaptations which appear throughout his work in all media. In *Les Deux Grâces* (cat. no. 70) of 1900, the pale, ethereal figures in white grow out of Redon's lithograph, *The Priestesses were Waiting* of 1886 which in turn is derived from the figures in the background of such paintings of Puvis as *Christian Inspiration*, which was exhibited at the Salon of 1886. They may also be compared with the figures in the centre background leaning against a tree in *The Woodcutters* (cat. no. 18) of *c.* 1870-75. The use of gold indicates an attempt to assimilate a kind of conscious archaism tinged with the exotic which stems both from the fifteenth century Italians and the legacy of Delacroix as carried on by Gustave Moreau. Nevertheless, the pervasive mood here is not dominated by this exoticism but conveys instead the cool, contemplative detachment of Puvis de Chavannes, together with a spare simplification in drawing which also finds its direct source in Puvis. Oil made to express restraint by way of its dry texture is a legacy of Puvis's shared by Maurice Denis and Redon: it establishes, in the work of the former, a means of contrast with the light-filled intensities of impressionism and, in Redon, with his bizarre, oriental, decorative exoticism. This contrast of the pale, delicate light-in-weight volumes is a major constituent of Redon's expressive individuality.

In *The Crown* (cat. no. 71), a pastel, the pose of the figure immediately recalls that of Puvis's *Euterpe* (cat. no. 27) of *c.*1885-90 and also the semi-draped Oceanid rising from the water in the left background of Puvis's *Dramatic Poetry* (fig. 35, p. 172) in the Boston Public Library. Puvis's *Le Rhône* of 1886 is another source of this figure and the numerous related nude figures which appear in Redon's work with increasing frequency after 1905.[1] Redon also makes extensive use of the Pegasus motif found on the rose-coloured wall in the background of Puvis's *Inter Artes et Naturam* (cat. no. 30).[2]

In *Red Tree not Reddened by the Sun* (cat. no. 72) of 1905, Redon's lush exoticism dominates but the nude figure clearly recalls types of nudes seen in Puvis's *The Woodcutters* (cat. no.18) and also somewhat the textures and colour density of *The Bathers* (cat. no. 31). That Redon had paid close attention to the nudes of Puvis de Chavannes is shown in his journal entry for May 14, 1888:

> That painter is not intellectual when the nude woman he has painted leaves us with the notion that she will get dressed again at once.
>
> The intellectual painter shows her to us in a nudity which reassures, because she does not hide it; she leaves it, without shame, in an Eden, for the gaze of others than ourselves, who are from an intellectual world, an imaginary world created by the artist where beauty moves and spreads and will never engender immodesty but, on the contrary, endows nudity with a pure attraction which does not debase us. The nude women of Puvis de Chavannes do not re-clothe themselves, like many others of past times, in the charming gynaeceum of a Giorgione or a Correggio.
>
> There is one, in Manet's *Déjeuner sur l'herbe* who will hasten to dress herself after her troubled uneasiness on the cold grass, beside these gentlemen with no ideals who surround and converse with her. What are they saying? Nothing very fine, I suspect.[1]

It should also be pointed out that along with Cézanne, Renoir, Toulouse-Lautrec and Puvis de Chavannes, Redon exhibited sixty-two works at the *Salon d'Automne* of 1904. He would then have had an ideal opportunity to study his own work side by side with a comprehensive selection of Puvis's. It is perhaps due to this circumstance that many of Redon's subsequent paintings and pastels reveal a subtle but discernible indebtedness to Puvis's art.

1. See, for example, *Pandora, c.* 1910 (Metropolitan Museum of Art, New York); *Andromeda,* 1912 (The Arkansas Arts Center, Little Rock); *The Birth of Venus,* 1912 (Kimbell Art Museum, Fort Worth).
2. See, for example, *The Fall of Phaeton, c.* 1900 (Josten Collection), *Apollo c.* 1904 (Yale University Art Gallery, given by the Phillip L. Goodwin Collection, formerly Collection of John Quinn) and *The Chariot of Apollo, c.* 1910 (Metropolitan Museum of Art, New York).

1. Redon, *A soi-même,* p. 91.

Pablo Picasso (Spanish, 1881-1973)

Lo que el Rusiñol le pensaba (*What Rusiñol was thinking*), *circa* 1901
Pen and ink on cardboard, 5¼ x 3½ in. (13.3 x 8.8 cm.)
Signed lower right: Picasso
Lent by Perls Galleries, New York

Catalogue no. 73

Ref. unpublished.

Pablo Picasso

Crouching Woman, 1902
Oil on canvas; 39⅞ x 26 in. (101.3 x 66 cm.)
Signed upper left: Picasso
Art Gallery of Ontario

Catalogue no. 74

Ref. Daix and Boudaille, VII.5

163

Pablo Picasso

Bonhomme assis, 1904
Pen and ink on paper; 11¹¹/₁₆ x 8¹¹/₁₆ in. (29 x 21.5 cm.)
Signed and dated lower right: *al amigo Pablo Gargallo muy afectuosamente Picasso Paris 6 Mayo 1904*
Ian Woodner Family Collection

Catalogue no. 75

Ref. Christian Zervos, *Pablo Picasso*, Vol. VI , *Supplément
      aux Volumes I à V*, Paris, Editions Cahiers d'Art,
      1954, no. 630, p. 77.

Pablo Picasso

Circus Family, 1905
Watercolour and pen on paper; 9½ x 12 in. (24 x 30.5 cm.)
Signed lower right: Picasso
The Baltimore Museum of Art, Cone Collection

Catalogue no. 76

Ref. Daix and Boudaille, XII. 18.

Pablo Picasso

The Swineherd (Prodigal Son among Pigs), 1906
Pencil and ink on paper; 8 x 7½ in. (20.3 x 19 cm.)
Signed upper right: Picasso
Collection of Mr. and Mrs. Daniel Saidenberg, New York

Catalogue no. 77

Ref. *Four Americans in Paris, The Collection of Gertrude Stein and her Family*, The Museum of Modern Art, New York, 1970, p. 168; *The Autobiography of Alice B. Toklas*, New York: Harcourt, Brace, 1933, pp. 108-109.

Pablo Picasso

La Toilette, 1906
Oil on canvas; 59½ x 39 in. (151 x 99 cm.)
Signed upper left: Picasso
Albright-Knox Art Gallery, Buffalo, New York, Fellows for Life Fund, 1926

Catalogue no. 78

Ref. Daix and Boudaille, xv. 34 (formerly John Quinn
    Collection).

167

As a source for Picasso's early work, Puvis de Chavannes has not so much been disregarded as discounted by the very students who, while acknowledging some vague debt to Puvis, have preferred not to draw conclusions consistent with the raw data of their observations. The reasons for this are various but obvious — Puvis de Chavannes is not as glamorous a source as El Greco or Cézanne, nor so esoteric for a young Spaniard as Nietzsche or the Pre-Raphaelites. Nonetheless, Picasso showed interest in a wide variety of sources and Puvis de Chavannes was surely one of the major — not minor — determinants of his "Blue," "Harlequin" and "Rose" period work. Alfred H. Barr, Jr. has written:

> Picasso's youthful classicism is informal, fresh, unacademic. He was influenced somewhat by Puvis de Chavannes and the idyllic figure compositions of Gauguin though it is possible that during his visits to the Louvre he had studied Greek sculpture and painting.
>
> Years later, during the twenties, when Picasso again tried his hand at the classic style, his references to the ancients were sophisticated. Perhaps by then he knew too much so that the results were less classic than neoclassic.[1]

Although it is not the purpose here to reconstruct the step by step evolution of Picasso's early work, we may trace the broad outlines of Picasso's familiarity with and his opportunities to acquaint himself with the work of Puvis de Chavannes and also cite some specific examples of where the influence can be demonstrated.

Picasso's awareness of Puvis de Chavannes dates from the crucial formative years in the late 1890s spent mainly in and around Barcelona. His initial source was his friend, the Catalan painter Santiago Rusiñol (1861-1931), an enthusiastic admirer of Puvis who had known his work firsthand prior to his friendship with the teenage Picasso. Rusiñol lived in Paris in the early nineties and became a *membre associé* of the *Société nationale des beaux-arts* in 1893 when he exhibited seven paintings at the *Salon du Champ-de-Mars*. This, in itself, would not be of more than passing interest if it were not for the fact that Rusiñol attended the banquet for Puvis in 1895 and left a vivid eyewitness account of that occasion:[2]

> The best of the arts and literature were around the large table to pay tribute to the most universal genius of the art of our time. An act of admiration to one of the few who has done the work which will remain; to a great artist and thinker, an honour to the sincere art so rare in our days.[3]

Rusiñol goes on at great length to describe the speeches, those attending — "The great hall was a forest of trees, the trees which have enriched the garden of France"[1] — and Puvis's art. That year Rusiñol showed five paintings at the *Salon du Champ-de-Mars*, none in 1896, three in 1897 and he again entered five in 1898. Thus, he would have been in a position to be thoroughly conversant with Puvis's art and hence to be able to relate his feelings about it to Picasso. It is known that Rusiñol, who had acquired two paintings by El Greco in 1894 in Paris,[2] introduced Picasso to the work of El Greco at his home, the *Cau Ferrat* in Sitges, south of Barcelona. Rusiñol surely did not confine his discussions to El Greco for, as Juan-Edouard Cirlot observes, "In 1899 and 1900 Barcelona became almost an antechamber to Paris."[3] At this time, Picasso frequented the *Club de san Luc*[4] and *Els Quatre Gats*, a café modelled on the Parisian type of which Rusiñol was one of the founders. He made a number of drawings of his friends, including several of Santiago Rusiñol. Apart from conventional sketches of Rusiñol,[5] a heretofore unknown drawing has come to light. In this small pen sketch, *Lo que el Rusiñol le pensaba* (*What Rusiñol was thinking*), catalogue no. 74, one of a series of the same format done around 1901, we see Picasso referring directly to Rusiñol's connection with Puvis de Chavannes. A flying figure of a muse with wings, labelled "*ARTE*," crowns the bowed head of Rusiñol with a laurel wreath on which is written "*Associé*." The muse is unmistakably Puvis-esque, recalling those in *Les Muses inspiratrices acclamant le Génie messager de lumière*, the mural for the Boston Public Library which Rusiñol would have known from the *Salon du Champ-de-Mars* of 1895. When we connect these elements with the fact of Rusiñol's status as a *membre associé* of the *Société nationale des beaux-arts*, something of which the painter was undoubtedly proud, the drawing assumes additional documentary significance. Although a lighthearted caricature, the drawing is a revealing example of Picasso's awareness that Rusiñol attached great importance to Puvis's art. Moreover, on one of his early visits to Paris,[6] very likely in 1901, Picasso made a sketch after one of Puvis's paintings. *Three Figures* (fig.

1. *Picasso: Fifty Years of his Art*, New York: The Museum of Modern Art, 1946, p. 40.

2. Maria Rusiñol, *Santiago Rusiñol vist per la seva filla*, Barcelona: Editorial Aedos, 1950 (in Catalan). The biography is based on Rusiñol's memoirs.

3. *Ibid.* Chapter II, "El amics del meu pare," p. 54.

1. *Ibidem.*

2. Rusiñol was deeply involved in the Catalan cultural revival. It is interesting that the man who attempted to reestablish the cultural autonomy, especially the indigenous language, of Provence, Frédéric Mistral (1830-1914) — and whose poetry would have attracted Catalans — was also an admirer of Puvis de Chavannes.

3. *Picasso: Birth of a Genius*, London: Paul Elek, Ltd., 1972, p. 98.

4. Anthony Blunt and Phoebe Pool, *Picasso, The Formative Years: A Study of his Sources*, London: Studio Books, 1962, "In 1898, when Picasso was living in Barcelona, a session of the Club of San Luc was held in his [Puvis's] honour."

5. See Cirlot, *op. cit., Portrait of Santiago Rusiñol* (1899-1900), no. 164.

6. We cannot entirely discount the possibility that Picasso had already studied Puvis at the time of his visit to Paris, October — December, 1900, during the *Exposition Universelle*.

29) is clearly annotated by Picasso, "*De Puvis en el Panteon*" [from Puvis in the Panthéon].[1] The three figures are copied from the lower left section of Puvis's *Sainte Geneviève ravitaillant Paris* (fig. 30) which was completed and installed less than a year before Puvis's death in 1898 and which Picasso sketched *in situ.*[2]

Two other aspects of Picasso's formative education can be related to the specific links with Puvis de Chavannes noted above. The first of these is the fact that Picasso, at the time of his June, 1901 exhibition at Vollard's, would have had the opportunity to see and study Gauguin's *Where do we come from? What are we? Where are we going?* (fig. 13, p. 124) which was at the dealer's gallery. Blunt and Pool have observed: "Reviewers of his exhibition at Vollard's in June, 1901 accused him of imitating Lautrec and this criticism may be partly responsible for the emergence of a new, more personal style towards the end of 1901. Gauguin had more to offer."[3] Indeed, what Gauguin had to offer in such a composition as *Where do we come from?* was a modernized version of Puvis de Chavannes's large scale murals. The simplifications and deep blue which pervade Gauguin's painting gradually began to manifest themselves in Picasso's work at the beginning of his "Blue" period in Paris at the end of 1901. Whether or not the combined impetus of Rusiñol and Gauguin's work led Picasso to go and look at Puvis firsthand cannot be

proven, but the fact that he did so around this time is documented by not only *Three Figures* but also by Picasso's companion, Jaime Sabartés, who in writing about the events in Paris during the late fall of 1901, specifically mentions a visit to the Luxembourg Museum with Picasso and also lunching with him regularly at a restaurant in the Place de la Sorbonne.[1]

The second connection to Puvis at this time is one that will always remain obscure in determining Picasso's development; that is, his experimentation with fresco. Barr mentions "some essays in fresco painting . . . perhaps in 1901 or 1902 after he had been in Paris. All traces of these experiments seem to have disappeared."[2] If our approximate dating of both the *What Rusiñol was thinking* and *Three Figures* sketches is

1. *Picasso: An Intimate Portrait*, New York: Prentice-Hall, Inc., 1948, pp. 61-62.
2. Barr, *op. cit.*, pp. 16-17. Joan Merli, *Picasso el artista y la obra de nuestre tiempo*, Buenos Aires: El Ateneo, 1942, p. 22, mentions romanesque Catalan frescoes as the source of Picasso's.

1. Museo Picasso, Barcelona (MAB 110.468), pen on paper, 14.6 x 18.1 cm., unsigned. Also inscribed, "*el cuadro de la hambre*" [a picture of the famine]; "*Mujer joven bien vestida*" [well dressed young woman]; "*Mujer vieja*" [old woman]; "*Hombre de el pueblo*" [man from the village]. Cirlot, *op. cit.*, reproduces the drawing (no. 957) without noting its connection to Puvis de Chavannes, dating it 1902-1903.
2. Picasso might also have seen the oil sketch final study for the same mural if it belonged at that time to the Luxembourg Museum. It was transferred from the Luxembourg to the Louvre in 1929.
3. Blunt and Pool, *op. cit.*, p. 13.

Fig. 29   Pablo Picasso, *Three Figures* (after Puvis de Chavannes), *c.* 1901

Fig. 30   Pierre Puvis de Chavannes, *Sainte Geneviève ravitaillant Paris* (left section), 1897

169

Fig. 31   Pablo Picasso, *Man with a Pack*, 1902

correct, they may well have been done while Picasso was experimenting with fresco. Although this must remain conjecture, subsequent to 1901-1902 Picasso's work becomes increasingly large in format and, as we shall point out, some of the compositions and individual figures bear striking resemblances to certain of Puvis's paintings in tonality, colour range, poses, as well as in mood.

Crouching Woman (cat. no. 74) of 1902 exhibits the limited colour range which stems mainly from Gauguin, but in its parallel hatchings it also reveals the influence of van Gogh and Cézanne; Picasso would have studied the latter's work at Vollard's. However, in mood the painting harks back to Puvis's *The Poor Fisherman* as well as to cloaked figures, both seated and standing in the *Allegory of the Sorbonne*, the kneeling women in the centre of *Charity* (cat. no. 35), and the woman at the extreme left of *Inter Artes et Naturam* (cat. no. 30). In a painting such as *Mother and Child in Profile*[1] of 1902, the simple division of the composition into flat bands, the pervasive blue tonality and the use of the boat, recall Puvis's *Sainte Geneviève veillant sur Paris* of 1898 and motifs from the centre panel of *Sainte Geneviève ravitaillant Paris*; the incorporation of the boat into the

1. Daix and Boudaille, VII. 20 (Private Collection, U. S. A.).

170

composition also recalls *The Poor Fisherman*. At this time Picasso also produced a series of drawings including *Man with a Pack*[1] (see fig. 31) which resembles the simplicity of Puvis's treatment of the same subject in the right hand section of *Sainte Geneviève ravitaillant Paris*. Another closely-related composition, *The Tragedy*[2] (see fig. 32) of 1903 carries many of the same features and in mood as well as in gesture and tonality recalls Puvis's *Epic Poetry* (cat. no. 38) and *The Poor Fisherman* (cat. no. 21). Actually, the Sorbonne mural was a mine of poses and gestures for Picasso's draped figures of the "Blue" period, as well as lending support to his subdued, nearly monochromatic colour. Many writers have sought to connect Picasso's work of this period with symbolism[3] or at least aver symbolic content in his work. In a composition such as *La Vie*[4] (see fig. 33) of 1903, painted in Barcelona, such conjectural interpretations have been applied. On this subject Picasso has stated:

> *La Vie* was not my title . . . . I did not plan to paint symbols. I simply painted the images which sprang up in front of my eyes: others can find hidden meanings there. For me, a painting speaks for itself; what is the good of adding explanations after the event? A painter has only one language.[5]

Rather than a literary or symbolic source for the composition, we would see visual material borrowed and adapted to suit Picasso's own purposes from, among other sources, figures in the *Allegory of the Sorbonne*, especially the cloaked figure of *Physics* on a pedestal at the far right.[6] In *Bonhomme assis* (cat. no. 75) of 1904, one of a number of drawings employing a similar motif, there is a distinct relationship to *The Prodigal Son* (fig. 28, p. 160) as well as to *The Poor Fisherman* (cat. no. 21).[7]

Apart from the abundant available resources at the Panthéon, the Sorbonne and the Hôtel de Ville, Picasso's greatest opportunity to saturate himself in the work of Puvis de Chavannes came during the latter stages of the "Blue" period. This was the exhibition of forty-three works by Puvis de Chavannes, some very

1. Zervos, *op. cit.*, Vol. I, p. 88., no. 179 (The Solomon R. Guggenheim Museum, Justin K. Thannhauser Collection).

2. Daix and Boudaille, IX. 6 (National Gallery of Art, Washington, D.C., Chester Dale Collection).

3. See for example, Ronald W. Johnson, "Picasso's 'Old Guitarist' and the Symbolist Sensibility," *ARTFORUM*, December, 1974, pp. 56-62.

4. Daix and Boudaille, IX. 13 (Cleveland Museum of Art).

5. Quoted in Antonina Vallentin, *Pablo Picasso*, Paris: Editions Albin Michel, 1957, p. 46. Blunt and Pool, *op. cit.*, point out that the magazine *Arte Joven* of which Picasso was the co-founder in 1900, "printed unsparing parodies of symbolism" (p. 14).

6. The simplified background in *Sainte Geneviève veillant sur Paris* appears to be the source of similar reduction in such works as *The Old Guitarist*, 1903, Daix and Boudaille, IX. 34 (Art Institute of Chicago).

7. See also Picasso's *Study of Male Nude with Arms Raised*, 1902-1903 (Paris), Daix and Boudaille, D. VIII. 1 (Musée des Beaux-Arts, Grenoble) with the nude child right of centre in Puvis's *The Sacred Grove* (cat. no. 25).

Fig. 32   Pablo Picasso, *The Tragedy,* 1903, National Gallery of Art, Washington, Chester Dale Collection

Fig. 33   Pablo Picasso, *La Vie,* 1903

large in scale, at the *Salon d'Automne* of 1904. It was this event, more than any other, which crystallized the Puvis influence on Picasso and perhaps helped to accelerate the transition into the "Harlequin" and what Barr calls the "first classic" period from mid-1905 to mid-1906. Blunt and Pool have written:

> Another influence on Picasso's painting at this time was Puvis de Chavannes, forty-three of whose works were shown at the Salon d'Automne of 1904. His strange mixture of naiveté and sophistication, the tranquil gestures of his figures, the broad cool areas of colour, the geometrical organization of his picture, and the simplified drawing appealed to Picasso as they had done to Seurat, Gauguin and Van Gogh.[1]

1. *Op. cit.,* p. 26. Unfortunately, the authors do not follow their observation with any specific examples of Puvis's influence and are generally not disposed to see such influence as a significant element in Picasso's development. They do, however, cite Picasso's *La Coiffure* (dating it incorrectly 1905 instead of 1906) stating that it "resembles Puvis' study for a scene from the life of St. Geneviève for the Panthéon

The works exhibited from October 15 to November 15 varied in type — paintings, pastels, drawings and

shown in the Salle Puvis de Chavannes at the Salon d'Automne 1904." But the painting they reproduce as the comparison is not the study for the Panthéon mural but rather a photograph of one of the frescoes painted on the outside walls of the stables of Puvis's brother's house between 1854 and 1858 and which were not published until 1914. See Achille Segard, "Fresques inédites de Puvis de Chavannes," *Les Arts,* no. 147, March 1914, pp. 4-16. The fresco illustrated by Blunt and Pool is reproduced on p. 16. Segard states, however, "One cannot claim that they have been unknown up until now since all scholars interested in the work of this great artist do know of their existence and some have gone to see them in the family home where they have been reverently preserved for more than fifty years" (p. 4). We know, for example, that Maurice Denis wrote to the family to ask permission to see the paintings and was refused (undated letter from A. Puvis de Chavannes to Maurice Denis, Centres d'Art et de Documentation, Association "Symbolistes et Nabis," Saint Germain-en-Laye). It would be interesting to know if Picasso had seen these frescoes or photographs of them, since one of them, also reproduced on p. 16 of Segard's article, closely recalls the subject and format of Picasso's *Composition* (Daix and Boudaille, XV. 62) of 1906, collection The Barnes Foundation.

caricatures—and ranged from small to monumental and from rough preparatory sketches to finished works. The display must have constituted a reinforcement of Picasso's previous knowledge of Puvis for it both revealed unsuspected aspects of Puvis's style and demonstrated his technical methods — especially the unfinished large scale oil studies. This type of large scale oil study is here represented by *Study for Charity, c.* 1893-94 (cat. no. 33).[1]

In *Circus Family* (cat. no. 77) of 1905, the entire spirit of the watercolour is pervaded by the influence of Puvis de Chavannes. In the subtle, delicate terra cotta, pink, pale blue and chalky white colour scheme, the poses of the figures and the simplified bands of the background, *Circus Family* transposes Puvis's *Pleasant Land* (cat. no. 23) into a lithe ballet-like sequence of rhythmic movements against a backdrop-like setting which takes its point of departure from the static and poised interplay of illustrative activity in Puvis's canvas. Specific simi-

1. The near abstract, geometric patterns of the block-like rocks in the left background are in themselves a re-use of a similar motif in the *Allegory of the Sorbonne* where they almost simulate, illustratively, modern cantilevered architectural construction.

larities include the delicate silhouetted trees against the broad flat planes of the background, the standing harlequin figure in the Picasso and the woman with hands on hips right of centre in *Pleasant Land*, the balancing of the acrobat on the ball and that of the two nude children in the foreground of Puvis's composition, the placement of the building with horse, landscape, tree and figures in a series of barely perceptible receding horizontal planes and the hill, tree, water, foliage and figures in the Puvis. In addition, the mother holding her child in the Picasso and the seated woman to her right, as well as the use of architectural elements, recalls Puvis's *Inter Artes et Naturam*. Compare these units with the mother and child in the centre and the seated woman third from the left, or the interplay between the seated

Fig. 34   Pablo Picasso, *Young Acrobat on a Ball,* 1905

Fig. 35   Puvis de Chavannes, *Dramatic Poetry,* 1895

172

and standing women at the far right of Puvis's painting. There is a glimpse of *The Prodigal Son* (fig. 28, p. 160) in the kneeling man in the foreground and a hint also of *The Poor Fisherman* (cat. no. 21) in his pose and the two infants in the left foreground. Picasso, it seems was attuned to reinterpret Puvis's ideas because they were also built upon an illustrative framework, taken from nature but simplified and subdued in both colour and line. Puvis was more deliberate in the placement of his figures and one always is conscious of the effort that went into their organization. In Picasso, the natural facility as a draughtsman to handle complex illustrative themes and his ease in spontaneously, even effortlessly, placing them in relation to one another, differentiates the expressive character of his results. But, as with Maurice Denis, Picasso's simplifications grow out of Puvis's experiments rather than Cézanne's, for as Picasso more consciously tries to incorporate Cézanne's means into his art, his colour scheme becomes less bright and subtle and he suppresses the natural decorative and illustrative tendencies which link his work to Puvis.

At the same time as *Circus Family*, Picasso painted several large scale works including *Young Acrobat on a Ball* (see fig. 34) and *Family of Saltimbanques*.[1] In *Young Acrobat on a Ball* we find a conscious re-working of Puvis's *Dramatic Poetry* (see fig. 35) which Picasso had seen at the *Salon d'Automne* (no. 10). The seated figure seen from the back played against the dancing figure of the acrobat girl poised on a ball is taken over from the figure of Aeschylus and a combination of the two dancing Oceanides with arms raised above their heads to the left in the middleground of Puvis's composition. The man is also adapted from *Saint Genevieve in Prayer* (see fig. 36) where the contrast between strength and delicacy from foreground figures to middleground with oxen in the background, served as a model for Picasso. A similar seated figure is also found in the man in the boat with back to the spectator in Puvis's *Childhood of Saint Genevieve* (fig. 8, p. 121) in the Panthéon. Picasso's painting is essentially a large black and white drawing tinted with wash. Its drawing is an exercise in contrasts — the terse anchored blocks of the man and the soaring swift flights of the girl are brought into harmony by subtle distortions of scale and pattern. The broad geometric shapes of the two main figures and the background setting against which they are played are closely interrelated in order to achieve the gentle monumentality of the ensemble. In *Family of Saltimbanques* the size and very summary treatment of the landscape area as well as the range of pale tonalities recall Puvis's *Three Cartoons for the frieze of the Panthéon* — approximately seven by eighteen feet in size — (see detail, fig. 37, p. 174) which was shown at the *Salon d'Automne* in 1904 (no. 16). The pale whites, blues, greys and tans of

1. Daix and Boudaille, XII. 35 (The National Gallery of Art, Washington, D.C., Chester Dale Collection).

Puvis's composition are taken up by Picasso and merged with a supple and expressive drawing that derives from Goya by way of Degas. The gentle weight and sense of individual isolation of the figures also appears to have been somewhat the result of his study of Puvis's groupings. Wilhelm Boeck has written that the paintings of this period " . . . seem to reflect Picasso's predilection for Puvis de Chavannes and mark the culmination of his tendency to linear expression which was clearly marked even in his Blue Period . . ."[1]

1. Wilhelm Boeck and Jaime Sabartés, *Picasso*, New York: Harry N. Abrams, Inc., 1961, p. 132.

Fig. 36 Pierre Puvis de Chavannes, *Saint Genevieve in Prayer*, 1887

Fig. 37   Pierre Puvis de Chavannes, *Three Cartoons for the Frieze of the Panthéon* (detail), *c.* 1877

Other paintings of 1905 which can be related to Puvis include *La Coiffure*[1] which probably draw upon Puvis's *La Toilette*[2] of 1883, exhibited in the *Salon d'Automne* retrospective (no. 11); *Girl with a Basket of Flowers* (fig. 38, p. 175) which recalls the wan model of Puvis's *Hope* (nude version exhibited in the *Salon d'Automne*, 1904, no. 23); *Woman with a Fan* which reflects both the pose of Puvis's *La Madeleine*[3] of 1897 (*Salon d'Automne*, 1904, no. 9) as well as the seated woman at the left holding a tray in *Inter Artes et Naturam*; and *Boy Leading a Horse*, about which Barr writes: "it has an unpretentious, natural nobility of order and gesture which makes the official guardians of the 'Greek' tradition such as Ingres and Puvis de Chavannes seem vulgar or pallid."[4] Nevertheless, Picasso continues to adapt motifs from the paintings of Puvis de Chavannes in his work of 1906. A large

composition such as *The Two Brothers* [1] (fig. 39, p. 176) directly relates to the striding youth in the right centre foreground of *Inter Artes et Naturam* (see cat. nos. 29 and 30).[2]

La Coiffure[3] and *La Toilette* (cat. no. 78), painted during the summer of 1906 during a three-month stay at Gosol in Catalonia, have a distinct fresco-like colour quality and monumentality which stems from Picasso's having studied Puvis's *Three Cartoons for the frieze of the Panthéon* (see above detail, fig. 37) and the murals themselves. The dating of *La Coiffure* has been the subject of discussion. It would appear that the drawing of the topmost part of the two figures which Picasso made in a sketchbook[4] he employed that summer would fix the

---

1. Daix and Boudaille, XIII. 3 (The Baltimore Museum of Art, Cone Collection).
2. Musée de Louvre.
3. Szepmuveszeti Museum, Budapest.
4. Barr, *op. cit.*, p. 42.

1. Daix and Boudaille, XV. 9 (Kunstmuseum Basle).
2. The frequent use of pottery, by itself and in conjunction with figures, may also have taken its point of departure from *Inter Artes et Naturam*. See Daix and Boudaille, nos. XV. 10, XV. 11, XV. 13 and XV. 35.
3. Daix and Boudaille, XIV. 20 (Metropolitan Museum of Art, New York).
4. See *Picasso: le Carnet Catalan*, facsimile edition of Picasso's sketchbook with preface and notes by Douglas Cooper, Paris: Berggruen, 1958.

174

date of the painting as summer or early autumn, 1906. What is perhaps of equal note in this drawing, in terms of our interest in Puvis, is the fact that Picasso's original concept for *La Coiffure* sets the figures in a landscape in the left background of which are two figures, women, one standing on a ladder and the other watching with a basket nearby on the ground.[1] In addition, the page on which this drawing appears and the one preceding, contains a description of a working method. Picasso wrote:

> After having painted the background white, before painting it pink and Veronese green and very pale emerald (mixed with white), draw the landscape, the very clear cobalt blue sky, but in any case painting it white first in order to give it the substance of porcelain, [so that] everything has the tone of enamel. It is a question of a technical process.[2]

Cobalt blue is a middle range blue which Picasso did on occasion mix with white, and Veronese green gives a soft, dull effect, especially if mixed with white. The admixture of white to colour in order to give a pale fresco quality to the colour is a characteristic of Puvis de Chavannes's colour technique, something to which Picasso had paid particularly close attention between 1901 and 1905. Do any of Picasso's paintings of the summer of 1906 correspond to his text? Perhaps *Gosol Landscape*[3] which would seem to have been painted under the direct influence of Cézanne, corresponds to the procedure outlined. Although we do not find a great deal of green in Picasso's work of this period, there is a conspicuous patch on the sash of the standing figure at the right in *La Toilette* (cat. no. 78) which is placed in conjunction with the greyish-blue of the figure's arm and the pale blue shades of the shoulder and front of the dress and the section beneath the sash. There is also a marked difference between the relative opacity, resulting from Picasso's use of oil to approximate gouache or tempera in *La Toilette* and the thin tints of colour and inky blacks on a fine grain surface found in *Young Acrobat on a Ball* of 1905 (fig. 34, p. 172). This technique of whiting the colours, especially on the scale on which Picasso employed it in the years 1905 and 1906, stood in marked contradistinction to what his contemporaries, the fauves and those adhering to the neo-impressionist method, were doing with colour.[4] The drawing of the women in the background harvesting fruit and the description of a "substance of porcelain" and "tone of enamel" might reflect an interest in the painting of Maurice Denis,

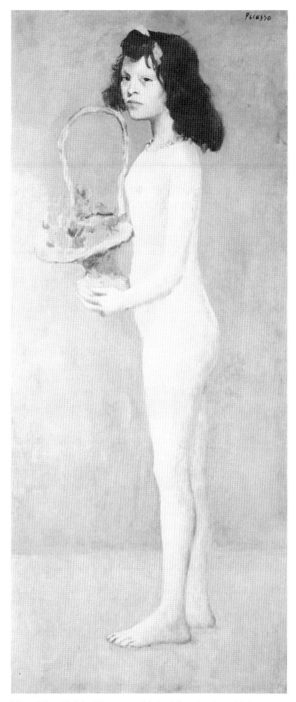

Fig. 38   Pablo Picasso, *Girl with a Basket of Flowers,* 1905

1. *Ibid.*, p. 19.

2. *Ibid.*, pp. 18-19. Again, on p. 37 of the same sketchbook, Picasso notes a recipe which involves the mixture of white with colour (original texts in Spanish).

3. Daix and Boudaille, xv. 48.

4. Signac used white as both a ground and in individual brushstrokes but it was not employed as tone or wash thinly applied as Picasso painted.

who himself had used Puvis's *Inter Artes et Naturam* as one of the sources for his pastoral compositions (see *L'Enfance ou la cueillette des pommes*, cat. no. 57).[1] On the other hand, with a knowledge of what had transpired in the preceding years, we cannot totally discount the possibility of Picasso's remarks having resulted from his direct observation of Puvis's technique but it would be wrong to see these notes as a formula for Picasso's work. The existence of such a text, taken together with the pastoral motif in the original conception of *La Coiffure*, should be noted in the overall context of Picasso's consciousness of Puvis de Chavannes.

In *La Toilette* (cat. no. 79) Picasso merges the expressive qualities of both his "Blue" and "Rose" periods as if it were a summation of the experiments of the past five years. The monumentality, classical dignity, grace, poise and subtle distortions of line and shape and space all contribute to the solid substance of the canvas. The scale and poses of the figures, especially the girl holding the mirror, derive from Puvis's above-mentioned full scale preparatory sketch for the frieze of the Panthéon (fig. 37, p. 174). Among other compositions by Puvis, such as *Inter Artes et Naturam*, the tonality, simplifications and flat modelling of the Panthéon study, had immense effect on Picasso. In *La Toilette*, however, figures are flattened without losing their basic sense of volume. The girl to the right is comprised of colour shapes ranging from the dramatic black of her hair and crisp profile of her face to broader striations made up of large strokes of blue, grey, green. Towards the bottom of her dress these modulate into roses and finally a distinct rose-terra cotta in the lowermost portion. Her legs appear crossed under her dress; her right leg appears in profile, pulled forward towards the spectator while the left leg is shown head on and appears in back of the right at the hip. These distortions render articulation which is anatomically impossible but such rearranged features are utilized to emphasize the close-to-the-surface, firm, sculpturesque bulk of the figure. Compare, for example, this figure and the standing woman at the extreme right in Puvis's *A Vision of Antiquity* (cat. no. 28). This is accomplished without loss of gentleness and with an intimacy which differs from the detachment and isolation of the "Blue" and "Harlequin" period pictures. In the solid proportions of the nude and the irregularity of her outline Picasso continues to keep in mind both the standing figures of Gauguin and those of Puvis in works such as *Pleasant Land* (cat. no. 23) and the *Allegory of the Sorbonne*.

1. The only other source which could be interpreted as corresponding to Picasso's notes is Renoir's painting of the 1880s which we have tried to show owed a debt of reinforcement to Puvis. We know from various sources that Picasso was most interested in Renoir's work of that period. (See Leo Stein, *Journey into the Self, op. cit.*, pp. 18-19. The specific painting Stein mentions is *Washerwoman and Baby, circa* 1886, The Barnes Foundation.)

176

Fig. 39   Pablo Picasso, *The Two Brothers,* 1906

During the period from 1919-1923 Picasso returned to classical influences and certain elements in his work at that time show residual interest in themes treated by Puvis, especially the groups of bathers by the shore. In Picasso's backdrop curtain for *Parade*[1], painted in 1917, and which is an expanded version of the pictorial ideas just seen in *Circus Family* (cat. no. 77) of 1905, he incorporates the broken archway and the Pegasus from the background of *Inter Artes et Naturam* (cat. no. 30). The scale of the stage setting also appears to have caused Picasso to revert to ideas he had developed out of Puvis's large murals. Although there is no single painting, drawing or pastel precisely akin[2], the woman leaning on the architectural fragment in front of the rose-coloured wall with the Pegasus motif in Puvis's above-mentioned mural in Rouen, her pose and the drawing have the rounded proportions and illustrative pose similar to Picasso's works of the period in question.

In conclusion, we are here not claiming Puvis to be the sole influence on Picasso and by emphasizing his impact we do not discount that of Gauguin, Daumier, Lautrec, Degas, El Greco, Cézanne, Redon and many

1. Zervos, *op. cit.*, vol. II (2), no. 951.
2. Zervos, *op. cit.*, vol. IV, nos. 237, 316, 328 and 385.

others whose importance to his formation has been universally recognized. But we do seek to underscore the fact that Puvis's influence was not inconsiderable, inconclusive, or peripheral to Picasso's natural inclinations towards large scale, fresco-like paintings with complex illustrative content. Puvis was a major figure when Picasso arrived in Paris, better known than Cézanne, infinitely more available for examination, and he was considered important enough in 1904 to be shown with Cézanne, Redon, Lautrec and Renoir which, in itself, would have encouraged a young artist to study his work. Picasso, ambitious as he was intelligent, with a knowledge of the old masters from the Prado and frescoes from Catalonia firmly in mind, found Puvis perhaps simpler to integrate than other of his contemporaries and he did so with a skill and ease, even a virtuosity, which was always the hallmark of his art. The failure to identify and study this important influence is one of the corollaries of Puvis's fall from grace in the past fifty years; it stems primarily from the fact that most of the critics who have devoted themselves to the investigation of Picasso's development have not been conscious enough of Puvis's accomplishments to discern and evaluate the influence he exerted.

Roger de La Fresnaye (French, 1885-1925)

Landscape with Woman, Cow and Dog (Marie Ressort), circa 1913
Oil on canvas; 78½ x 62¾ in. (200 x 160 cm.)
Signed lower right (partially covered): R. de . . .
Lent by Gwen Weiner

Catalogue no. 79

Ref. Germain Seligman, *Roger de La Fresnaye* (with a catalogue raisonné) Neuchâtel: Editions Ides et Calendes, 1969, no. 125, p. 152 (*Marie Ressort avec ses Vaches, La Bergère*). A study for this painting is in the collection of the Albright-Knox Art Gallery, Buffalo, New York (Seligman, no. 124).

La Fresnaye studied with Maurice Denis at the Academy Ranson in 1908 when Denis was painting mural decorations such as the series of five panels for the Russian collector Morosov (see La Fresnaye's *Eve*, 1909-1910, Seligman, *op. cit.*, no. 30, p. 122).

In *Landscape with Woman, Cow and Dog*, the positioning of the dog and cow is very reminiscent of Puvis (see *Normandy*, cat. no. 33). The scale of the painting, the pastoral theme[1] and the rugged versus crisp outlines all recall Puvis. The silhouette of the tree illustratively indicates a *repoussoir* but the planes are flat and very shallow, a lack of deep space which is also characteristic of Puvis. The flat planes of the units below, including the cow in textured pale grey-white and the white clouds above, combined with the Cézanne-esque blues in the sky played off against the figure in red all convey a sense of the static, gently monumental compositions found in Puvis's murals in the Panthéon. La Fresnaye's classicism would have found Puvis as well as Cézanne a congenial source of inspiration. In an article on Cézanne, published in 1913 (approximately at the same time as *Landscape with Woman, Cow and Dog*) La Fresnaye wrote:

Cézanne's opinion of the painters whom he knew may appear a little unexpected. He liked neither Gauguin nor van Gogh, but he admired the great impressionists and also *L'Orgie romaine* of Thomas Couture of which he possessed a reproduction. He admired Delacroix, Courbet, Manet and Puvis de Chavannes but he seems not to have appreciated Ingres, whom he called a harmful classicist and a painter of very little note.[1]

This intelligently written article, containing numerous insights into Cézanne's art and especially in the manner in which Cézanne's statements and writings should be evaluated, is intriguing for it is the only source known (albeit secondhand) of Cézanne having expressed admiration for Puvis's art. La Fresnaye would have gleaned at least some of his information from Denis who met Cézanne and would undoubtedly have sought his ideas on Puvis. Their aims differed, for Cézanne's "classicism" consisted of striving for a solid monumentality. The flat and pale figures of Puvis's large scale, but not truly monumental, murals recalled aspects of Poussin whom Cézanne valued highly, although Puvis's adaptations were diametrically opposed to Cézanne's interpretations. Cézanne's one recorded comment about Puvis's art as quoted by Joachim Gasquet is: "what bad literature!"[2]

---

1. "Paul Cézanne," *Poème et Drame,* Paris, January 1913 (Seligman, *op. cit.*, p. 276).

2. *Cézanne,* Paris, Les Editions Bernheim-Jeune, 1921, p. 47. Gasquet's statement carries more weight than La Fresnaye's and he prefaces the above-mentioned quotation by saying, "Cézanne detested Puvis de Chavannes, to the point of wanting to throw the reproduction that I had of the Sorbonne hemicycle out of my house" (*ibid.*).

Another acquaintance of Cézanne and one of the first critics to write about him, Gustave Geffroy (1855-1926) met Cézanne for the first time in November, 1894 and the following Spring posed for several months while Cézanne worked on a portrait of him which the artist never completed. (See John Rewald, *Cézanne, Geffroy et Gasquet suivi de Souvenirs sur Cézanne de Louis Aurenche et de Lettres Inédites*, Quatre Chemins-Editart, Paris, 1959.) Geffroy, a great admirer of Puvis, attended the Puvis banquet. (See, for example, Geffroy, "Puvis de Chavannes", *La Vie Artistique*, series 6, chapter 31, October 15th, 1894: Paris, E. Dentu and "Puvis de Chavannes," *Revue des Beaux-Arts et des Lettres*, May 1, 1899, p. 226 where the author makes it clear that he considers Puvis a great genius.) Cézanne, in Paris at the time, did not attend.

---

1 The theme could also have been adapted from Picasso's *Composition* of 1906 (The Barnes Foundation) which La Fresnaye could have seen at Vollard's.

Balthus (French, born 1908)

The Window, 1933
Oil on canvas; 63¼ x 44¼ in. (166 x 132.6 cm.)
Unsigned
Lent by the Indiana University Art Museum

Catalogue no. 80

Ref. *Paintings from Midwestern University Collections, Seventeenth-Twentieth Centuries*, 1973, p. 138, no. 57.

The art of Balthus is one of detachment and introspection executed with a control over compositional alignments, texture and a relatively narrow range of colour harmonies which link him to his predecessors in the traditions. Indeed, his use of sources, especially Piero della Francesca, Poussin, Seurat, Courbet and Chardin, is so forthright that at times the compositions are little more than updated versions of their ideas. A sombre colour note, deriving in part from Géricault and Courbet as well as from Derain, pervades many of his interiors with figures. *The Window*, dating from the same year as the artist's large version of *The Street* (private collection, U.S.A.) which incorporates features borrowed primarily from Piero, Seurat and Carpaccio, also conveys some of the fixed geometric simplicity of Puvis's broadly patterned illustrative settings for figures whose psychology remains intentionally enigmatic. In this, Balthus, as does La Fresnaye in his own way, carries on the austere side of classical tradition in French painting, both by conscious recourse to its sources and by predisposition toward its restraint in the use of pictorial means.

Albert Pinkham Ryder (American, 1847-1917)

The Sisters
Oil on panel; 11½ x 5⅝ in. (29 x 14 cm.)
Unsigned
Vose Galleries of Boston, Inc.

Catalogue no. 81

William J. Glackens (American, 1870-1938)

Orestes pursued by the Furies, 1896
Watercolour and tempera on cardboard; 14¾ x 8⅜ in. (37.4 x 21 cm.)
Unsigned
Inscribed and signed on *verso: Orestes pursued by the furies; the composition does not consider the story litteraly [sic], but more as representing conscience in the abstract/Glackens*
Philadelphia Museum of Art, Given by Mr. and Mrs. John Sloan

Catalogue no. 82

182

Fig. 40   William J. Glackens, *Justice*, 1896

A precocious draughtsman since childhood, William Glackens became a newspaper reporter-illustrator in 1891, one year after his graduation from high school (he was a schoolmate of John Sloan) where he had followed courses in perspective, foreshortening, mechanical and engineering drawing as well as "decorative and historical ornament" and "shades and shadows." Glackens drew for various Philadelphia newspapers until 1895. Between 1892 and 1894 he enrolled part-time in classes at the Pennsylvania Academy of the Fine Arts, studying mostly at night. In 1892 at the latest, he met Robert Henri (1865-1929) and shared a studio with him in 1892-1893. Henri stimulated Glackens's desire to become a painter and strongly influenced his painting in the direction of the realism derived from the Spanish-Dutch school, as exemplified in America by Frank Duveneck and in France by Manet. Glackens's work from the early 1890s until 1907 reflects these basic influences as well as that of Whistler.

From 1888 to 1891 Henri had been to Europe and by the time he met Glackens he had worked through an impressionist phase, rejecting that style in favour of the direct realist approach. In June, 1895, Glackens and Henri sailed for Paris where Glackens remained for fifteen months. Unlike most of his contemporaries, he did not attend any art school.[1] He painted, visited the

museums and investigated contemporary art at the galleries and Salons. Glackens's companions in Paris were Henri and Charles Wilson Morrice. Morrice had been an intimate of Maurice Prendergast from 1891-1894 when Prendergast lived in Paris and had introduced him to a great deal of contemporary French painting. It is probable that he did the same for Glackens although no indication of this exposure can be found in Glackens's work either in Paris or after he returned home. In 1896 Glackens made a bicycle trip with Henri visiting museums through northern France, Belgium and Holland, thus underscoring their interest in the Dutch masters.

Henri is known to have admired the work of Puvis de Chavannes, especially the mural in the ampitheatre of the Sorbonne,[1] and Glackens was also probably encouraged to look at Puvis's work by Henry Thouron, his composition teacher at the Pennsylvania Academy and an admirer of A.E. Abbey.[2] Abbey was at that very time engaged in his mural frieze, *Holy Grail*, for the Boston Public Library which, along with those of J.S. Sargent (*The Dogma of the Redemption*) and Puvis de Chavannes, decorated various walls within the building. Abbey in turn held Puvis in high esteem and was

1. E.g. Maurice Prendergast studied at the Académie Julian in 1891-1892, as did Ernest Lawson in 1893, both with Jean-Paul Laurens.

1. See William I. Homer (with the assistance of Violet Organ), *Robert Henri and his Circle*, Ithaca and London: Cornell University Press, 1969, p. 62.
2. Glackens also knew fellow illustrator and Philadelphian, Henry McCarter who had studied with Puvis (see p. 17).

183

delighted that he had been prevailed upon to undertake the Boston commission. In fact, Puvis's Boston commission undoubtedly was one of the active topics of conversation among young American artists in Paris, and Glackens would have seen the five upright panels destined for Boston at the *Salon du Champ-de-Mars* in 1896. The combined circumstances of his having been a student of Thouron and his having been able to study Puvis's murals firsthand in 1895-1896 led to a heretofore unknown interlude in Glackens's career.

When Glackens returned to Philadelphia in the early fall of 1896, John Sloan was engaged in painting a commissioned mural for the auditorium of the Pennsylvania Academy of the Fine Arts. This commission was to be one of a series of nine assigned to pupils from the school, mainly those studying under Thouron, although Sloan himself had never been his student. The idea was probably initiated during Glackens's absence, but the project may have been a long-standing one. If so, Glackens may have had specifically in mind to do research in Paris in preparation for work on a mural of his own. Sloan was at work on his mural by the summer of 1896, since Thouron urged him in a letter to get on with the "decoration."[1] Either through the intervention of Sloan or by an agreement made prior to his departure or even after his return, Glackens undertook a segment of the auditorium decorations. His mural, measuring six feet six inches by ten feet eight inches, was to illustrate the subject "Justice" (fig. 90, p. 183). Thouron had given Sloan a set of typewritten directions, guidelines with which we can surmise Glackens was also familiar. They tell us, incidentally, something of the nature of the instruction at the school at that time.

The Mural Paintings will extend in a broad, unbroken frieze, entirely around the Lecture Room.

The character of the building, and the customary uses of this particular room, have decided the choice of subjects, and their relative positions on the wall.

Each and all, at once suggest dignified, and beautiful treatment.

The effect of colour upon entering the room, should combine richness with delicacy, resembling that produced by a great parterre of many-tinted flowers.

The spaces, divided by a simple gold moulding of sufficient width, are quite varied in size, and proportion. The distribution of the upright panels (the Muses) giving an appearance of symmetry.

Electric lights, concealed as much as possible, will be introduced, and the strong reflections from the ceiling, and walls will so diffuse the light that no place will be undesirable.

The panels are to be about ten feet from the floor.

General coloring of room — a creamy white, with slightly greenish tendency, relieved by dull gold bronze, but without design or ornamentation of any kind.

General tone of the subject-panels — light and brilliant, with yellows and greens prevailing, but introducing any or all other colors in an agreeable proportion according to individual taste.

Stronger colors, with reds, blues, violets, etc. should be used in the upright panels, occupied by the Muses. These figures will have a flat background, either of white or gold, or perhaps both, combined by a stenciled Greek pattern of gold on white.

The full-size figure of a man standing in the immediate foreground of a composition, must not exceed 9 feet 6 inches in height, which will allow 11½ inches for division above and below. The figures of the Muses, all posed standing [?], are on the base edge of the panel, must be six feet, three inches in height, allowing the same distance, eight inches, above the top of each head.

The difference of nine inches between the height of these figures and that of the largest figures in the subject panels, should give the impression of heroic size desirable in that of the former.

Flatness being one of the essential qualities of good mural painting, the modelling of the flesh should be greatly simplified. The contours, however, should be kept firm, with due appreciation of the value of a strong line.

Draperies should be very broadly painted, and too exact costuming, or localizing by dress in one or two panels, might injure the general effect of the series.

Should an interior (Architectural) setting be chosen for the figures, it might be well to include a glimpse of out-doors in the composition. On the other hand, if the surroundings be landscape, the corner of a building, or some architectural necessary [necessity] would go far towards unifying the effect of the series.

"Sacred Music" might illustrate the first, "Pastoral Music," the second suggestion.

Very strong effects of light-and-dark, are not desirable.

Small details are to be avoided.

[There follows the handwritten additions:]

1. Letter from Thouron to Sloan, August 18, 1896 (John Sloan Trust, on deposit at the Delaware Art Museum, Wilmington, Delaware, Courtesy of Mrs. John Sloan).

mented upon sources in the traditions. Among these, Puvis de Chavannes is both the most pervasive and imaginatively integrated into Prendergast's own inherently joyous vision of humanity.

Prendergast lived in Paris from 1891 through 1894 where he studied with Gustave Courtois at Colarossi. He also studied at the Académie Julian with Jean-Paul Laurens, Benjamin Constant and Joseph-Paul Blanc. At Julian he met Charles Wilson Morrice (1865-1924) who introduced him to Charles Conder (1868-1909) and Aubrey Beardsley, both admirers of Puvis de Chavannes.[1] Morrice, Conder and Prendergast painted together in the early nineties at St. Malo and Dinard. Similarities in style have been noted between the small oil on panel sketches of Morrice and Prendergast but the relationship of both men to the work of Conder has yet to be systematically investigated. Conder had been working on small nine by five inch cigar box lids in the late 1880s in Australia and had exhibited his colourful oil sketches in Melbourne in 1889 prior to leaving for France where he was at Julian's by October 1890. Prendergast must have known his work of this period, which predates Conder's paintings on silk which begin in 1892-93.[2] Certain of Conder's later oils — he did no painting after 1906 — (see *Four Ladies on Terrace, c.* 1905; see fig. 42) in their pale grey tonalities and poses stemming in part from contact with Puvis, may also have had their effect on Prendergast. All three young artists were under the pervasive influence of Whistler at this time and also cannot have failed to study Puvis's work in Paris. Prendergast, upon his return to Boston, was acquainted with the murals in the Public Library there. However, it is not until after 1905 that we find concrete evidence of Prendergast's interest in Puvis and it was several years later before it appears to have manifested itself in his work.[3]

In a sketchbook which can be dated *c.* 1904-05, we find a pen and ink drawing (see fig. 43) after *Pleasant Land* (cat. no. 23).[4] This coincides with Prendergast's

1. In mid-1892 Beardsley visited Puvis in Paris with a letter of introduction from Burne-Jones and presented him with one of his drawings, "Children Decorating a Terminal God!" (see Brian Reade, *Aubrey Beardsley*, New York: Bonanza Books, 1967, pp. 16, 319 and 359). This occurred at the very time Prendergast was associating with Beardsley.

2. See Ursula Hoff, *Charles Conder: His Australian Years*, Melbourne: The National Gallery Society of Victoria, 1960 (especially cat. nos. 21 and 33) and David Rogers, *Charles Conder: 1868-1909*, Sheffield: Graves Art Gallery, 1967.

3. Prendergast did not paint extensively before this time, concentrating on his watercolours and colour monotypes which he exhibited as early as 1900 at the Art Institute of Chicago.

4. Museum of Fine Arts, Boston, Sketchbook no. 13, p. 44. In the same sketchbook are references to Italian art periodicals of 1904 and the *Gazette des Beaux-Arts* on January 1, 1905. Also noted is Morrice's address, 45 Quai des Grands Augustins. The drawing would appear to have been copied from a reproduction.

Fig. 42   Charles Conder, *Four Ladies on Terrace, c.* 1905

shift from watercolours and monotypes to pastels and oils and marks a decisive turning point in his development. In 1909 Prendergast went to France where he remained approximately a year and where, in addition to Cézanne, he closely studied the work of Denis, Vuillard, Roussel and Redon, all, as we have noted, artists who were influenced by Puvis de Chavannes. Hedley Rhys comments about his work of this period:

In France in 1909-1910 he started to combine pastel with watercolor and opaque Chinese white. These mixed media he used with greater frequency in the next ten years than pastel alone. Work of this type done in Paris is somewhat grayer than the pure water colors, but eventually he used the combination to

Fig. 43   Maurice B. Prendergast, *Copy after "Pleasant Land" by Puvis de Chavannes, c.* 1905

189

Fig. 44 Maurice B. Prendergast, *Copy after "Summer" by Puvis de Chavannes, c.* 1912

Fig. 45 Maurice B. Prendergast, *Copy after "Girls by the Seashore," c.* 1912

produce a suffused, bright . . . luminous effect.
. . . This is an effect that often accompanied the tapestried surface of his late oils.[1]

These are techniques and effects which may have been adapted from Vuillard, Denis, Roussel and Redon and the inclination toward dense, decorative patchwork of luminous colour probably also stems from this collective source.

However much Prendergast studied and was influenced by the colour constructions of Cézanne, his aims were primarily decorative and illustrative rather than monumental. The fact that his compositions were made up primarily of colour relationships links him to Cézanne. Barnes and de Mazia in their analysis of Cézanne's influence on Prendergast observe:

The successive strokes of color . . . make up the pattern of overlapping patches [and] coalesce into a series of receding planes, which build volumes and define spatial intervals as they do in Cézanne. The constituent planes, however, are actually fewer in Prendergast's masses and less accentuated, with the result that figures are usually flattened and trees, especially when placed in compact space, appear as parts of a screenlike pattern, with little three-dimensional extension.

. . . Prendergast's space-compositions render a frieze-like or panoramic sequence of rhythms.[2]

The specific influence of Cézanne, however, has generally been overestimated in the sense that other parallel sources such as Puvis have been disregarded in tracing

the origins of Prendergast's decorative form. Prendergast's figures and figure groupings have something distinctly idealized, pastoral, gentle, even naive, as opposed to the thumping rhythmic force of Cézanne's compositions. Prendergast drew incessantly from nature and in his pencil sketches he sought to preserve the immediacy of the moment observed and to transfer some of this fresh, spontaneous liveliness into the sparkle and fluidity of his paint surfaces done in the studio. Moreover, in his search for pastoral figure compositions, Prendergast knew exactly what type of model he was looking for in the traditions and this led him to intersperse, between his drawings of teeming outdoor scenes at the beach or in the park, more formal figure groupings carefully copied from such pictures as Giorgione's *Concert Champêtre*,[1] Poussin's *Echo and Narcissus*,[2] nudes by Titian[3] as well as such compositions by Puvis de Chavannes as *Summer* (see fig. 44) and *Girls by the Seashore* (see fig. 45).[4] The last two drawings appear in a sketchbook which can be dated around 1912 and were undoubtedly done from reproductions rather than from

1. Rhys, *op. cit.*, p. 48.
2. *The Art of Cézanne*, New York: Harcourt, Brace and Company, 1939, pp. 139-140.

1. Museum of Fine Arts, Boston, Sketchbook no. 66, p. 73.
2. Museum of Fine Arts, Boston, Sketchbook no. 54.
3. *Ibid.*
4. Museum of Fine Arts, Boston, Sketchbook no. 46, pp. 34 and 35, pencil on lined paper.

life. And it is in Prendergast's oils from around 1912 on that we can trace the unmistakable application of ideas adapted from Puvis to his painting. At the Armory Show in 1913, Prendergast would have had the opportunity to study Puvis's work[1] and we know that he looked at Matisse and Gauguin among others, since, either in New York or when the show travelled to Boston, he made sketches of several Matisses and Gauguin's *Faa Iheihe*[2] (fig. 14, p. 125), thus underscoring his apparent interest in exploring frieze formats. Prendergast also was closely associated with John Quinn at this time[3] and shortly after he and his brother Charles moved permanently to New York in October 1914, Quinn commissioned two large, mural-size paintings from the artist. These connections would have brought him into contact with such paintings as Puvis's *Cider* and *The River* which were placed on exhibition at the Metropolitan Museum of Art early in 1915 (see p. 28).

All of these circumstances would mean little if it were not for the evidence of the paintings themselves, in their formats, colour tonality, texture, mood, pattern and space composition. Indeed, as early as 1925, Dr. Barnes, Prendergast's most perceptive critical and financial supporter, described his colour scheme as including "lilac-pinks, yellow, pale blue, chalky whites, pale greens and roses."[4] These are precisely the colour qualities of Puvis de Chavannes, especially the chalky white tonalities, but the lilac-pinks and pale blues and greens as well. Barnes also states that at times Prendergast's pictures have "the charm and delicacy of the finest of early tapestries and frescoes. Another claim to distinction is that the composition in his easel pictures often yields the effects of murals to a larger degree than the work of any mural painter since the Renaissance."[5] In a painting such as *Figures in a Park* of 1914, the elongated distortions in drawing of the figures, the dusky, scumbled impasto, the chalky tonality of the paint and the fixed poses of the figures all point to adaptations from Puvis. The size and scale of the canvas suggest interest in the large scale murals of Puvis and their early Florentine sources. Compare *Figures in a Park* with Puvis's *Charity* (cat. no. 35) of 1894 in their pale tonalities, light-absorbing textures, their subtle range of greys, tans, pinks and blues within a restricted chromatic range.

1. Durand-Ruel in New York had shown some of his paintings from December 18-31, 1912 shortly before the show opened.

2. Museum of Fine Arts, Boston, Sketchbooks nos. 21 and 38. Among the Matisses copied were *Goldfish and Sculpture* (Museum of Modern Art), *Nasturtiums and the "Dance"* (Worcester Art Museum), *Le Luxe II* (Royal Museum of Fine Arts, Copenhagen) and *The Hairdresser* (Staatsgalerie, Stuttgart).

3. He and his brother Charles made frames for Quinn at the time of the Armory Show. Maurice shares in the tendency to render poses consciously archaic, even naive, similar to those found in the carved, gilded and gessoed panels of his brother.

4. *The Art in Painting*, 1st edition, *op. cit.*, 1925, pp. 298-299.

5. *The Art in Painting*, 3rd edition, *op. cit.*, 1937, p. 340.

Fig. 46   Maurice B. Prendergast, *Bathers, c.* 1915

The impressionist and neo-impressionist colour has been toned down in the interest of uniting the figures into a one-piece tapestry effect. The distinctly placid mood is also derived from Puvis.

In a composition such as *On the Beach no. 3* (cat. no. 84) of 1918 which represents Prendergast's oils at their most complete stage of development, the frieze-like disposition of figures across the composition, the jutting out of the landscape elements in the middleground at the right, the trees as dense compositional pattern units taking their place in the overall tapestry-like decorative scheme, the use of the horizontal bands of sky and water to establish a contained deep, rather than infinite, recession into space — all of these have their source in such works by Puvis as *A Vision of Antiquity* (cat. no. 28) of *c.*1887-1890 and *The Shepherd's Song* (cat. no. 32) of 1891, with which Prendergast was undoubtedly familiar, since it was at the Metropolitan Museum. The subordination of posed figures, "awkwardly" articulated like colourful rag dolls, set up and assembled in groups, to a well-planned colour, compositional and textural ensemble, is so much like Puvis in conception that it is difficult not to credit Puvis as one of Prendergast's fundamental sources of inspiration.[1] A watercolour such as *Bathers* (see fig. 46) of *c.* 1915 reverts to Puvis-esque thematic content as well as compositional features and one has only to compare this with Prendergast's copy of Puvis's *Summer* (see fig. 44) and any one of Cézanne's *Bathers* compositions to discern how much of the borrowing is from the former and how much from the latter. The sinuous drawing of outlines, broken, yet with no emphasis on the underlying structure but rather the decorative surface, is dependent on Puvis's

1. In oils such as *Figures at the Beach*, also *c.*1918, The Barnes Foundation (see *The Barnes Foundation Journal of the Art Department*, vol. III, no. 2, Autumn, 1972, plate 39), the frieze motif becomes even more explicit. See also *Summer Day* (watercolour, eight by eighteen inches), *Paintings and Water Colors by Maurice Prendergast*, New York: The Knoedler Galleries, 1966, fig. 48.

late oils and perhaps even such watercolours as *Sacred Grove* (cat. no. 24).[1]

Puvis de Chavannes had a demonstrable and significant influence on the work of Maurice Prendergast, whose intelligent adaptations from numerous sources in the traditions constructively enhanced Prendergast's unique decorative vision of the world he portrayed.[2]

1. An oil such as *Idyl* (The Barnes Foundation, ill. in *The Art in Painting*, 3rd edition, *op. cit.*, p. 99), in addition to revealing influences as diverse as Gauguin, Renoir and perhaps even van Gogh, clearly recalls similar usages in Puvis's *Pleasant Land* (see cat. no. 23 and Prendergast's copy, fig. 43 p. 189), in the pair of standing figures at the left and the semi-draped seated figure to their right. See also *Eight Bathers*, *c.*1916-18 (Museum of Fine Arts, Boston) for strong colour, compositional and textural overtones of Puvis and *Waterfall* of 1911 (Rhys, no. 22, formerly collection John Quinn) in which the pose and colour tonality of the nude recall Puvis's figures such as the standing woman second from the right in *A Vision of Antiquity* (cat. no. 28).

2. Two additional sources of Prendergast's art: Monticelli and Moreau. Monticelli's ruggedly-textured, updated *fêtes galantes* were extensively exhibited in America during Prendergast's formative years in the early part of the century. The interest in the Frenchman's work was reinforced by the respect of the younger generation for Ryder whose work shows certain affinities with Monticelli. Prendergast's processional friezes and also his still lifes owe something to Monticelli in their prominent use of texture and brightness of colour to secure primarily decorative effects. (See Rhys, *op. cit.*, cat. nos. 14 and 34.) It would also be reasonable to assume that Prendergast was familiar with Moreau's work and probably visited the Moreau museum on one of his later trips to Paris. Moreau's watercolours and mixed media watercolour pastels appear to have led Prendergast to both intensify his colour and loosen his application in the watercolours painted from about 1910 on. Such Moreaus as *Eve* (Musée Moreau, no. 302) and *Eve* (Musée Moreau, no. 315) have the broad bright splotches and blobs in watercolour over chalk, colour areas and patches which are randomly placed but with a specific compositional structure in mind. Prendergast's splotches make up the figure whereas Moreau's are employed as a setting — a conservative's venturesome setting — for basically academically drawn figures. These two aspects are separated and never unified in Moreau into a picture theme. Colour is used lavishly but over a resolutely academic and literary framework.

Arthur B. Davies (American, 1862-1928)

Free of the World, 1918
Oil on canvas; 14½ x 28 ⅜ in. (36 x 71.8 cm.)
Signed lower left: A. B. Davies
Lent by M. Knoedler and Company, Inc.

Catalogue no. 85

Ref. *Arthur B. Davies: A Chronological Retrospective*, March 11-April 15, 1975, New York, M. Knoedler & Company; p. 53, no. 84 (introduction: Joseph S. Czestochowski).

Arthur Bowen Davies was born in Utica, New York in 1862. He studied art at the Chicago Academy of Design in 1878 and, after a trip to Mexico City in 1880, at the Art Institute of Chicago in 1882. He moved to New York and from 1887 to 1891 worked as an illustrator for *The Century Magazine*, for which also at that time worked Kenyon Cox, a great admirer of Puvis de Chavannes. Davies had the opportunity to see Puvis's work as early as 1888 at the National Academy of Design where Durand-Ruel exhibited a number of works including the reduced versions of *War*, *Peace*, *Work* and *Rest*. The study for the mural in the Sorbonne, acquired by the Havemeyers in 1889 from Durand-Ruel, was on loan to the Metropolitan Museum of Art in 1890.[1] Davies ex-

1. See *The Art Amateur*, December 1890, "The Atelier;" *Puvis de Chavannes*, p. 5. This article also indicates that the painting in question was "touched up since the completion of the work," an observation which appears to coincide with our analysis of the painting. Therefore, although signed and dated 1889, in our view, at the time of this retouching, we cannot agree with the observation that the painting is "a reduction, done after the completion of the mural" as stated by Sterling and Salinger, p. 229. It is rather a slightly retouched definitive preparatory sketch painted *circa* 1887.

hibited at the National Academy of Design in 1893 and subsequently William Macbeth became his dealer. In 1893 Benjamin Altman financed a trip to Europe where the artist visited Italy. It is not certain that Davies went to Paris, but he returned in time to see the Puvis de Chavannes exhibition at Durand-Ruel in New York (December 15 — 31, 1894). The installation of the Boston Public Library murals in 1896 would have provided a further basis for firsthand study of Puvis's art.

Davies's work early inclined towards the transcendental landscapes so popular in the latter part of the nineteenth century in America. The work of Blakelock, Inness and Ryder (see cat. no. 81) was the basis of his style in terms of colour and texture. This was applied throughout his career to subjects encompassing figures which appear in reverie and dreamlike trances, an ethereal and rather transparent mystery which also draws heavily upon Whistler. His frieze-like motifs, pale handling of flesh and the sequential motifs of figures disposed in various related poses across the surface of his compositions are fundamentally derived from Puvis. The lyrical pastorals of his later years, including *Free of the World* of *c.* 1918 (cat. no. 85), *A Thousand Flowers, c.* 1922 (Hirshhorn Museum and Sculpture Garden, Washington D.C.) and *Heliodora*, 1926 (Museum of Fine Arts, Boston) characterize his use of Puvis's pale tonali-

193

ties and floral settings. Davies participated in the exhibition of "The Eight," 1908, at the Macbeth Galleries but his style was in no essential ways related to the other artists shown. Following his efforts in organizing the Armory Show in 1912-13, together with Walt Kuhn, Davies adopted a quasi-cubist style which he never fully assimilated. Shortly thereafter he returned to his academic drawing style which was closely based upon Botticelli and Pollaiuolo and which, in addition to his paintings, he applied to drawings, pastels, etchings and lithographs, his main pre-occupation at the end of his life.

Milton Avery (American, 1893-1965)

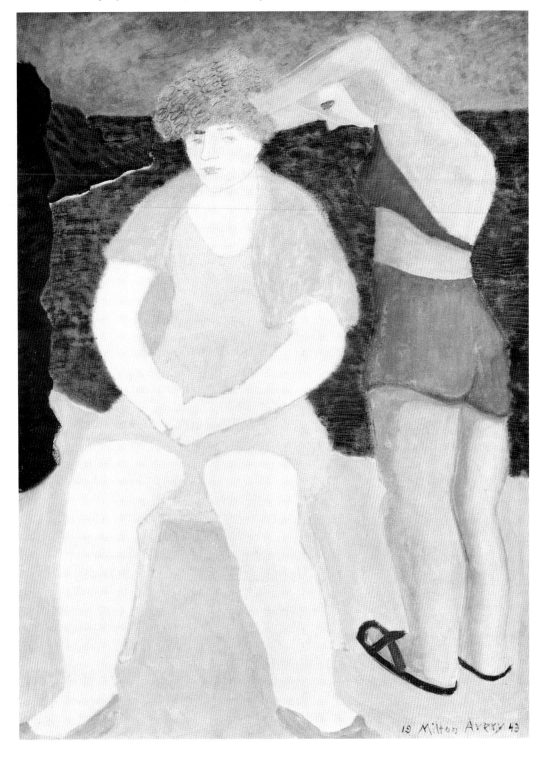

Haircut by the Sea, 1943
Oil on canvas; 44 x 32 in. (111.7 x 81.2 cm.)
Signed and dated lower right: 19 Milton Avery 43
Memorial Art Gallery of the University of Rochester

Catalogue no. 86

Milton Avery was born in the town of Altmar, upper New York State in 1893. His family moved to Hartford, Connecticut in 1905 where he became interested in painting. In 1925 he came to live in New York where he worked, with summer vacations in New England and Canada, until the end of his life. Since he did not visit Europe until he was nearly sixty years old, his acquaintance with the traditions of art, including contemporary art, came through his visits to galleries and museums throughout the United States. We have no way of documenting that Avery saw the murals in the Boston Public Library at any time in his career, but it appears more than likely that he did so. The major formative influences on his mature style were Matisse, Marsden Hartley and Abraham Walkowitz. These artists tended to flatten volumes into shapes and employ broadly decorative areas of colour to portray figures, still lifes, land and seascapes and interiors, never losing sight of the human content of the illustrative facts before them, even though simplifying and distorting to considerable degrees. Matisse's interiors of the mid and late twenties had particular attraction for Avery. There were also a number of paintings by Puvis hanging at the Metropolitan in the late twenties and early thirties. Apart from *The Shepherd's Song* (cat. no. 32), the museum acquired *Cider* and *The River* (see Sterling and Salinger, pp. 225-227) from the Quinn Collection in 1926; *Tamaris* (cat. no. 22) entered the collection in 1930; *Sleep* (Sterling and Salinger, pp. 227-228) came in 1930 and may have been on exhibit prior to that time. In addition, Avery could have looked at Puvis's work on display at the memorial exhibition of Quinn's collection held in January, 1926.

In *Haircut by the Sea* the compositional arrangement of figures with a backdrop of curving shoreline and rocky outcropping reduced to flat planes, although internally mottled as colour units, stems directly from Puvis de Chavannes (cf. *The Bathers*, cat. no. 31 and *Girls by the Seashore*, Musée du Louvre, fig. 11, p. 122). In addition, the pale blues, lilacs and greyed tonalities throughout strongly recall Puvis. The simplifications of patterns by way of varied, overlapping outlines, neither crisp nor flowingly arabesque in movement as in Matisse, point to a careful study of Puvis's work.

Placing Avery's work in this context is important for two other reasons: first, through his simplifications of pattern and subdued tonalities, friends such as Mark Rothko and Adolph Gottlieb came to develop their mature styles in the nineteen forties. Although at first one would not connect Puvis de Chavannes with these men, Milton Avery can be seen as the link between the Frenchman and those later and even more radical simplifiers who carry Puvis's means to their furthest state of extension. This is not so far-fetched when one considers the second link between Avery and a number of European painters, aspects of whose aesthetic forms are close to his in quality. Giorgio Morandi, Marie Laurencin and Albert Marquet were all masters of the understatement, with subdued tonality, modulated colour and pattern harmonies. These features stand in direct opposition to most of the qualities found in the predominant movements of this century — fauvism, cubism, constructivism and expressionism. The pervasive calm, method without rigidity, and gentleness, attributes which all these artists share in common with Milton Avery are, I believe, a legacy of the flexible classicism and broad simplifications so much a part of Puvis's expression.

196

Catalogue designed by Olive Koyama.
Printed on Lustro Offset Enamel and
bound by The Hunter Rose Company,
Toronto, Ontario. Text composed in
Baskerville by Howarth & Smith
Limited; colour separations made by
Colorgraph Reproduction Incorporated.
Printed in Canada.